SECRET DIPLOMACY

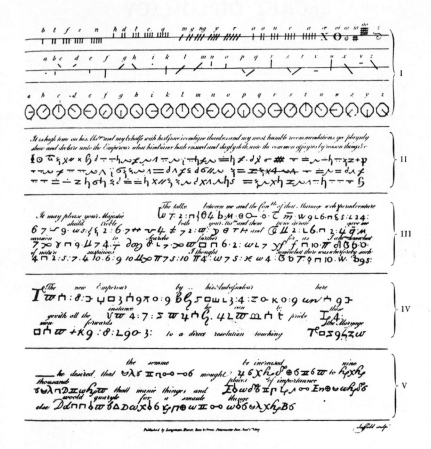

SIXTEENTH- AND SEVENTEENTH-CENTURY CIPHERS

(I) Oghams. (II) The cipher of the Marquis of Worcester. (III) The cipher of Cardinal
Wolsey. (IV) The cipher of Sir Thomas Smith. (V) The cipher of Sir Thomas Chalmer.

SECRET
DIPLOMACY

Espionage and Cryptography
1500-1815

JAMES WESTFALL THOMPSON
and
SAUL K. PADOVER

FREDERICK UNGAR PUBLISHING CO.
NEW YORK

Second Printing, 1965

Copyright 1963 by Saul K. Padover
First Edition 1937

Printed in the United States of America

Library of Congress Catalog Card No. 63-11844

PREFACE TO THE NEW EDITION

In the Preface to the first edition, my collaborator, the late Professor James Westfall Thompson, explained how this book came to be written:

> "Years ago . . . , while working in the *Archives nationales* and *Archives des affaires étrangères,* I not infrequently came upon diplomatic documents written in cipher. Sometimes a decoded translation or a key accompanied the original; but every once in a while I would come upon an uncoded document which had either to be deciphered or passed over. Not only did the cipher of each country's ambassador differ from that of other ambassadors, but also the ciphers of every diplomat were frequently changed, usually because of suspicion that the key had been discovered. These ciphered dispatches, when taken in connection with other evidences of a wide web of secret diplomacy spread over Europe in the sixteenth, seventeenth, and eighteenth centuries, interested me deeply. Accordingly much of my professional research and a large portion of my leisure reading for years past has been in diplomatic history and the fascinating memoirs and letters pertaining to those periods."

By the time I became his Research Associate at the University of California in 1933, Professor

5

Thompson, whose primary field was medieval history, had in his files a rare collection of assorted materials on espionage and "double-dealing." My own interest was then in diplomatic history, especially of the eighteenth century, and so we pooled our resources. It was a complementary collaboration. Professor Thompson supplied his accumulation of uncommon data and general guidance; and I contributed much of the writing and the more recent materials.

We also supplemented each other in our respective linguistic skills—a necessary combination, since the core data came from foreign sources: Latin, Italian, Spanish, German, French, Polish and Russian. Between us, as it happened, we could read all of those languages. As an example: the Russian correspondence of Count Vorontzov yielded us the solution to the old diplomatic mystery of how Prime Minister Canning learned about the secret articles of the Treaty of Tilsit.

The appended bibliographic apparatus, brought up to date for this edition, indicates the range and variety of the sources on which this book is based. They are public and official, private and obscure. We found our materials in contemporary manuals and guidebooks, government reports, police dossiers, memoranda of ministers, personal letters, memoirs of diplomats, official correspondence, scholarly histories, biographies and autobiographies of participants.

There are two facets to this book. One is entertainment, and the other serious history. Some of the authentic episodes here recounted surpass fiction. At the same time this is documented history. It is a study of the development of a relatively neglected aspect of diplomacy, that of institutionalized spying and coded communication. The chapters on the techniques of diplomacy and cryptography deal with subjects that are not easily found elsewhere.

The original title of this book was *Secret Diplomacy, A Record of Espionage and Double-Dealing: 1500-1815*. It was published in London by Jarrolds, in 1937. Two editions appeared before World War II. Then came the London Blitz, which destroyed many publishing houses, and among the victims were the plates and remaining copies of this book. Since then, it has been all but impossible to obtain a copy of *Secret Diplomacy* either in London or in New York. This new edition owes its existence to the enterprise of Mr. Frederick Ungar, whose patient efforts to locate Professor Thompson's widow and to obtain our respective clearances for republication were finally rewarded with success.

SAUL K. PADOVER

The New School for Social Research
New York, June, 1963

CONTENTS

LIST OF ILLUSTRATIONS

INTRODUCTION

PERHAPS the earliest diplomatic service was that of Egypt under the Eighteenth Dynasty (1580–1350 B.C.). In the time of Sesostris I there was a regular messenger route between Egypt and Syria. The Egyptian Royal Messenger became the connecting link between the king and his provinces.

The Royal Messenger's functions were those of courier and diplomat. The Messenger—wowty ny-śwt —had military and clerical training and was treated with great respect. Of forty-eight messengers listed, two became kings, two viziers, five viceroys. The duties of a Messenger ranged from buying horses or precious stones for his king to making treaties or pacifying native rulers.

Ancient diplomacy relied upon deputations rather than upon correspondence. An embassy would be sent to conclude certain affairs and then return home. Resident ambassadors were unknown. In Athens envoys were appointed by the assembly and in Sparta by the ephors. As a general rule only those were selected for the embassy who were known to be *personæ gratæ* to the states to which they were sent. In some cases envoys were given specific instructions ; in others they were told to do their best.

The functions of ancient ambassadors included those of negotiator and spy ; they were to send home pertinent facts and news, to make alliances, to negotiate with disloyal minorities in enemy states. Generals in the field also acted as ex-officio ambassadors. Such powers were held by the Spartan kings when in the field.

Ambassadors had to have not only a knowledge of the political situation but also the ability to present their case effectively. Athenian diplomats were trained in rhetoric and oratory. Plato tells that the rhetorician Prodicus made a great impression on the Council of Five Hundred when he came to Athens on a mission from Cos. Thucydides criticizes the oratori-

13

cal deficiencies of Spartan diplomats who spoiled their case by an ineffective presentation, for the diplomacy of the period was usually open and depended upon its psychological appeal.

Communication in antiquity was always difficult and ingenious means had to be devised. Diodorus of Sicily relates that Medea and Jason made use of the old Chinese and Persian method of lighting fires on the hills as signals. According to Æschylus, Agamemnon informed Clytemnestra of the fall of Troy by means of such fire signals. When Harpagus conspired with Cyrus against his uncle the King of Medea, he put his letters to Cyrus in the belly of a hare which, together with nets, he sent through a faithful servant disguised as a hunter. When the Spartan King, Demaratus, who was an exile at the Persian court, learned that Xerxes was preparing for war against Greece, he hastily wrote a message on a tablet of wood, covered the letters with wax, and sent it through a servant to the magistrates of Lacedæmon. Aeneas (*Poliorcet.*, cap. 3) mentions a message written on tree leaves which covered the putrid ulcers of a disguised beggar. Ovid refers to secret messages inscribed on the bearer's flesh.

Herodotus relates that when Hystiœus visited Darius in Persia he wished to communicate with his ally Aristagoras in Greece about revolting from the Persians. The message being of a dangerous nature, Hystiœus employed an ingenious device to transmit it. Pretending to cure one of his servants who had sore eyes, he shaved the man's head and imprinted the message on the skull. When the servant's hair was grown, Hystiœus told him that for a perfect recovery he should go to Aristagoras who, by again shaving his head, would cure his eyes.

Messengers were often dressed as beggars, sometimes concealed in coffins, and occasionally disguised as beasts. At times a message would be engraved on thin plates of lead and fastened to the thigh of an expert swimmer. According to Frontinus (*De Stratag.*, lib. 3, ch. 13), when Lucullus wished to inform a besieged city that he was coming to its relief he put the communication into two bladders, between which a soldier, disguised as a sea-monster, swam into the city. If there was no river, messages were tied to pigeons, swallows, or arrows.

There was, of course, reason for all this secrecy in communication, for most rulers had their spies, and some even a well-developed intelligence service. Procopius, the sixth-century Byzantine historian, tells that before the time of Emperor Justinian spies were an important part of statecraft.

" The spies," Procopius writes, " were organized in the following manner : A number of men used to be supported at the State's expense, whose business it was to visit hostile countries, especially the court of Persia, on pretence of business or some other excuse, and to observe accurately what was going on ; and by this means, on their return, they were able to report to the emperors all the secret plans of their enemies, and the former, being warned in advance, took precautions and were never surprised. The system had long been in vogue amongst the Medes. Chosroes, by giving larger salaries to his spies, none of whom were born Romans, reaped great benefit from this precaution. Justinian, having discontinued this practice, lost considerable territory, especially the country of the Lazes, which was taken by the enemy, since the Romans had no information where the King and his army were."

King Hakim, an eleventh-century Moslem ruler, had an omnipotent secret police system, including women spies. At the battle of Bouvines (1214), both King Philip Augustus of France and Emperor Otto IV had organized intelligence service to report on the movements of the opposing armies. During the Anglo-French war (1293–1298) an English knight, Sir Thomas Turberville, was a spy in the service of the

French King Philip IV. Turberville had been captured by the French and imprisoned at Rheims. King Philip, offering the knight a grant of land to the value of one hundred pounds but requiring Turberville's two sons as hostages, sent him across the Channel to incite the Scotch and Welsh against King Edward I. In the summer of 1295 Turberville appeared in England and, as a supposedly escaped prisoner of war, was favourably received by Edward who made him a member of his Council. Turberville was caught when a letter of his to the Provost of Paris was intercepted by the English Government.

Spies swarmed everywhere and messages had to be cautiously worded. Statesmen preferred oral communication. " Besides what we have written," Pope Gregory VII (1073–1085) once added in a postscript, " there are many details about which the bearer is authorized to give you full explanation." Spying and lying in the interest of any service were accepted practices. Anna Comnena, the daughter of the Byzantine Emperor Alexis, tells that her father hated lying; but she praises him for sending letters to Bohemund's officers, thanking them for their letters to him which they had never written, in order to compromise them with their chief. Anna unblushingly admits that her father deceived the Crusaders at the taking of Nicasa; and she relates with admiration how he invited the Bogomile heretic, Basil, to a private interview, telling him that he admired his virtue and urging him to make a full statement of his doctrine, while all the time a secretary behind a curtain took down the unsuspecting Basil's confessions which were used as evidence against him to send him to the stake.

SECRET DIPLOMACY

CHAPTER I

WAYS AND MEANS

" There is something in the history of diplomacy which
inclines to be cold and forbidding, and lacks the full-blooded
leap of the larger story of human lives. Like the history of
institutions it will tend to concern itself with the development
of a system, abstracted from its human context ; it will aspire
to the mathematical theorem. There is a balancing of forces,
and adjustments of interests ; there is much that proceeds out
of the logic of a situation, there is much that seems to come by
a kind of automatic interaction. Sometimes, in rationalization,
one can almost forget that human beings are at work, with play
of mind and mood and impulse ; acts will not seem to cry out
for an explanation in personality, but will be referred to some
logic of policy. And history will fall to her greatest temptation
—hearing the tick of the clock, but forgetting to feel the pulse."
—H. BUTTERFIELD, *The Peace Tactics of Napoleon* (1806–1808)
(Cambridge, 1929), 232.

MODERN diplomacy was born in Venice.
The Republic on the Adriatic was the first
European state to protect its interests
abroad through the medium of ambassadors. According to a regulation of 1268, Venetian ambassadors
were required to give a report of their mission within
fifteen days after arrival at home in such a fashion as
to be *ad proficuum et honorem Veneciarum*. The envoys
had to deliver in writing a full and exact report of
their mission, as well as a written statement of their
answers to questions asked by the government to
which they had been accredited. The ambassadors
were forbidden to talk about politics with any person ;
nor could they accept gifts, although once, in 1523,
Ambassador Suriano at London was permitted to
keep the 500 crowns which King Henry VIII gave him.
The diplomatic missions—the envoys were known
as *legati*, *nuncii*, and in Italian, *ambasciadori*—were at
first occasional, of special purpose and short duration,

generally of a commercial nature. But the extension of Venetian domination to the Italian mainland, followed by French intervention there in 1494, caused a political revolution in Italy and compelled new changes in the diplomatic machinery. As the dynasts of Spain, France, England, and Austria developed their programmes of national aggrandizement, most of which pivoted on Italy, they found it desirable to establish embassies in the Italian courts. From the time of Louis XI of France—who, incidentally, kept himself informed of the doings of other states by means of paid secret agents—we find Venetian, Tuscan, and Milanese ambassadors in Paris. By the sixteenth century the Italian states had envoys in Spain, Austria, Rome, Burgundy, and England.

Italy thus became the pioneer in modern statecraft, with Venetian diplomacy serving as the model for all Europe. The Republic's envoys were carefully selected and their despatches, regularly addressed to the Doge and Senate, became secret histories of every country in the Occident, including the Turkish Empire. Upon their departure the ambassadors were given detailed instructions which were supplemented from time to time ; the diplomats, in turn, sent home not only political reports but also news-letters. These ciphered accounts found their way to the public and took the place of newspapers, of which there were none in Europe at that time. Some of these despatches were printed and had wide sales.

Latin was the language of the diplomatic correspondence up to the end of the fifteenth century, when Italian began to be used by the Venetians. In 1524 Ambassador Gaspar Contarini presented Emperor Charles V with a Latin letter. " I am a bad Latin scholar," the Emperor replied, " I will have it read to me bye and bye." Queen Elizabeth corresponded with the Venetian Republic in Italian. French was not introduced into European diplomatic discourse until the following century.

Closely connected with diplomatic technique was the foundation of archives, for the important documents—treaties, despatches, agreements, letters—had to be preserved for reference. The earliest European power to develop a systematic use of archives—the so-called Papal Registers—was the Papacy, which had inherited the method from the Roman Empire. Among modern states Venice was the first to establish a repository for all State documents. In fifteenth-century Spain, for example, the ministers of State kept the current papers at home ; upon the death or retirement of a minister, an inventory was made in the presence of two notaries and the documents were then delivered to the Government. These State papers were placed in *arcas* (this may be the origin of the word " archives "), chests, and deposited in the various royal castles throughout Spain. Some of these *arcas* have been preserved ; wooden chests of moderate size and beautiful workmanship, carved and gilded, heavily locked. Important personages, such as governors and ambassadors, had their own *arcas* in every palace. When travelling, King Ferdinand of Spain deposited State papers even in foreign countries, which often caused great inconvenience, as business could not be transacted without a reference to the documents. Emperor Charles V finally began to gather all State papers throughout Spain and deposited them in the castle of Simancas, where they still are—about 10,000,000 documents.

Diplomatic correspondence was mostly in cipher, sometimes so complicated as to defy analysis for centuries. The cipher of Michel, the Venetian ambassador to England in the time of Mary Tudor, was not unravelled until 1868 when two scholars, after years of independent research, found the key to the 374 signs. Even cipher, however, was not always safe, for clerks in embassies could be bribed. Noailles, the French ambassador in London, paid Michel's secretary sixty crowns a month to read the Venetian reports. A still

better way of getting at despatches was to intercept or
steal them, methods which were universally practised.
In 1515, Giustiniani, the Venetian ambassador in
London, discovered that his letters were being inter-
cepted by the English Government. Indignantly he
went to Cardinal Wolsey, the all-powerful minister of
Henry VIII, and complained. He reports to the
Doge :

" The letters received by me from your sublimity,
had been taken out of the hands of the courier at
Canterbury by the royal officials, and opened and read :
the like being done by private letters from the most
noble, the ambassador Badoer of France and others.
. . . After this preamble, I communicated to him by
word of mouth the contents of the aforesaid letters,
but varying the passages written in cipher, lest (as I
believe they have kept a copy of the opened letters)
my words might serve them as a key to the
interpretation."

Interceptions, theft, and bribery were approved
methods of diplomatic craft ; there was not a chancel-
lery in Europe, large or small, that did not practise
such means. Pope Adrian VI (1522–1523), for
example, had in his employ a young secretary named
Cisterer who was in the service of the ambassador of
Emperor Charles V to whom he betrayed all the
Pope's private affairs.

Despite the wretched roads and the danger of
travel, the expedition of despatches was frequent
and regular. Communications of great importance
were sent by couriers ; less important letters were
entrusted to the great banking houses, most of
which had Italian correspondents. Machiavelli, when
on a mission in France, sent his official despatches
to Florence through the Florentine bankers Dei, who
had a branch in Lyons. But couriers were not
always safe.

" Here," Bernardo Navagero, the Venetian ambassador in Rome, wrote to the Doge in 1556, " they

have imprisoned a courier who was on his way from the King of Spain to Naples, seizing his despatches, to retaliate for what the Imperialists did by the post, saying, that if they stopped the post because he had no licence, and that a clause in the truce forbids the post to enter garrisoned places without a licence, they detained the courier for the same cause, as he had no licence to pass through Rome, and that on the release of the post they would release the courier."

Considering the primitive method of travel and the often impassable roads, the speed of the couriers is a matter of surprise. In 1474 a courier sent from Rome by the French ambassador covered the distance to Paris in thirteen days. In 1498 the news of the death of King Charles VIII of France at Amboise reached Venice within a week, at a moment when Doge Antonio Barbarigo and the Signory were debating the question of war against the French monarch. A breathless courier, having worn out thirteen horses on the way, dashed into the Signory and blurted out: "Most Serene Prince, the King of France is dead, and to assure yourself of the truth, read this letter." In 1509 the courier of the Venetian ambassador in France rode from Blois to Venice in seven days. The Queen of Hungary—a "virago," according to Roger Ascham—once rode from Augsburg to Flanders in thirteen days, a distance "that a man can scarce do in seventeen."

The most distinguished diplomatic post in Venetian service was the Bailage. The office of the Bailo was established during the Fourth Crusade in 1204, when Venice captured Constantinople. Two and a half centuries later, when the capital on the Bosphorus fell into Turkish hands, Venice was the first Christian power to make a treaty with the Ottomans, gaining thereby the exclusive privilege of trading in the Moslem Empire. The Bailage was revived and the Bailo became the protector of Venetian commerce, exercising full civil and criminal jurisdiction even over non-Venetian foreigners.

The importance of the Bailo was so great that he was the only diplomat appointed by the Grand Council instead of the Senate. His salary was 180 ducats monthly, supplemented by 300 ducats for outfit and from 300 to 900 ducats for travelling expenses. The Bailo also carried a fund for gifts and bribes. His salary was not exorbitant, considering that he was compelled to support ten servants, one physician, an apothecary, a major-domo, and a barber. His office staff consisted of a secretary, a coadjutor, an accountant, and two or three dragoman students acting as clerks.

The duties of the Bailo were essentially those of a modern consul. Important diplomatic negotiations were not carried on by him but by an ambassador-extraordinary who went on a special mission and returned home as soon as it was accomplished. The ambassador-extraordinary was usually accompanied by fifteen servants, fifteen horses, and four grooms, all on a salary—as long as the mission lasted—of 200 ducats a month and 1,600 for expenses.

When the Bailo and his suite were ready to sail, the Government put two galleys at their disposal, with the right of calling upon escorts from the Adriatic fleet, should there be danger from pirates. As for routes, the Bailo could choose either the sea to the Aegean or, more often, one of the two land routes, both starting from Alessio. He could go the northern way through Uskiup and Adrianople or the southern way through Monastir and Saloniki. The Bailo himself, usually an elderly gentleman, travelled in a litter, while his suite rode horseback; the baggage was carried by mules and horses.

The journey to Constantinople was always hazardous. In 1599 Vicenzo Gradenigo was chosen Bailo and took the southern route through Lepanto and Saloniki. In Lepanto twelve of his servants fell ill from a " surfeit of fruit, the bad air, the ice-cold

water and the burning sun." Within four days three
servants died and twelve more sickened. By the time
the company arrived at Platamona two more servants
had died and all but five fell ill with fever ; there were
no medical facilities and no drugs. While waiting for
a ship the Venetians were attacked by brigands but
were saved in time by Turkish janissaries. By the
time Gradenigo reached Constantinople, three months
after he had started out, eighteen of his suite were
dead. He himself had a renewed attack of fever
which " rendered me so weak that I can hardly sit up
in bed." He died soon after.

When the Bailo—that is, if he was not dead—
entered Pera, where the embassy was located, he
donned a *duliman*, a close-fitting silken tunic reaching
to his ankles, and either a *ducale* (fur coat) or a long
crimson cloak of satin lined with velvet. His shoes
were of gold-embroidered crimson velvet and his
bonnet of jewel-adorned damask. The horse he rode
was draped in a crimson tabard which reached to the
ground. Thus accoutred, the Bailo was received by
the diplomatic corps and by the Turkish dignitaries.

On the day appointed for the interview with the
ministers, the Bailo went to the Divan, which was held
three times weekly, and met the Grand Vizier, three
or four Pashas, the Capudan Pasha, the Beglier Beys
of Greece and Anatolia, two Chief Justices (*Cadiles-
kiers*), three Treasurers (*Deftarders*), the Chancellor
(*Nisangi*), and the Chief of the Janissaries (*Aga*).

On the day of the first audience, the Bailo, splen-
didly robed, accompanied by his suite and his servants
bearing presents, crossed the Golden Horn from
Galata to Stambul. Upon landing, they were received
by an escort of Spahis, Janissaries, and messengers
(*Chaushes*). The cavalcade galloped up hill to the
palace. The entered the first court of the Seraglio
where the cavalry was drawn up in order. Here the
Bailo dismounted, left his suite behind, and walked
into the turfed second court. Six or seven thousand

Janissaries stood there in absolute silence, rigid and attentive. At the extreme end of the court was the Chamber of the Divan, with pillars and tasselated marble pavements. The Bailo seated himself among the Pashas, while the servants unpacked the presents, consisting of cloth of gold, silk damask, silver plate, scarlet robes, Piacenza cheeses, confectionery. The gifts were distributed among the Janissaries who carried them along the windows of the Sultan's chamber, whence His Majesty might or might not cast an indifferent glance at the goods, and then deposited the offerings in the Treasury (*Cazna*). Incidentally, the Sultan's revenue from gifts—for no one dared approach His Majesty without presents—amounted to 8,000,000 ducats, or about as much as the income from all other sources.

In the inner court of the Seraglio, surrounded by delicate marble pillars, was the Sultan's chamber, guarded by ushers in robes of gold and silver. The ceremony required that the ambassador, or Bailo, pay his respects to the Sultan by kissing his skirt. At the door two attendants seized the envoy's arms and wrists, and introduced the pinioned man to the sacred presence. His Majesty sat on a divan covered with silk wrought in gold thread and strewn with pearls, rubies, diamonds, and other precious stones ; on the floor were spread lush Persian carpets. A brazier of solid gold, inlaid with precious stones, stood in the middle of the chamber. The Sultan, wrapped in a stiff golden robe, sat on downy pillows, perfectly motionless, his eyes on the ground, his hands in his lap. The pinioned ambassador kneeled and kissed the imperial robe ; then the breathless envoy was made to retreat backwards step by step. At the opposite end of the chamber, near the exit, the diplomat made his quavering address to a motionless, bored, and cold Sultan. If His Majesty was pleased he deigned to murmur in reply : *Giozel* (very well).

For Europeans it was always difficult to deal with

the unsophisticated and victory-flushed Turks. In 1554 Ogier Ghiselin de Busbecq, the Imperial Ambassador, was sent on a mission to Constantinople. He stopped at Buda, the capital of Hungary which was then held by the Turks, and demanded from the ruling Pasha the restitution of those places which had been seized in violation of the truce.

" I either did not promise to restore these places," the Pasha replied artlessly, " or I did promise to restore them. In the former case, a man of your intelligence must comprehend that I made a promise which I have neither the right nor the power to keep ; for my master has assigned me the duty of enlarging his dominion, not of diminishing it, and I have no right to impair his estate. . . . When you see him you can ask him for whatever you like."

But before Busbecq was admitted to the sacred presence of the Sultan he had to undergo some harrowing experiences. The pashas, " in accordance with their usual practice," wanted him first to reveal his mission to them. When they learned that the Emperor refused certain concessions to the Turks, the pashas' wrath " knew no bounds," insisting that they could not enter the Sultan's presence with such despatches. Busbecq pressed them for the interview, but the pashas angrily asked the ambassador " how many spare heads we thought they had got, that we expected them to introduce us to their master's presence with an answer of this kind ? " The Turkish officials warned Busbecq that " his wisest course was to keep quiet, and not arouse his (Solyman's) anger ; there was no need to hasten the evil day ; it would come quite soon enough." The other Turks with whom the ambassador and his suite spoke were no more encouraging : " for the mildest punishment they treated us with was, that two of us would be thrust into a noisome dungeon, while the third (Busbecq himself) would be sent back to his master, after being first deprived of his nose and ears." For six months the Imperial embassy was held prisoner, " although," Busbecq reports sadly, " we were ambassadors."

Busbecq did not, after all, lose his nose or ears. Instead, he had an amusing experience. A courier arrived from Vienna with despatches for the ambassador. The Turks, who were fast learning Occidental ways, seized the courier, who succeeded in concealing the Emperor's despatches but had to hand over the private letters. The pashas knew from their interpreter Ibrahim, a Pole by birth, that European governments did not write secret messages in ordinary characters but in cipher. They picked up one letter, held it to the light, and because the paper was thin, they could see the words. " I have found it," exclaimed the delighted Ibrahim. The pashas told him to break the seal and read the message. Ibrahim, however, could not make out a single word. Had Ibrahim forgotten Christian characters ? the pashas demanded angrily. The interpreter replied that it was the sort of writing known only to confidential secretaries. " But if so," the pashas said, " why do you delay ? Why don't you hurry off at once to the Secretary of the Venetian or Florentine Bailly ? "

The Italian diplomats noticing that what Ibrahim brought was a private letter to Busbecq from a Burgundian friend, shrugged their shoulders and blandly informed poor Ibrahim they could not read it without a key. The crestfallen interpreter returned to the pashas ; they held a conference. Suddenly one pasha had a brilliant idea. " There is the Patriarch," he exclaimed, " who is acquainted with many kinds of characters ; if he, being an old man and a Christian, cannot read them, no one else can." Ibrahim dashed off to the Patriarch. The venerable man was pious, and probably holy, but European languages were a greater mystery to him than the Godhead. Shrugging his ancient shoulders in perplexity, and with a deprecatory gesture, he said the characters were neither Greek, nor Latin, nor Hebrew, nor Chaldee.

Ibrahim returned more dejected than ever. Then Ali Pasha said to Grand Vizier Roostem : " *Cardassi* (brother), I remember I had a slave, by birth an Italian, who knew all languages and characters. Were he still alive I feel no doubt that he could have read and interpreted these characters ; but he died some time ago."

Constantinople had exhausted its learning, and the letter (probably in French) remained unread. The pashas decided to deliver the mysterious epistle to Busbecq. Ibrahim brought it. Busbecq pretended to be enraged : It was a violation of international law to intercept and open his private correspondence ! Poor Ibrahim told Busbecq of his misadventures with the letter; the ambassador said he would read him passages from the epistle. When the interpreter returned, the pashas wanted to know whether Busbecq could read " those characters." " As easily," Ibrahim replied, " as his own name." Roostem was struck with admiration. " The ambassador," he opined, " is a young man, and yet he understands what the old Patriarch cannot so much as read ; he will certainly turn out a great man, if he attains old age." The qualifying clause, coming from a Grand Vizier in Turkey, did not sound so good ; but Roostem's heart was filled with respect. Such a man as Busbecq deserved a better fate than to be a dog of a Christian. Roostem tried to convert the ambassador to Mohammedanism. Busbecq politely refused.

" But," Roostem asked sadly, " what is to become of your soul ? "

We have seen how ambassadors were received in Constantinople. It may be of interest to contrast it with a reception in England, where Sebastian Giustiniani represented Venice in the time of King Henry VIII. The description is from the famous diary of the Venetian official, Sanuto :

" On St. George's Day the ambassadors were escorted by two lords and a numerous retinue in a large barge to a place called Richmond. Having landed with about 200 persons we went into the palace, and on entering a very handsome and lofty hall a collation was served of nothing but bread and wine, according to the custom here. And this being ended, we passed through some other chambers, where we saw part of His Majesty's guard, consisting of 300 English, all very handsome men in excellent array, with their halberds; and by my faith I never saw finer fellows."

The ambassadors were then ushered into the royal presence and found the King (Henry VIII) gorgeously attired in the robes of the Garter. After the introductions came an oration in fine Renaissance Latin, then Mass, followed by a sumptuous dinner. May Day came and the court went to celebrate the festival in Greenwich. Two English lords called on Ambassador Giustiniani to conduct him to the monarchs. "Her Majesty," to quote again from Sanuto's diary, "was most excellently attired and very richly, and with her were twenty-five damsels, mounted on white palfreys with housings of the same fashion most beautifully embroidered in gold; and these damsels had all dresses slashed with gold lace in very costly trim, with a number of footmen in most excellent order." Then the festivities started.

Diplomatic ceremonial was rigidly observed. Early in the seventeenth century the English ambassador at Venice caused some surprise when he introduced his secretary, Albertus Morton, to the Doge in Council, "a thing he had never done before." The ambassador explained that the Spanish envoy, Don Francesco de Castro, had introduced his secretary, "and if that was done as an indication of superiority the Ambassador of England could not let it pass unnoticed."

There was little change in diplomatic procedure with the passing of the centuries. In the eighteenth century Lord Northampton, the British ambassador, was received at Venice by sixty senators who led him

to the door of the Collegio. The Doge and College
rose ; the ambassador uncovered, bowed thrice, and,
leaving his suite behind him, mounted the dais, seating
himself on the Doge's right. The envoy then covered
his head and handed his credentials to the chief of the
state ; while the Doge read, the ambassador took off
his hat and then put it on again. The Doge rose,
made a brief reply, and welcomed the ambassadors ;
each time the King's name was mentioned the envoy
raised his hat. The ceremony over, the diplomat made
three bows and retired, accompanied by sixty senators.

An English ambassador-extraordinary had certain
privileges, which were not established, however, until
the seventeenth century. He was lodged and maintained at the Republic's expense, at a cost of from
500 to 600 ducats ; he had a free box in each Venetian
theatre, and, upon his departure, the Senate voted him
a gold chain and medal valued at 2,000 scudi.

CHAPTER II

THE AGE OF CHARLES V

" Cui licit finis, illi et media permissa sunt."—JESUIT MAXIM.

I

SIXTEENTH-CENTURY governments, especially those of the Italian states, were personal and capricious. Their foreign policy was unscrupulous and amoral, and, particularly that of the Italian despotisms, short-sighted. Even the popes were no exception ; they played the same game as their secular rivals and competitors. A pontiff like Leo X, for example, was as false and double-dealing as any *condottiere*, being a Medici who had learned guile at the Florentine court. Leo X blandly made treaties with rival kings at the same time, without intending to be faithful to any of them. According to a famous Catholic historian, Leo acted on the principle " that the conclusion of a treaty with one party need offer no obstacle to the conclusion of another in an opposite sense with his opponent."

The aggressions of the great powers in their attempts to consolidate their dominions brought about close international contact, with the balance of power principle becoming a reality if not a formulated concept. The sixteenth century saw the growth of diplomatic treachery and political artifice on a hitherto unheard of scale. Violence and duplicity replaced whatever moral bounds still prevailed from the Middle Ages. There was a moral revolution in European society.

" Courtesans," Sir John Cheeke reported from Venice in July, 1554, " in honour, haunting of evil houses noble, breaking of marriage a sport ; murder, in a gentleman, magnanimity ; robbery, finesse if it be clean conveyed—for the spying is judged the fault and not the stealing ; religion, to be best that best agreeth with Aristotle's *de anima ;* the common tenant, though not in kind of tenancy, marvellously kept bare, the gentleman, nevertheless, yet bare that keepeth him so ; in speech cautious, in deed scarce ; more liking in asking than in giving. The farther they go into Italy it is said to be the worse."

Early in the sixteenth century the Venetians were ominously gaining ground on the Italian mainland. Rumours had it that the Republic was aiming at an Italian monarchy and that it would spare neither papacy nor communes ; the Venetians were, in fact, claiming Faenza and Rimini, then held by the Pope.

Pope Julius II, lining up behind him Florence, France, and the Empire, and acting in deepest secrecy, formed the League of Cambrai against Venice, the allies binding themselves to fall upon the Republic suddenly without a declaration of war. In January, 1509, news of this " unprincipled treaty of spoliation " reached the Republic. Time was pressing and the Signory decided to despatch an ambassador to England, to urge King Henry VII to attack France. The roads were everywhere blocked by the allies " the fire was raging most fiercely in every quarter." The government searched all over Venice for one " who had the heart to venture through such a hurricane." Finally Andrew Badoer, a veteran diplomat in his sixties, was chosen for the perilous mission.

Badoer hesitated to undertake the dangerous journey but he finally succumbed to the " certain promise of 100 ducats per month," and the persuasion of the Doge. " Knowest thou not," the Doge said to him, " how those whom the Council of Ten sends on similar errands of need are rewarded ? "

" In short," Badoer relates, " I allowed myself to be persuaded, and in six days got ready ; and departed in so auspicious an hour, that after riding twenty-six days I reached London . . . ; nor do I know what more could have been expected of a man at my age." The trip was full of disasters. " I rode incessantly day and night," Badoer continues, "in disguise, crippling and laming myself so, that I shall never again be as sound as I was previously ; for when on the Mount St. Gothard, my horse fell under me, whilst riding over ice and in the dark, I received such a wound on my right leg, that it was bared to the bone two inches deep, and by good fortune he fell to the right ; for had he slipped on the other side, I would have gone down a precipice." With bruised body and swollen legs Badoer reached the Rhine where he embarked on a boat. "The bottom of this boat struck upon some sedges under water, in the middle of the stream, near a shoal, past which the water rushed with great violence ; the boat went over on its side, and there we were, between the sedges and the shoal, when from the shock, the planks of the boat separated, and she was carried to the shoal, on which we all jumped immediately."

Suspicion was everywhere alive, and when Badoer reached Strasbourg, he had to be careful not to be caught by the Emperor's spies. "It behoved me to give account to everybody of what I was doing, and not change colour whilst telling my tale ; so sometimes I passed for an Englishman, and sometimes for a Scotchman, whilst at others I thought it safer to make myself out a Croat, and subject of the Emperor's, saying I was on my way to the court (the Emperor was then in Flanders). . . . With this pretence, I went on for some days, having made my face very black according to a device of my own ; and when I had passed the territory where he was, I replied to all inquiries that I was a messenger of the King of England."

Badoer's exertions were in vain. Having braved innumerable perils in traversing Europe to reach " the end of the world," as England then was to a cultivated Italian, he arrived at London only to find Henry VII dying.

Foiled in her first attempt, Venice decided to buy

off the Pope, and granted him his claims to Imola,
Cesena, Cervia, Ravenna, and portions of Romagna.
The Holy Father, however, had to maintain publicly a
hostile front, while secretly working against the
coalition which he himself had created. Venice was
defeated at the very moment when her publisher
Aldus Manutius gave the first printed edition of Plato
to the world. Pope Julius finally allied with Venice
against France and expected England to join the
alliance. When the furious Pope heard that England
and France had made peace, he prepared galleys at
Ancona for flight, and exclaimed: "You are all
scoundrels."

II

Emperor Charles V and his son Philip II cast their
shadows over sixteenth-century Europe. Charles was
born in 1500 and his son and successor died in 1598 ;
together the two men spanned and affected the whole
century.

The grandson of Emperor Maximilian I on his
father's side and of Ferdinand and Isabella of Spain on
his mother's, Charles, at the age of sixteen, inherited
the two most powerful monarchies in Europe and
vast colonies in America. Men said that the sun
never set on Charles' dominions.

Charles' grandmother, Isabella of Spain, has often
been praised for her virtues. In truth, both she and
her husband Ferdinand were perfidious and brutal,
when judged even by sixteenth-century standards.
Isabella took greatest pleasure, she admitted, in four
things. *Hombre d'armas en campo, obisbo puesto en
pontifical, linda dama en la cama, y ladron en la horca.* Out
of piety and rapacity the Spanish Queen introduced
the Inquisition in her dominions. The cruelty of the
Inquisition caused such an outcry that the Pope was
compelled to send a legate to investigate its activities.
Hotly denying the charge that she instituted the
Inquisition in order to confiscate the victims' property,

Isabella bribed the legate to make the inquiry innocuous —on condition that the Pope absolve her from simony. " I have caused great calamities," the devout Queen, who identified her own interests with those of God, admitted, " and depopulated lands, provinces, and kingdoms " ; but she did it, she said, for the love of Christ and the Holy Mother.

Charles' paternal grandfather, Emperor Maximilian I, was a no less pious person. When his second wife died he decided to remain celibate in order to qualify for the papacy. " He would," Maximilian impersonally informed his daughter, " then be ordained a priest and afterwards canonized as a saint; his daughter, therefore, would after his death be obliged to venerate him, whereat he should feel very much glorified. With 200,000 or 300,000 ducats he hoped to carry his point with the cardinals." The letter was signed : " Your good father, Maximilian, Pope that is to be."

Alas for his ambitions, Maximilian, having no money to bribe the cardinals, was deprived of sainthood. He pawned his best jewels with the opulent Fuggers to raise the large sums needed to " refresh the parched throats of the cardinals," but in vain. In the sixteenth century the papal throne cost more than an Emperor could afford to pay.

But ambition was not extinguished in Maximilian. If he himself could not be Pope then his young grandson should be Emperor. The Holy Roman Empire was a medieval vestige, without form or unity, a loose congeries of states held together by tradition, a skeleton whose breath had expired in the thirteenth century. The title of Holy Roman Emperor, however, was coveted by every monarch in Europe, for it implied titular supremacy over Christendom.

Unfortunately Maximilian was old and poor and deeply in debt to the Fuggers. Jacob Fugger—" this man is learned and hath gathered such a library of Greek and Latin books as is thought no man else to have "—loaned the impecunious Emperor 2,000 florins, for he had " nothing to eat." Young Charles borrowed 94,000 from the same banking house, promising to pay after his election ; but his grandfather informed him that at least 450,000 would be necessary to buy the Electors.

The Habsburgs, however, reckoned without their French enemy, for King Francis I maliciously entered the market as competitor for the Imperial crown. Francis I was ready, he said, to buy the glittering title even if he had to spend half of his kingdom's annual revenue, which was estimated at 3,000,000 livres. But that was only a boast, for the French King was short of cash and when he asked the Genoese bankers to loan him 80,000 scudi he was politely refused. The Lyons and Antwerp branches of the Florentine bankers likewise rebuffed the French King. Only Francis' rich mother trusted her son by loaning him 100,000 écus, which was insufficient to buy the title.

The Italian and German moneylenders showed greater confidence in the Habsburgs than in the Valois. In January, 1519, the bankers formed a pool, the house of Anton Welser contributing 110,000 florins, the house of Filippo Gualterotti adding 55,000, and two Genoese firms participating with 110,000. The Habsburgs did not get cash but notes payable in Augsburg and Frankfort, to be liquidated after Charles' election. The notes were deposited in the safety-boxes of Jacob Fugger.

The French king asked Fugger for a loan of 300,000 écus, but the Augsburg banker thought it better to refuse, wishing, he said, to remain a " good and faithful subject of our king and lord." If the bankers would not trust the French King there was little likelihood that the Electors would. Nevertheless, King Francis offered the Electors double the price the Habsburgs were willing to pay. The Electors were practical business men ; although they did not take the French King's offer seriously they increased their demands on Charles who was furious at the hold up.

By March the price of the crown had risen to 850,000 florins and the Habsburgs had to borrow another 543,000 florins from the Fuggers, 143,000 from the Welsers, and 165,000 from the Italians. The seven Electors were paid at the moment they handed in their votes, about 100,000 florins per Elector. Councillors, princes, nobles, and servants all shared in the loot. The Swabian League and the hero Franz von Sickingen received no less than 171,000 florins. The Imperial cities, members of the supreme court, the Swiss Guard, the deputies all received good Rhenish gulden. Finally Emperor Charles V had to borrow 125,000 pounds at Antwerp to celebrate his pompous coronation at Aachen.

III

The thirty-six years during which Charles V reigned (1519–55) were filled with interminable wars, for the Emperor possessed more power than was good for his soul and less humanity than was good for his subjects. He fought the Pope and the German Lutherans, the English and the Turks, the Italians and the French, especially the French.

Charles' duel with Francis I was of long standing. The two monarchs, fighting for the supremacy of Christendom, neglected no weapon of war or diplomacy. Their particular pawns were Venice and Turkey.

In 1537 Venice declared war on the Ottomans, having been promised the active aid of Charles V and the Pope. The Republic, however, received no support from either Christian sovereign and was badly defeated by the Turks. Venetian embassies were rudely rebuffed by the Ottomans. In despair the Republic appealed to King Francis I to mediate and the French King instructed his ambassador, Antoine Rinçon, to do what he could for the Venetians. Rinçon bribed the pashas with 67,500 livres' worth of

FRANÇOIS I

gifts and the Turkish Government promised to receive
the Venetian envoys.

Luigi Badoer, burdened with two sets of contradictory instructions, was sent to Constantinople. On
the one hand the Senate supplied the ambassador with
30,000 ducats to bribe the Turks, instructing him to
make peace only on the basis of the *status quo* and
under no condition to cede any territory. The Council
of Ten, on the other hand, told Badoer to relinquish
the cities which the Turks demanded.

Though handicapped by contradictory instructions,
Badoer might have slipped out of this diplomatic
tangle if he had not been betrayed by two Venetian
brothers, one of whom was secretary to the Senate
and the other to the Council. These two secretaries
sold the information to Bishop Guillaume Pellicier, the
French ambassador in Venice, who hurriedly transmitted it to Constantinople. Thus, when the unsuspecting Badoer arrived in Turkey the Sultan and
pashas knew exactly what his instructions contained.

Prepared to bargain, Badoer was shocked by the
sudden rudeness of the pashas. They told him that
he was a " liar and impostor " and that unless he
" produced all his instructions " the Turks would
destroy Venice " with fire and sword." The helpless
ambassador, tricked and intimidated, was compelled
to sign a disastrous peace, relinquishing the Venetian
possessions in the Archipelago and the Peloponnesus.

This peace was favourable to France, since a weak-
ened Venice could no longer be of much help to
Emperor Charles V. His Imperial Majesty, therefore,
was furious and resolved to revenge himself—not on
King Francis I, but on the French ambassador Rinçon
who was responsible for Venice's diplomatic defeat.

The Emperor's hatred was to cost Rinçon his life.
It is a strange and sanguinary story.

After the treaty was concluded Rinçon left Turkey for
France to consult with the King about plans for a new
war against the Emperor. The latter watched Rinçon's

movements with anxiety and ordered his spies to track him on his way to Italy. The French Government, knowing that the Imperialists were out "to get" Rinçon, took measures to protect the ambassador's life by circulating a rumour that he was taking the route through Switzerland. Wherefore the Spanish governor of Milan prepared an ambuscade along the Po River.

Rinçon and his companion Fregoso took the river route, despite the pleas of Du Bellay, the French governor of Piedmont, to travel at night through Papal territory. Rinçon was half-minded to agree, but Fregoso refused to be persuaded that there was danger. In the end they both decided to continue on the road which, they said, was *le plus aisé, non le plus sur*.

Near Verolino a courier arrived from Du Bellay with urgent advice that the two men change their route. If they remained obstinate they should hand over " their instructions, letters of credit, and papers," which he, Governor du Bellay, would safely transmit to Venice. Du Bellay, it seems, was sure that the men were to be ambushed. Rinçon gave up the papers and sailed down the river. Neither he nor Fregoso was ever seen again.

Weeks passed and not a trace was found of Rinçon and Fregoso. When the Imperial ambassador in Venice was asked whether he knew anything about the two missing men, he replied blandly that in all probability they were being held for ransom by bandits. Another Imperial dignitary, the Governor of Milan, expressed himself as " amazed at this affair."

For three months French diplomats and agents searched all over Italy. Then the French ambassador Pellicier informed Du Bellay that he had found one of Rinçon's boatmen. " He told me," Pellicier wrote, " that those poor gentlemen had arrived slain on the boat, and that he himself had carried them to a little island where their supplies were." The other boatmen were kept in a Spanish dungeon in Piacenza. With the aid of Du Bellay they escaped to Turin and told that armed ruffians had attacked the boat and killed Rinçon and Fregoso.

Even the Pope was scandalized, for no one doubted that the murder was committed by the Emperor's emissaries. The French King lodged a formal protest before the Imperial diet at Regensburg. The Emperor was coldly disdainful. " That," Francis I said, " was carrying things too far." . . . And he declared war on Charles V. " I shall show him that I am King of France."

CHAPTER III

THE AGE OF PHILIP II

"No great country was ever saved by good men, because
good men will not go the lengths that may be necessary."—
HORACE WALPOLE.

I

IN 1556 Philip II succeeded his father in the kingdom of Spain, the Netherlands, and Latin
America. Together with the lands he also took
over the Habsburg ambition to dominate Christendom
and to advance the cause of Catholicism. The situation
in Europe was such that there was little to hinder
Philip from carrying out his schemes. France was
torn by factions and disrupted by civil war. Italy
was not united. The Germanies were split. Russia
had not yet emerged. England under Elizabeth,
whose right to the crown was contested by the
Catholics, was then just beginning to rise as a great
power.

The reign of Elizabeth can be understood only in
terms of personal and political insecurity. If her vacil-
lations seem bewildering and her contradictions incom-
prehensible, one must remember that she was in
constant danger of losing not only her throne but also
her life. She lived in a period of political instability
and social brutality and soon learned that wiles and
flattery were good things, but coercion and bribery
better. She became a master of diplomatic technique
and played the game like the best of men.

The English Queen's training and background
fitted her to be a successsful adversary of Philip II.
She could lie and bribe as deftly as her royal contem-
poraries. Her court and capital swarmed with Spanish
spies who reported to their master that England was
on the verge of ruin, being "without money, men,
armour, fortresses, practice in war, or else good
captains." The Spanish King never relaxed in his
efforts of conquering the country and humbling the
heretic Queen. But Elizabeth fought Philip with

every conceivable weapon. She not only bribed and flattered and wheedled, but also corrupted Spanish officials in the Netherlands and paid Sir Jasper Schetz, " factor and councillor to King Philip," to manipulate the Antwerp money market in favour of London.

Although England was a poor country, a large part of the exchequer went for the support of foreign embassies. From 1572 to 1602 the English Government spent almost £120,000 sterling on ambassadors, averaging about £4,000 annually. Ambassadors learned that to serve the Queen well they had to be more than merely good diplomats. Elizabethan diplomats added a touch of gallantry to their reports. When Sir John Smith described the French court he was careful not to praise the beautiful women. " I assure Your Majesty," the wise Smith concluded his despatch, " that there is more beauty in Your Majesty's little finger than there is in any one lady that there was, or in them all."

The conflict among the sixteenth-century dynasts was complicated by religious passions. Violence embittered both rulers and peoples, and it begot greater brutality. Murder, both of individuals and of groups, became an accepted technique of political activity.

There is no moral to be drawn from the fact that the two most famous women of the age, Catherine de Medici of France and Elizabeth of England, were responsible, the one directly and the other indirectly, for the mass murder known as the massacre of St. Bartholomew.

Catherine's position in France was more precarious than that of the English Queen. The French Queen-Mother's role was the most difficult in Europe. Religious factions endangered the throne and Spanish hostility threatened the State. By her cleverness and gift for intrigue Catherine not only ruled her royal offspring but managed to play one party against the other. She had to preserve the crown for her children, to pacify the Huguenots, to placate the Catholic factions, to keep Philip II at a distance, to be on good terms with Queen Elizabeth.

This tightrope walking led directly to the massacre of St. Bartholomew. In April, 1572, Catherine's son, Charles IX, concluded an alliance with Elizabeth, directed against Spain. Philip discovered what was going on, and war between France and Spain seemed imminent. Paris was frightened. What if Elizabeth backed out ? This was precisely what the vacillating English Queen did ; at the crucial moment she gave up the alliance and left the Protestants of the Low Countries as well as France in the lurch. Catherine and Charles were in terror. How save themselves from the wrath of the Huguenots and at the same time appease Philip ? The Queen-Mother hit upon the terrible idea of sacrificing the Huguenots to propitiate the King of Spain.

The murder of several thousand people had to be hushed up somehow. France still desired friendship with Protestant England and the Government did its best " to make it appear that the massacre was a for- tuitous occurrence." It is significant that the reports of the Venetian ambassadors at Paris in this period (February 24, 1572, to April 6, 1573) were stolen from the Venetian archives.

Political assassinations did not stop with St. Bartholomew. In 1580 one Best, a secret agent of Ambassador Cobham at Paris, having killed another Englishman in a duel, decided to represent himself to the Spanish ambassador as dissatisfied with his master and to offer his services to Spain. The Spaniards became suspicious and Best was killed at the door of the English embassy.

At the same time Pope Gregory XIII ordered the assassination of a man who refused to recant his religious opinions. " And as for the Pope," the English agent Lloyd wrote to Walsingham from Paris on May 30, 1580, " he has already begun to play his part

by a massacre committed by his command." The
story is this : M. de Patris, major-domo of Cardinal
d'Armagnac at Avignon, turned Protestant. Pope
Gregory XIII invited de Patris to Rome " for some
special service." Both de Patris and his master, the
Cardinal, being suspicious, refused the invitation and
the Pope wrote to the Mayor of Avignon " to find
some means to put him (de Patris) to death." The
Mayor got busy, and a hired assassin stabbed the major-
domo to death. The news of the murder made the
townspeople take up arms, " some against the Mayor,
some with him, so that the slaughter is reported to be
great among them."

The greatest centre of violence was the Low Countries, then under Spanish rule. A letter of Philip II
to his sister Margaret, who governed the Netherlands,
will illustrate the Spanish governing mind. " His
Majesty is resolved never to suffer any change in
religion in his estates . . . ; he recommends that new
means of punishing the heretics be discovered, not
that he approves that the death penalty cease—such an
idea is far from his intentions ; he does not believe
that such an indulgence would be agreeable to God
or useful to religion, but something should be done
to deprive the heretics of that species of glory which
they attach to capital punishment and which makes
them face death with an impious fanaticism."

This letter is typical of sixteenth-century statecraft.
Here is an identification of politics with religion, and
the advocacy of violence as a means of governing.
Philip II, to be sure, had the misfortune to be the ruler
of the Low Countries at a time when they were the
burning-glass of Europe. The provinces were divided
among themselves, Catholic against Calvinist, noble
against burgher. Here every European problem found
its reflection in intensified form. The crown was
challenged ; the Church was attacked. Philip II's
hold on the Netherlands threatened to break when

the nobles joined the middle classes in their opposition to his autocratic government, hoping to wrest power for themselves. Philip at first tried to seduce the aristocratic leaders, especially Counts Egmont and Horn, but the Spanish plans fell into the hands of the English ambassador, who had bribed a Spanish secretary, and warned the rebels.

Revolutionary sentiments spread among the lower classes and the rebels submitted a compromise to the Duchess of Parma who, out of fear, promised to cease persecuting the Protestants. Encouraged by the concession, the repressed masses rose in revolt in the cities, established the reformed religion, and attacked the Catholics. The privileged aristocracy, considering their quarrel with the King a private affair between gentlemen and dreading a victory of the common people, combined with the Government in a ferocious suppression of the revolt.

At Madrid King Philip was outraged at the insurrection. He sent the Duke of Alva, an experienced soldier, proud, astute, and brutal, with a small troop of· picked men to Brussels. Alva took over the government, instituted a reign of terror, and executed two of the leaders, Counts Egmont and Horn. The Prince of Orange, a distinguished Protestant chief, wisely retired to Germany, where he attempted an unsuccessful invasion of the Netherlands.

" We continue to arrest," Alva announced triumphantly to Philip in April, 1568, " the devastators of the churches, the consistorial ministers, and those who have taken up arms against Your Majesty. On Ash Wednesday we took more than five hundred. . . . I shall soon proceed against the refractory cities."

As the opposition increased, so did Alva's brutality. " The fright," he informed Philip, " is so great here, and the executions which have taken place have inspired such a terror that there is a belief here that the bloodshed will never cease." Even the hardened soldier was uneasy at the results of his slaughter.

" Commerce," he wrote to his King, " begins to decline because foreigners dare not entrust anything to the natives here, believing that their goods might be confiscated any day, and the inhabitants themselves have no confidence in each other, neither father in sons, nor brother in brother."

The Prince of Orange's attempted invasion of the Low Countries only increased Alva's ferocity. Feeling against the Spaniards was so bitter that Orange offered a perpetual pension of 1,000 écus to anyone who would assassinate Alva. King Philip retaliated by publishing a ban against Orange, offering gold and a patent of nobility to whoever " should deliver this pest to us, dead or alive."

Orange escaped a number of attempts on his life. In 1584 a Burgundian named Balthazar Gérard approached the Prince as he entered his chamber and shot him with a pistol under the breast. Orange dropped dead and Gérard, shouting : " *Sauve moi la vie, je conterai tout*," fled towards the ramparts where he was caught. " What is the matter," the murderer asked, " have you never seen a man killed before now ? It is I who have done the deed, and would do it if it were still to do." Upon being teased that he had not killed the Prince, Gérard " regretted that more than the punishment which he should receive." For two weeks the murderer was tortured. " His right hand was pressed and burnt off with a hot engine made to that end, afterwards the flesh pulled from his legs, arms and other parts with fired pincers and then his body cut open and quartered alive." But he remained resolute and would not repent.

II

In the inextricable web of international intrigue which constituted diplomacy in the sixteenth century, it was difficult for ambassadors and agents to avoid suspicion of corruption. The case of Sir Edward Stafford, for example, still remains a puzzle.

Stafford, a descendant of a distinguished family and a relative of Queen Elizabeth, was made ambassador to France in 1583. He was inexperienced in diplomacy and worked under the double handicap of being disliked by " Mr. Secretary " Walsingham, to whom he had to send his despatches, and left unprepared by Sir Henry Cobham, whom he replaced at Paris.

Cobham, Stafford complained to Walsingham, " has not shown me so much as the copy of a letter or anything else which might instruct me what course to take ; or what humour the men of this Court are of." When the inexperienced Stafford begged Cobham to enlighten him about the personnel of the French court, the departing ambassador told him that it was " no purpose " for Stafford to know anything about that, " for that which is to-day is not to-morrow." Nor would Cobham inform Stafford about the confidential agents or those well disposed towards England. " I desired him," Stafford concluded sadly, " to deal franklier with me, for no returning ambassador ever left his successor so bare. He answered that Sir Amyas Paulet left him worse, without paper, discourse or man."

To make a good impression on Elizabeth, Stafford sent his despatches frequently and regularly. Instead of receiving thanks, however, he was gently warned by Walsingham not to be so zealous. Her Majesty, the Secretary informed the ambassador, " is many times so offended with the charges of often posting as I dare not make her privy of all the despatches I receive from you." When he himself, Walsingham added, was ambassador at Paris he " did not oftentimes hear from hence once in two or three months," and concluded with the advice that Stafford should " not write but upon occasions of good importance."

Stafford began to suspect that Walsingham was deliberately concealing his despatches from Elizabeth in order to get him in trouble with the Queen. " I know," Stafford complained of Walsingham, " that by his means the Queen has had false advertisements of preparations here from his factors and has been incensed that news of importance should come from others, and some have come from me and he has kept them a day and delivered his first."

Despite obstacles, Stafford established an intelligence system at Paris for the purpose of acquiring secret information about Spain. His friend the Venetian ambassador, he said, " serveth my turn willingly," but unfortunately the Venetian's information was insufficient. The ambassador of Savoy was more difficult to win over, being in " disposition altogether Spanish." But Stafford did his best to gain the Savoyard's confidence " by my wife's well usage of his wife, who hath found herself beholding unto her."

For reasons known only to himself, Walsingham never trusted Stafford, who was an indifferent Protestant and had friendly contacts at Paris with Mary Stuart's agents, Charles Paget and the Archbishop of Glasgow. Walsingham sent one Rogers (*alias* Nicholas Berden) to Paris to keep an eye on the ambassador. Rogers discovered that Stafford forwarded Catholic letters to England, aided the papists, and revealed to them valuable secrets. The most serious charge against Stafford was that he was bribed by the Duke of Guise to show him the English despatches. If that was true, the French would realize Elizabeth's double policy towards the Netherlands, the English Queen urging her ambassador to work for the preservation of " these Low Countries, . . . either from conquest by the King of Spain or intruded into by the French King." Among Stafford's papers one could also read a letter of Walsingham in which the Secretary disapproved of Elizabeth's policy in the Netherlands ; " for we neither help these poor distressed countries ourselves, nor yet suffer others to do it."

Perhaps because he distrusted the reports of a spy,

Walsingham took no action against Stafford. Yet
there is some evidence that the English ambassador
betrayed his Queen. In 1585 Bernardino de Mendoza,
Spanish ambassador at Paris, reported to his government that he believed Stafford could be bribed to give
information to Spain. We must keep in mind that
Spain was at this time the bitterest enemy of England.
In May, 1586, Mendoza again wrote to King Philip II :
" Charles Arundel, an English (Catholic) gentleman,
to whom Your Majesty granted eighty crowns pension
a month, in respect of the Queen of Scotland, was
constantly in the house of the English ambassador
here when he was in Paris, which Muzio (the Duke of
Guise) assures me was at his instructions, as the
English ambassador was needy, and he, Muzio, had
given him 3,000 crowns. In return for this the
ambassador gave him certain information through this
Charles Arundel."

Stafford was indeed needy ; he was a lavish nobleman and a gambler, and his ambassadorial pay was
insufficient to keep him in pompous state. The
Protestant Henry of Navarre (the later Henry IV) who
was at war with the French Catholics, complained to
Elizabeth of Stafford's doings. When Stafford heard
of this, so reports the Spanish ambassador who had it
from Arundel, he " flew into a terrible rage . . . and
swore he would never be satisfied until he had been
revenged on Béarn (Henry) and the other too, no
matter by what means ; and that now was the time
for Your Majesty (King Philip II) to make use of him
(Stafford) if you wished any service done." Stafford
then urged Arundel to find out from the Spanish
King " in what way he might serve." " And," concludes the Spanish ambassador in his letter to Philip II,
" you should see by his acts how willing he was to do
so. . . . This ambassador is much pressed for money,
and even if he had not made such an offer as this, his
poverty is reason enough to expect from him any
service, if he saw it was to be remunerated." At that

moment news arrived that an English fleet was to be sent against Portugal; any information the English ambassador would sell might be extremely useful. Hence Mendoza urged his King that it was desirable to bribe Stafford, who was " ready enough to give intelligence." The Spanish King replied that Stafford should be given the " 2,000 crowns, or the jewel you suggest."

Henceforth Stafford came to be known in the secret Spanish diplomatic correspondence as the " new friend." Mendoza gave the English ambassador the jewel and money, and Stafford regularly supplied the Spaniards with valuable information. Stafford also appropriated public funds, being at least 15,000 crowns behind in his accounts.

When Drake went on his famous expeditions to " singe the beard " of the King of Spain, the latter was informed by Stafford of all the movements and activities—ships, armaments, equipment—of the doughty English sailor. When in June, 1588, the great Spanish Armada sailed for England, Stafford supplied Spain with precise news of Admiral Howard's and Drake's fleets. Stafford also betrayed Elizabeth's attempt at allying herself with Henry III of France. The ambassador hoped to make his fortune when Elizabeth " disappeared," as he phrased it, thinking that Philip II might succeed her.

Stafford was never exposed or punished. Perhaps Walsingham was not sure of his information. At any rate, his penalty was neither death nor obloquy. He returned to England unmolested, and died a respectable gentleman in 1605.

Stafford informed Spain of his country's preparations against the Armada, but he also reported to Walsingham about the Spanish fleet. " The Spanish party here," he wrote from Paris in July, 1586, " brag that within three months Her Majesty will be assailed in her own realm, and that a great army is preparing for it." Four months later an agent informed Walsingham that " King Philip manifestly has some great design against us, having made the agreement with the Focchers (Fuggers) for money payable here in a special place."

Thus England had knowledge of the Armada two years before it sailed. Early in 1587 an Englishman, Richard Gibbes, informed Walsingham of his observations in the Spanish ports. He noticed about one hundred and fifty ships and heard " talk of 300 gallies." At Lisbon Gibbes gave himself out for a Scotsman and was therefore favourably received by the Spaniards. He was taken before the " Markease " and questioned closely :

" He asked me . . . what good havens or rivers were in Scotland for a navy to come in. I answered him the Frith (Forth ?) in these parts of Scotland, for that was a fair river without danger. Also, ' whether one might ride over between England and Scotland.' I answered Yea. Then he demanded of me what parts I did ' occupy ' most. I answered Denmark, Danske, Hambrow, and all these parts, France, England and Spain. Then he asked me whether I had been at Bristo in England, or in any good harbour thereabout. I made answer, No, I was never in that part of the sea. Then . . . what good harbours or rivers were in the West part of Scotland. I answered him, I have heard there be good harbours, but I was never in them, nor about that coast. Then—whether I had been at London or in that river. I answered, Yea we came now from thence. Then—what manner of river it was to bring in a navy. I answered him, It is a very ill river, full of sands within and without sight of land, and not possible to bring in a navy."

At the same time the Spaniards sent agents to England to discover the possibilities of an insurrection. The instructions issued to one agent B show with what thoroughness Philip prepared his destruction of England.

B was to discover :

" The causes and grounds of the late division between the puritans and the protestants. Who are the heads of each party and their adherents. How the Council is divided in that point and whether of the two parties were best and fittest for the cathol(ics) to deal or join with.

" Whether they could be contented to give ear to a peace. . . .

" Whether they would doubt that the King of Spain will attempt any invasion. Where according to their judgments they fear most, if he should go about it, and which part of the realm they account weakest and worst able to resist such attempts. . . .

" What numbers of men they have ready within the realm to defend any invasion; how appointed; in what order each part shall give correspondence and succour to the other; what leaders in every part. . . .

" Whether of late they have made any new fortifications on the sea coast, where and in what order. How the new and the old is defended.

" To procure familiar acquaintance with some officer in the Queen's ships or belonging to the Admiralty; to see if any there might be brought to serve a turn (cancelled).

" To learn the cause the Lord Admiral is not employed. Whether he be ' disconted ' and poor.

" What ships of the Queen or other are at sea or in readiness at the present; in what order, how appointed and under whose charge. What number of ships they could set to sea of all sorts; how prepared, also how many out of every town and seaport.

" To learn what nobleman is ' disconted ' and poor and wherefore " (cancelled).

III

Henry III of France was pious and weak, unable or unwilling to cope with either Spain abroad or the Catholic factions at home. When Prince Alexander of Parma, acting in the name of Philip II, was sweeping the Netherlands in a series of bold conquests, the United Provinces—Brabant, Flanders, Holland, Zealand, Guelders, Zutphen, Utrecht, Friesland, and Mechlin—sent an embassy to the French King and offered him the sovereignty of the provinces under the French Crown. Such an offer would have dazzled any French king, but it terrified Henry III.

"It is mentioned in Scriptures," the quaking Henry III replied, "that one of the Jewish kings was ruined through evil counsel : may not this lesson find an application to the King of France. The goodwill of our subjects is lost, and we are diverging farther from the way in which it might be regained. From the pressure of debts there is no relief to be obtained even in times of peace. The very circle nearest to the King swarms with heretics ; attempts against the State are as common as eating and drinking : the number of discontented exceeds computation, and is daily increasing ; every one, except those who preserve their truth and fidelity, most carefully makes his own party, and the whole system of the nation is shaken. I think I see very clearly what would be of advantage to us, but I am like those who, out of obedience, would rather be drowned than save themselves. I might be, too, the only one who entertained such views, and I may be deceiving myself."

The King adorned the ambassadors of the Netherlands with gold chains and declined the proposal.

No one in Europe had any respect for the pusillanimous King of France. "*Jesus !*" Queen Elizabeth stormed at Henry III ; "*ayt il jamais esté veu qu'un prince fust jamais si espris par lacs de traistres sans avoir ou courrage ou conseil pour y respondre ? Pour l'amour de Dieux, ne dormées plus ce trop long sommeil.*"

Even the Pope was indignant at Henry's cowardice. In 1587 the hard-pressed King sent Cardinal Joyeuse to Sixtus V for aid. The Pope "held a long discourse" on "money and severity," pointing out how important it was for a "prince to be always well provided with money." "The Pope," he said of himself, "in comparison with the King of France, must seem like a fly to an elephant; yet I have, in a short space of time, collected much money, and shall soon lay by a good deal more."

In that case, the Cardinal argued, it would be easy for the Holy Father to loan the King of France some money. His Majesty, Joyeuse explained hastily, would not apply for a loan if he were not forced by necessity. "Necessity!" the Pope interrupted angrily. "Why then has the King fallen into this necessity? Why has he not laid by money for such chances. Nothing has befallen him which he should not have foreseen. *A prince without money is nothing.*"

The Pope, Joyeuse insisted, was in duty bound to help a Catholic King, for the Protestant Henry of Navarre received aid from Elizabeth and other heretics. "I should be ashamed," the Holy Father answered, "to lend the King so small a sum as 300,000 crowns."

Unable to get money or to maintain his authority against the League, Henry III invited Duke Henry of Guise, the leader of the Catholics, to his castle at Blois and had him assassinated. Half a year later, in the summer of 1589, a fanatical Dominican monk slew King Henry with a knife. Only the third Henry, King of Navarre, remained as the claimant of the French throne; but, being a Protestant, Henry of Navarre had to fight for a number of years before he became Henry IV of France.

Henry IV, to whom Paris was well worth a Mass, was both a great gallant and an astute politician. Having won a French throne, he determined to give his country the peace it needed. There were two vital problems to solve, the question of the Netherlands and peace with Spain. Philip II was old, frustrated, and weary. Henry decided to come to terms with the Spanish King even though he had to do it without the knowledge or consent of his ally, Elizabeth. In 1597 the French and Spanish plenipotentiaries met at Vervins and acted with such secrecy that neither the English, Dutch, nor Venetian representatives knew what was taking place.

The French and Spaniards came to an agreement. Fearing such an eventuality, Queen Elizabeth sent Robert Cecil to Paris to offer aid if the King continued war against Spain. Henry IV, however, was not in his capital. In the meantime, Alexander de Medici, the Cardinal who represented France at Vervins, hastily concluded the peace in order to forestall the English. The treaty gave England and Holland the right to accede, provided they did so within two months. But the Dutch refused outright and the English agent, Thomas Edmondes, hurriedly left for London.

At the news of the Franco-Spanish treaty, Queen Elizabeth blustered and threatened the faithless Henry IV with war. " If I am once free of the lion's paw," the witty French King remarked, " I'll easily save myself from the cat's claws."

The content of the Treaty of Vervins was kept in complete secrecy. English and Dutch agents tried in vain to learn what was in the document. It was the clever Venetian ambassador in Paris who succeeded where the others had failed. " At last," Ambassador Contarini reported to Venice, " hearing the Grand Ecuyer was to be sent to Spain with the articles, I succeeded, through the man who has charge of his papers, in procuring a copy."

Over one hundred and fifty years later the German historian Leopold Von Ranke, when working in the Venetian archives, found this communication of Contarini to the Senate, and folded within it was the transcript of the Treaty of Vervins with an account of how it was procured. The courier was drugged in an inn in the south of France, the proprietor having been bribed. How delicate the operation was may be appreciated by the fact that the text of the treaty was within a soldered and sealed metal tube within the courier's pouch, which also was sealed and the pouch chained to the person of the courier. After the copy was made the text was restored and tube and pouch resealed with forged seals so perfectly fashioned that not even the Foreign Office in Madrid had any suspicion that the contents had been tampered with, when the courier turned it in to the chief clerk.

Four months after the Peace of Vervins, on September 13, 1598, Philip II of Spain died, and with him the sixteenth century came to an end.

CHAPTER IV

STATECRAFT

"If there were no knaves, honest men should hardly come by the truth of any enterprise against them."—WALSINGHAM.

THE seventeenth century, one of the great epochs in European civilization, was an age of grandeur in politics. France had her Richelieu, Mazarin, and Louis XIV. Northern Europe saw the emergence of Gustavus Adolphus and the Great Elector. England had her Cromwell, and Russia her Peter the Great. It was a new Europe that was being organized on the feudal ruins and the birth of a new order threw up men of genius whose impress was felt by later centuries.

A few words about the general set-up. Europe was divided into five great monarchies—Spain, England, France, Austria, Russia—and two small ones, Sweden and the United Provinces. Two states, Bohemia and Italy, ceased to exist as independent political entities. The Protestant powers—Holland, England, Brandenburg, Sweden—successfully maintained themselves against the major Catholic states, although Spain, a country already dying from exhaustion, continued to lead the struggle against the "heretics." Spanish agents were to be found in every European court. At one time there were no less than four Spanish ambassadors in Vienna, each plentifully supplied with letters of credit.

Internally, the larger states were consolidating themselves as administrative monarchies on the Continent and as a parliamentary monarchy in England. The history of the smaller states, especially the German and Slavic, was determined by the encroachments made upon them by the great powers.

All the states were expanding, and therefore in conflict. This was a century of almost continuous wars, commercial and dynastic in nature. The pressure and play of power-politics were open, brutal, and fascinating. It was in this period that diplomacy was developed, especially by the French, to a fine art and perfected to a degree which made the old and experienced Venetians envious. From that day to this the technique of diplomacy has been what the seventeenth century has made it.

The best way to illuminate the subject is to trace the functions of the ambassador. These may be described in three words : lie, spy, bribe. " An ambassador," to quote the famous words of Sir Henry Wotton, written in the album of a friend at Augsburg, " is an honest man sent to lie abroad for the good of his country."

The job of an ambassador was not easy. His pay was usually small and his expenses great. Under James I English ambassadors received £3 6s. 8d. a day and an additional sum of £400 for expenses, couriers, and secret service. On this income the ambassador had to support his staff as well as his household, the latter consisting generally of a steward, cook, usher, chaplain, and sometimes a physician.

Ambassadorial positions were not infrequently dangerous, particularly in Venice and Turkey. In Venice, where the Government punished with life-long imprisonment or death any dignitary or official seen conversing with a foreign minister, the ambassador had to watch his step very carefully. There were many temptations, the chief one being the acceptance of bribery from foreign princes. The brilliant Wotton, who was English ambassador in Venice, considered such venality a good way " to ease an indiscreet enemy of his money " and, practising what he preached, he accepted a pension from the Duke of Savoy, while he applied for another one from Spain. (Even Lord Robert Cecil, Queen Elizabeth's minister, was a Spanish pensioner.)

The practice of bribing was a universally accepted diplomatic method. In Brandenburg under the Great Elector it was impossible to transact any business without preliminary payments to the Electoral minister and often his wife (who grew rich from this source). A list of European bribes in this period would fill a good-sized volume. In 1612, to give but a few examples, the Spanish viceroy of Naples spent 50,000 ducats on " secret " expenses ; from 1616 to 1619 the sum for *spese segrete* reached the astonishing figure of 380,000 ducats. In 1672 Louis XIV, preparing for war with Austria and Holland, spent 80,000 livres monthly in buying the goodwill of Germanic princes.

Only a portion of the " secret " funds set aside by every government was used for direct bribery. Much of the money was spent on spies and secret service. The case of Sir Henry Wotton is in point. He was a perfect diplomat who knew and practised all the arts of diplomatic chicanery, including an occasional telling of the truth. (He once advised a young diplomat to speak the truth, for " you shall never be believed ; and by this means your truth will secure yourself . . . ; and 'twill also put your adversaries to a loss.") While in Venice, Wotton practised, as he said, the " arts though not the ends " of his enemies. His house was full of diplomatic underworld figures, venal spies and corrupt intrigants. Knaves, Wotton found, were indispensable, although expensive. Italy was full of them. Wotton established secret communication with Fitzherbert in Rome and acquired all kinds of confidential news. He robbed the posts and stole Jesuit letters. The Jesuits' seals were known to him, as well as their agents and methods. Wotton had agents in Rome, Turin, Milan, and Venice and intercepted Jesuit letters in order to " light upon some of their plots and practices." After copies were made, the originals were sent on. " I must confess myself," this expert

British ambassador wrote humorously, "to have a special appetite to the packets that pass to and from these holy fathers." Wotton did this with relish, for he knew that James I found "very much sport" in reading the correspondence of the Jesuits. Sometimes (for a price, one presumes) Wotton handed over confidential information about the Society of Jesus to the Venetian Government.

It was inevitable that so much diplomatic activity should give rise to a few books on the subject. The seventeenth century saw the appearance of a number of manuals on diplomacy, and these are of considerable interest. There was Albericus Gentilis' *De Legationibus*; Jean Hotman's *L'ambassadeur* (English translation, 1603); James Howell's *Discourse of Ambassadors* (1664). A treatise on diplomacy, published in 1716, but written by a seventeenth-century French diplomat, deserves more careful attention. It was written by François de Callières and entitled: *De la manière de négocier avec les souverains;* two centuries later it was translated into English (by A. F. Whyte, *The Practice of Diplomacy*, London, 1919). De Callières was quite a personage. He was councillor to Louis XIV, private secretary to His Majesty, ambassador-extraordinary and plenipotentiary of the French King, entrusted with the treaties of peace concluded at Ryswick, and one of the Forty of the French Academy. In short, De Callières was fitted to speak of diplomatic practice with authority.

The brief manual covers every function of an envoy. An ambassador, De Callières writes, must clothe himself with care and magnificence. He should entertain frequently and well, and enter into the spirit of his environment, "but always in a light, unconstrained, and agreeable manner. . . . He must on no account neglect any opportunity of placing himself and his master in a favourable light in the eyes of these ladies (at court), for it is well known that the power of feminine charm often extends to cover the weightiest resolutions of State. The greatest events have sometimes followed the toss of a fan or the nod of a head." But at the same time the diplomat should not lose his own heart, for " Love's companions are Indiscretion and Imprudence."

A good diplomat " must reinforce his own good manners, his insight of character, and attraction of person by certain expenses." But the money should be used with care. " Wherever large gifts are offered, the giver must take care beforehand to know that they will be received in the right spirit," for " a gift presented in the right spirit, and at the right moment, by the right person, may act with tenfold power upon him who receives it." Every diplomat ought to be aware that " at every court there are certain persons of greater wit than fortune who will not refuse a small gratification or secret subsidy which may bring in large results." Among such persons are dancers, " who by the fact of their profession have an entrée less formal and in some degree more intimate with the prince than any ambassador can perhaps possess." Then there are certain officers of low rank who have close contact with the master, and with them, " a timely present aptly given may reveal important secrets." And finally, " even great ministers of State themselves may not be inaccessible by the same means."

Nor should a diplomat neglect spies. " Well-chosen spies contribute more than any other agency to the success of great plans. . . . And as there is no expense better designed . . . than that which is laid out upon a secret service, it would be inexcusable for a minister of State to neglect it." The Spaniards, De Callières points out, never neglected their espionage system ; the Spanish court established the " wise custom " of giving ambassadors an extraordinary fund called *Gastos Secretos*. " The ambassador has sometimes been called an honourable spy because one of his principal occupations is to discover great secrets."

A diplomat must have *sang froid*, and know how to dissimulate. Mazarin, De Callières says in admiration, excelled in this. Once Mazarin was sent on a mission to the Duke of Feria, Governor of Milan, to discover the duke's true feelings on a certain matter, " and he had the cunning to inflame the duke's anger and thus to discover what he would never have known if the duke himself had maintained a wise hold over his feelings." Mazarin, the crafty Italian, " made himself absolute master of all the outward effects which passion usually produces, so much so that neither in his speech nor by the least change in his countenance could one discover his real thoughts."

But all this, while important, is not enough. A diplomat should also be educated in history. He should know all the important treaties of Europe ; he should read the memoirs of great men and the instructions given to the ablest negotiators. Most valuable in this connection are the letters of Cardinal d'Ossat, that keen man who had reconciled Henry IV with Clement VIII. Likewise Mazarin's instructions given to his agents during the negotiations leading up to the Treaty of Münster (1648), in which " the Cardinal examines the interests of each European Power." In private archives the diplomat may find important books, such as those by De Noailles, Montluc, and the letters of President Jeannin.

Diplomacy, De Callières insists, is a profession and requires careful training. " The diplomatic genius is born, not made. But there are many qualities which may be developed with practice." Men of small mind should never be sent abroad, for their errors are irreparable. The Duke of Tuscany once complained to the Venetian ambassador at Rome that the Republic's agent at Florence was a person of no value. " I am not surprised," answered the ambassador ; " we have many fools in Venice." " We also have fools in

Florence," the Tuscan duke retorted, " but we take care not to export them."

An ambassador must be well versed in history and in letters. When he makes an address he should be careful and avoid the famous mistake of the ambassadors of the Isle of Samos who made a long speech to the Spartans. " We have forgotten the beginning of your harangue," the Spartans replied ; " we paid no heed to the middle of it, and nothing has given us pleasure in it except the end."

Although an envoy's business is that of an honourable spy, he should not spy himself. " Most of the great events in recent diplomatic history have been prepared by ministers sent in secret." The intricate Peace of Münster, " was not really the work of that vast concourse of ambassadors and envoys which met there and appended their signatures to the document. The essential clauses of that treaty were discussed and drawn up by a secret agent of Duke Maximilian of Bavaria sitting at a table in Paris with Cardinal Mazarin." Likewise, the Peace of Pyrenees (1659) was concluded as a result of secret negotiations at Lyons between Mazarin and the confidential Spanish agent, Pimental. " And finally, the Peace of Ryswick, to which I am a party throughout the negotiation, was devised by the same secret diplomacy before its public ratification in Holland in the year 1697."[1]

De Callières concludes with a warning for the need of permanent vigilance. The diplomat should always take great care that his despatches do not fall into hostile hands. Each ambassador should have his own cipher. " A really effective cipher is literally worth far more than its weight in gold."

[1] The Treaty of Ryswick in 1697 was dedicated to Europe by an agreement privately arranged between William III and Louis XIV, in spite of the elaborate show staged by the ambassadors and the multitudinous array of documents in evidence ; Trevelyan, *England under Queen Anne*, II, 181.

It is interesting to compare De Callières' manual
with a similar booklet written contemporaneously by a
Spanish diplomat whose name is not known.   The
Embajada Española appeared at the end of the seventeenth century and reflects Spanish diplomatic practices.   The anonymous author pays special attention
to the training of ambassadors, insisting that they must
have a knowledge of foreign languages, be aware of
the importance of precedence, and know how to value
dignity.   The author's definition of diplomacy is not
unlike Wotton's :   " *Un honrado modo de enganar.*"

" The ambassador who wishes to understand the
origin of affairs in the kingdom where he is to reside,"
the author points out, " must spend his spare time in
reading its histories or chronicles, must gain a knowledge of its laws, of the privileges of its provinces, the
usages and customs of its inhabitants, the character of
the natives, their temperament and inclination :   and
if he should desire to serve in his office with the goodwill of his own and of a foreign people, he must try
and accommodate himself to the character of the
natives, though at cost of doing violence to his own ;
he must listen to them, talk with them and even flatter
them, for flattery is the magnet which everywhere
attracts goodwill. . . . Anyone who listens to many
people and consorts with them, sometimes meets one
who cannot keep a secret and even habitually makes a
confidant of someone, in order to show that he is a
man of importance, trusted and employed by the
heads of the Government. . . . Should he lack
friends and ability to discover the truth and to verify
his suspicions, money can help him, for it is and always
has been the master-key to the most closely-locked
archives."

In all the courts of Europe, the unknown writer
points out, there are busybodies—" conduits and
gutter-spouts of political gossip."   These people spend
their lives hunting for news.   They deceive everyone.
" Money is their only love and they hate natives and

foreigners alike." An ambassador, the author warns,
should exercise extreme caution when dealing with
these " moths and woodlice," who are " a plague and
epidemic from which the body politic suffers on all
sides."

CHAPTER V

THE DYNASTS

" Les grands desseins et notables enterprises ne se vérifient jamais autrement que par le succès."—RICHELIEU.

I

JAMES VI of Scotland was worried about his chances of succeeding to the English throne upon the death of Elizabeth. His mother, the executed Mary Stuart, had been a Catholic and he himself was an indifferent Protestant. James, a descendant of the Tudors, was the rightful heir to the English crown, but he was not sure whether England would prefer a Protestant or a Catholic monarch. Good politics dictated that the aspirant for the crown have friends in both camps. King James therefore carried on secret negotiations with Grand Duke Ferdinand of Tuscany, an influential Catholic who had been the mediator between Henry IV of France and the Pope. If Paris was worth a Mass to Henry, why not London to James ?

Elizabeth's secret service discovered the intrigue, but before action could be taken the Queen died and James, having won over the powerful Cecil, was assured of the English throne. " Na, na, gud faith," the Scottish King said, " wee's not neede the Papists now."

But the King, now James I, was plagued by his former Catholic sympathies. In his defence James had recourse to authorship and composed a *Premonition to all Most Mighty Monarchs, Kings, Free Princes, and States of Christendom.* This he bound in velvet with arms and corner pieces of solid gold stamped with the rose, the thistle, the lion, and the lilies, and sent copies to every court in Europe. When Henry IV, who had once been a Protestant, received the curious book he flung it on a table with the remark that " those who held their tongues knew better how to preserve their authority and dignity." Turning to the

English ambassador, Henry said bitingly : " Writing books is no business for a king, my peer; he had better have done something else."

Upon coming to the throne James had to solve a series of problems in foreign affairs. The questions of Venice, France, Spain, and the Netherlands waited a settlement. James sent Sir Henry Wotton to Venice with instructions to establish commercial relations and to come to an agreement about English piracy in the Mediterranean. But Wotton was immediately confronted with a delicate diplomatic problem. Could he, a Protestant, enjoy the same prerogatives and immunities as a Catholic ? Up to the last quarter of the sixteenth century Venice had been " the freest part of Italy " ; but the Catholic counter-reformation had a disastrous effect on the once-powerful Republic. " None can remain there," an English agent wrote, " but such as will ' reform ' themselves to the Roman religion, which is duly and surely executed towards all men." When Wotton arrived, the Pope warned Venice to have no " dealings with the English." " Take care," the Holy Father said to the Venetian ambassador in Rome, " what you are about. . . . I promise you that, if you let the English open a change house in Venice, I will never submit to it, even though I ended by being flayed alive in that city."

Nor did the Venetian ambassadors, Molin and Duodo, fare much better at London, although for different reasons. They came to complain to King James of the depredations of the English buccaneers in the Mediterranean. James replied that " none detested such actions more than he did," but that he was helpless. He was, he frankly confessed to the Venetians, " still new to the government of England, and compelled to employ the old ministers, and, therefore, was unable to attend to everything at once, the more so that he feared his naval officers were somewhat interested in the matter." Which was a diplomatic

OLIVER CROMWELL
(1599–1658)

HENRI IV
(1553–1610)

way of saying that piracy was too profitable a business for the British Navy to be given up easily.

Henry IV of France also sent an embassy to James. The French King wanted England to aid the Dutch in their conflict with Spain and he chose his famous Protestant minister, the Duke of Sully, for the mission. In June, 1603, Sully boarded an English man-of-war at Calais; he had with him ninety gentlemen and three hundred servants, and was escorted by two French vessels. There was trouble from the start, for the French ships wanted to show their pride and began to sail ahead of the British man-of-war; promptly the English admiral ordered the bombardment of the presumptuous French vessels. Only " with great difficulty " did Sully persuade the British to stop shooting, which they did when the French commander " took in his flag."

Sully's instructions were to establish an Anglo-Dutch-French alliance directed against Spain, for which purpose he was to play upon the English prejudices against Catholic Spain and the intrigues of the Jesuits. The French plenipotentiary knew that the Dutch envoy could get no audience with James; it was therefore arranged, perhaps with the King's connivance, that Barneveld should be secretly introduced into one of the galleries at Greenwich through which James was passing. Barneveld thus met James and the two had a long conversation.

Henceforth Sully and Barneveld, who lived close to each other, worked together. Their intimate consultations aimed to give a satisfactory answer to James' question: " How can you ask me to go to war in order that you may live at peace? " In less than two weeks the two envoys had worked out the proper formula to please James, and Sully, satisfied with the results, was ready to leave London.

Sully kept Paris informed of his London activities by a triple set of despatches; one in plain writing; one in cipher to which the Council had the key; and one in cipher to which Henry IV alone had the key. The reports to Henry were brief, for the King found it as hard to read the ciphered reports as Sully to write them.

Sully was not altogether successful, for King James insisted upon an offensive and defensive alliance with France against Spain before he would undertake to aid the Dutch. After much negotiation James and Sully signed a provisional treaty, the defensive part of which was to be made public and the " offensive shall remain secret." The treaty was not achieved without heavy bribery on the part of the French statesman. The Queen of England was given jewels to the value of about 13,000 crowns ; members of the Privy Council were offered 1,000 crowns a piece, " in the King's name." Some of the councillors, Ambassador Molin reports, " made a difficulty about accepting the gift, and the question was discussed in the presence of the King of England, who declared himself content that each shall take all that was offered him."

Don Juan de Taxis, the Spanish ambassador in England, and Prince John de Ligne, the Imperial envoy, watched Sully carefully. They were fully informed of the secret negotiations and tampered with the French minister's correspondence. A French clerk in the Paris chancery was in the pay of Spain and betrayed the negotiations. When his treason was discovered he fled and was drowned in the Marne. His body was embalmed and put on trial as though he were alive.

Ambassador Taxis at London took advantage of the English minister's hostility to Sully and spent much money to purchase friendship for Spain. Taxis received from the Spanish King bills of exchange " to the amount of one hundred thousand crowns, to buy jewels and presents." Taxis, however, was hardly a success, for he had antagonized the touchy King James by presenting credentials to the British monarch

which left out his title " King of Ireland," an omission
which was probably due to Spain's desire not to offend
the Pope who claimed " that Ireland, like Naples, is a
papal fief." Taxis also outraged the Protestant populace by his secret dealings with the detested English
Catholics, among whom he distributed amulets, medals,
and crosses. Since no one dared openly take Spanish
gold, the Spanish ambassador offered to bet 100 to
1000 that peace between the Dutch and Spain would
not be concluded.

Despite the opposition of Holland and Zealand, two
provinces which were growing rich by war, peace
was ultimately concluded. France and England were
the mediators, although King James was so half-
hearted that the exasperated Henry IV called him a
" double-faced fellow " and a " fraudulent trickster."
James pursued a tortuous policy, for he was torn
between desire for peace between the Dutch and the
Spaniards and the " fear that the growing power and
commerce of the Dutch by sea will eventually
seriously damage the trade of England." The English
King well knew, as the Venetian ambassador pointed
out, " that if commerce is thrown open to the Dutch
the trade and the revenue of this kingdom would
greatly diminish."

The peace treaty was signed at Antwerp on March
30/April 9, 1609, and was guaranteed by England and
France. No one was aware that the treaty was to be
the prelude to the Thirty Years War, as both London
and Paris committed themselves to a war policy
against the Imperial House of Austria. In Germany,
where the disastrous war was soon to be fought, the
Catholic League and the Protestant Union already
faced each other in arms. Archduke Leopold seized
Juliers and the Protestant Elector of Brandenburg
took Cleves, two parallel acts which created an international crisis. Henry IV wanted to know what
James of England intended to do about it. James'
reply was that he would follow France's " counsel in

the matter of Cleves." But the English King had no
desire to be entangled in an European war; he
procrastinated and finally sent 4,000 soldiers.

Aided by Sully and dreaming of the abasement of
the Habsburgs, the vigorous Henry IV massed war
supplies and munitions at Châlons, while at Dauphiné
he prepared for the expulsion of the Spaniards from
Italy. The French King was not motivated solely by
political considerations. Personal passion also played
its role. Henry had made love to the Princess Condé
and her resentful husband had carried her off to
Belgium where the Condés were received with marked
attention. Spinola, the Spanish representative, gave
the Condés a ball where the princess danced the
" *bransle de la torche* and there were forty Spaniards that
kissed her." This was duly reported to the inflam-
mable Henry. The furious French King summoned
the faithful Sully from his bed and raged up and down
the room; then he sent three agents to demand the
princess back, declaring that the French King would
consider the lady's detention as a *casus belli* and that he
would march with 50,000 men to recover her. One
of Henry's emissaries tried to carry the princess off by
force, but was stopped by the Brussels city guards.

The Archduke who held Brussels sent an ambassador to conciliate Henry. " The King replied,"
according to the report of Ambassador Contarini,
"that . . . if fifty (thousand) were not enough he
would take a hundred thousand; and used other
violent expressions; whereupon the ambassador said
the Archduke would use all diligence to find out
where the Prince was and would induce him to return
on the understanding that the King would pardon
him."

But this comedy was a waste of time all around.
The lecherous Condé who, incidentally, was hated by
his wife, was forced to flee from Belgium and was
arrested in Milan. And the amorous Henry IV did not
long enjoy his victory. He was stabbed to death, not,

as one should have expected, by a jealous husband, but by a religious bigot.

II

About the time when France was again sinking into anarchy and Germany was preparing to commit suicide in the Thirty Years War, Muscovy's czar died and the land was without a head. The boyars were casting about for a new ruler and took an oath to choose a non-Russian czar.

In the Swedish army in Russia there was an English captain, Thomas Chamberlain, whom his compatriots who were trading in north Russia authorized to present a petition to King James I to accept the Muscovite throne. A number of influential Russian nobles were willing to accept the English King as the ruler of a country, " the revenue of which Crowne is eight millions of pounds sterlinge per annum."

Chamberlain saw profit in the enterprise and went to London where he submitted an illuminating memorandum to " my Lord Dorchester, Principall Secretarye of State." The captain pointed out that the " safety and wealth of this island dependeth principally upon the shipping thereof," and that the " number of shippes " and commerce " breedes our wealth." He described the " miserable and distressed estate of the people of Muscovia " who were " without a head and in greate confusion."

In order to make an irresistible appeal to James' covetousness, Captain Chamberlain took care to describe the potential wealth of Muscovy, " which lyeth between the Archangell and river Volga." The offer of the throne was the " greatest and happiest ouverture that ever was made to any King of this realme, since Columbus offered King Henry VII the discovery of the West Indies." Chamberlain proposed that King James should send envoys to Russia " to treat with that people " and the Russians would also send representatives. " In this project," the captain concluded, " there is no injustice or wrong to any men, nor any breach or straining of treaties concluded with any other prince or state. Contrariwise there is in yt (in my opinion) much glory to his Magestie, much charity towards those oppressed people, with whom wee have had long commerce, much pollicy in regard of the increase of our shipping and trade, which must needes augment both our strength and wealth."

All the motives are there : wealth and power, and influence and " much charity " to the " oppressed." Kipling, in truth, was not the inventor of the " white man's burden."

James was not unwilling to make himself wealthy and others happy. He sent two agents to Russia to discuss the project, but it was too late. When the English representatives arrived they found that a new Czar, Michael Romanov, had already been elected (March, 1613). The Englishmen kept their mission to themselves and congratulated Czar Michael. Thus Russia escaped the clutches of the Stuarts only to fall into the claws of the Romanovs.

On the eve of the Thirty Years War, James of England was the head of Protestant Europe. Catholic France was traditionally opposed to the Spanish and Austrian Habsburgs, but in this period the country, ruled by an intriguing woman and an Italian camarilla, was at the point of disruption. Royal and rebellious troops both plundered the land. " They have devastated a great part of the country," Ambassador Foscarini wrote in 1616, " which has suffered this one year more than in three or four of the past wars." Seventy thousand armed men ravaged France ; the infant King could get no recognition. The chaos was so great that, in the words of the Venetian ambassador, " if a remedy be not applied, the monarchy may speedily be reduced very easily to a number of separate princes and free towns, as is the case in Germany." When the English King was asked to take advantage of the weak situation of France, he replied that God had created him absolute ruler and therefore he could not encourage rebellion.

Nor was Spain in a better position. The King was a weakling and the country had no able statesmen; Spanish viceroys at Naples and Milan acted as independent princes. Sarmiento, the Spanish ambassador at London, confessed to a Venetian diplomat that the Madrid Government made " faulty decisions " and that the preservation of Spain " ought to be attributed to the grace of God," because the country was " governed by so many private interests that serious mistakes are made."

In the imminent politico-religious conflict in Germany, both anarchic France and weak Spain were forced to seek English aid. Ambassador Sarmiento, following the example of his predecessors who spent about 35,000 crowns annually on " pensions " in England, tried to buy the leading courtiers at London. Although many English nobles thought it a " glory to be the pensioners of another king and always to render ill service to their own natural sovereign," Sarmiento soon discovered that his gold was wasted and decided that " the money given here does no good and would be better employed in arming galleons." He confided to his Venetian colleague, Foscarini, that " the amount spent by his King here since the accession of the present sovereign, so large that it passes belief."

King James, too, found it necessary to spend money among his allies on the Continent, but he did it with poor grace. In 1615 he sent 50,000 ducats to the Duke of Mayenne to give military aid to the Duke of Savoy. No sooner was the money despatched than James repented and ordered his agents not to pay it; he was, however, outwitted by Mayenne's emissary who pocketed the gold himself. King James was disliked not only for being parsimonious but also a great babbler. No diplomat trusted him. No one had any confidence in him. " The King," to quote the Venetian ambassador in London, " is accustomed to be as liberal to his favourites with his secrets as with his riches." Riches James distributed only among his favourites, but State secrets among everybody. Whatever was imparted to the English King, a diplomat relates, was " immediately brought to the knowledge of the Spanish ambassador."

III

" *Væ tibi terra cujus est rex puer,*" exclaimed a Venetian diplomat about France when that country was under the regency of Catherine de Medici. The words could be even more justly applied to France during the minority of Louis XIII, when the turbulent nobility, now that the vigorous hand of Henry IV was no longer there to restrain them, again burst forth in all their audacity and mendacity, defying the weak royal authority and ruling the provinces as independent lords.

At the French court there was an aristocratic and erudite young Capuchin, François Le Clerc du Tremblay—famous in history as Father Joseph—who acted as mediator between the factions. It was on one such occasion that he met Richelieu, a young bishop who was ambitious to bring order out of the French chaos, and the two became friends. For seven years Richelieu performed his episcopal duties in his see, impatiently waiting for a call from the court at Paris where the loyal du Tremblay with infinite subtlety managed the greedy regent, Marie de Medici, guided the profligate Gaston d'Orleans, and insinuated himself into the mind of the taciturn young Louis XIII. The Capuchin always kept Richelieu in mind, and in April, 1624, the bishop and future cardinal entered history through the door of the French Cabinet.

Until the end of his days—he died in 1638—Father Joseph was Richelieu's closest collaborator, friend, and adviser. Both men, although so dissimilar, had the same goal : to make France united and powerful, regardless of means. Joseph was a peculiar mixture of religious zealot and astute politician, qualities which resembled those of Cromwell. Richelieu's tool in the most complicated political intrigues, Joseph yet found time to occupy himself with the salvation of souls, the conversion of heretics, and the expulsion of the Turks from Europe for the greater glory of Jesus. Although the priest had no directive influence on the Cardinal, he sometimes succeeded in modifying Richelieu's policies. The Cardinal never permitted religion to interfere with politics. His aim was to break the power of the Catholic Habsburgs in Spain and Austria, a policy which required Protestant aid; Richelieu invited the Lutheran Gustavus Adolphus from Sweden to Germany to check Austria. Although Father Joseph tried to moderate his chief's inveterate hostility to Austria and Spain, he always remained essentially a French patriot rather than a Catholic priest.

Father Joseph was always there to encourage and invigorate the Cardinal. In 1636 Richelieu's policies seemed to fail; when the Imperialists were threatening Paris, the Cardinal was hissed, pasquinaded, lampooned, and fiercely assailed. For once His Grey Eminence, that iron man, lost his nerve; he asked bitterly whether life was worth living. "What culpable weakness," Father Joseph reproved the Cardinal. "Is this the way to earn the divine compassion? Is it not rather calculated to call forth the wrath of God and to awaken His vengeance?"

Upon coming to power in 1624 Richelieu promptly revealed his masterly hand. His first act was to drive the Imperial, Spanish and Papal troops from the Valtelline, an act of tremendous strategic importance, for the Valtelline was one of the vital "gates of Italy." Then the new minister turned his attention to Germany, where he astutely exploited the misunderstanding that existed between the Elector of Trier and the King of Spain. This was followed by a treaty with

Holland and a *rapprochement* with England. In less than a year Richelieu had united Europe—Venice, Turkey, Hungary, and the German and Danish Protestants—against the Habsburgs.

But without England any anti-Habsburg coalition was ineffective. Yet England could not be managed. Richelieu was exasperated and kept on complaining that the English were " treating us badly." It must be said that Richelieu's diplomacy in England was bad. His envoy, the Savoyard abbot Scaglia, who went to London to " leave nothing undone " in order to achieve an alliance, had failed to do so. But when Richelieu's rival, Marshal Bassompière, in the following year succeeded where Scaglia had failed, the French minister, jealous of the soldier's reputation, used his influence to break the treaty. Richelieu, so observed a Venetian diplomat, " wants to rule this kingdom alone and cannot support the growing fortune of the Marshal Bassompière." Even Richelieu was not above personal pettiness.

For the Cardinal was determined that nothing should happen without his having " a hand in it." Such vanity was costly to France. The English fleet swept the seas, seized French ships, ruined French trade. " The merchants here," the Venetian ambassador Zorzi wrote from Paris, " cry out aloud and if matters go further and the Cardinal does not give way, this may break the neck of his greatness." Commercial pressure humbled the Cardinal's pride and once more he sued for peace with England. It was a mistake, he decided, to have opposed Bassompière's treaty out of spite. So Richelieu sent an emissary to England, a man named Seton, who was captain in the French King's Scottish guard. This was another blunder, for when Seton arrived in England he was arrested as a spy.

The strange thing was that no formal war existed between the two countries. Nevertheless, French and English sailors, merchantmen and fishermen, acted as if there were. English ports were closed to French commerce and English ships attacked French vessels. Such piracy was encouraged by the Government in London, particularly Buckingham, King Charles I's favourite, who was thereby acquiring supplies for the fleet which he was fitting out against France. Moreover, Buckingham incited insurrection in France, though not with much success ; even the Protestant city La Rochelle arrested the English agents. Buckingham then resolved upon *force majeure*. He gathered a fleet of ninety sail, more than half of which, however, was merchantmen, and prepared to ravage the French coast. The expedition contained 4,000 regulars and 4,000 ill-trained men pressed into service. The foppish earl's own flagship was encumbered with " musical instruments of every kind, bedding, coaches, horses for tilting and other hindrances to warfare."

In July, 1627, Buckingham's fleet landed near St. Martin on the French coast. When Richelieu heard of the British fleet he tore his beard in despair, not realizing that the fatuous English commander with his ludicrous knightly-romantic trappings was no more formidable than Don Quixote. Buckingham, having sailed gallantly, found himself in a desperate position. He received no supplies from home, was running short of ammunition, and quarrelled with his officers. The French found it easy to defeat such an expedition. When Buckingham finally sailed back to England, he had with him only 500 men, the rest having died of illness. The losses were so great that the officers were warned not to speak of them in public. Such reckless waste of human lives and so ludicrous a political action probably went far to discredit the Government of Charles I, who was to lose his head within some twenty years.

Richelieu's blundering in regard to England has been described here merely because it was so exceptional. Ordinarily the Cardinal was a superb diplomat who rarely met with failure. From 1624 to 1642, the year he died, His Grey Eminence had a hand in every European event. He fought, successfully, with words and gold. " Putting his hand on the purse and not on arms," Richelieu defeated Spain all along the line, in Germany, in Italy, in Flanders. He allied with any European power that was hostile to the Habsburgs. No instrument was too mean or too small in this relentless war against France's great rivals. Richelieu planned the Portuguese revolution in 1640 and took advantage of the Catalan revolt. He negotiated with the African Moors and instigated revolution in Bohemia. So ruthless was the Cardinal in his enmity, and so successful was his gold-diplomacy, that when he died, Spain, the greatest power in Europe for a century and a half, was practically reduced to the level of a third-rate State. France, on the other hand, took her place as the foremost power on the Continent.

IV

On October 26, 1630, the Spanish and French armies faced each other, ready for battle, before the walls of Casale. The long and complicated negotiations centring about the Mantuan succession had been made abortive by the well-known duplicity of the contracting parties, until the patience of Louis XIII was exhausted and he issued orders for an attack ; the battle would have meant a French victory and a march on Milan. Just as the guns went off, a captain in the Papal army galloped between the opposing lines, waved a white flag, and shouted : " *Pace, pace, alto, alto !* " The captain was no other than Jules, later Cardinal, Mazarin. He had kept the treaty in his pocket for a week, in order to produce it at the sensational moment. It was thus that the dramatic Italian entered history.

When Richelieu died in 1642, his assistant Mazarin, then forty years old, succeeded him in office. The handsome Mazarin who was of Sicilian parentage, was educated in a Jesuit college at Rome where he took the degree of Doctor of Laws at the age of twenty ; afterwards he entered the service of the Papal army, where he learned more diplomacy than military craft.

After a long apprenticeship under Richelieu, the Italian succeeded his master and continued his policies. Mazarin's aims, which coincided with French nationalism, were succinctly set forth by him in instructions given to the French envoys at Münster :

" The acquisition of the Spanish Low Countries will form an impregnable boulevard to the city of Paris. This may truly be called the heart of France . . . , *inasmuch as we will have extended the frontiers up to Holland, and, on the side of Germany, up to the Rhine through the retention of Lorraine and Alsace and the possession of Luxemburg and Franche Comté.*"

Mazarin did not quite succeed in this ambitious programme, but he left a powerful kingdom to Louis XIV, who spent his life in trying to execute this project.

The imperial election of 1658 was a characteristic example of Mazarin's money-diplomacy. Emperor Ferdinand III died in April, 1657, and the Imperial crown, which had been in the Habsburg family for over two centuries, was again open to purchase. Vienna, however, was so desperately poor that there was not enough money to bury the Emperor. " It was necessary," according to the Venetian ambassador, " to hold a council over his body before the breath had left it to find wherewith to clothe the court in mourning." Mazarin thought the time opportune " to carry the empire into some other family," and asked the Habsburg-hating Cromwell to help him. The Lord Protector of Britain was sympathetic, but he did little about it.

The Habsburg candidate was Archduke Leopold, then a boy of seventeen. The opposing candidates were Charles X of Sweden, the nephew of Gustavus

Adolphus, and the nineteen-year-old Louis XIV of France. Leopold had the powerful backing of Pope Alexander VII, Spain, Denmark, and Poland; but of the eight Electors, only one, Saxony, was favourable to the Habsburgs. The Archbishop-Elector of Mainz was wavering; the Electors of Trier and Cologne were hostile to Vienna; the Count Palatine was in secret alliance with France. Elector Ferdinand Maria of Bavaria was ambitious to get the crown for himself, at least his wife was ambitious for him. Frederick William, the Elector of Brandenburg, although secretly allied with France, was inclined to bargain with Vienna. It looked, in those fifteen months of interregnum, as if Leopold had little chance.

Mazarin at first supported the Bavarian's candidacy. Wagnée and Gravel, the French agents in Germany, were busy working for Ferdinand Maria. For a while there was a third candidate, Duke William of Neuburg. But William was terribly poor, and was also blessed with seventeen children; "to maintain him as an emperor," a contemporary wit said, "it would be necessary to take up a general collection." So Papa Neuburg could get no backing and dropped out. The Elector of Bavaria ultimately decided to oppose his wife's ambitions. Not being a fool, he preferred, as Nani said, "to remain a rich elector rather than become an impoverished emperor." Thus, at once, Leopold found himself without a rival.

But Mazarin had not yet played his trump card. Why could not nineteen-year-old Louis XIV be Emperor of Germany? Had not Charlemagne, Louis' predecessor, been Emperor? French emissaries became active. The powerful Archbishop of Mainz was approached first. The Archbishop's councillor, Boineburg, was favourable. "We shall have, if it please God," he said, "a Louis V." Mazarin then informed Mainz that Louis XIV reluctantly agreed to accept the honour of the Imperial crown and that he would treat his friends generously, insinu-

CARDINAL DE RICHELIEU
(1585–1642)

CARDINAL MAZARIN
(1602–1661)

ating that the Elector of Mainz would be the real ruler of Germany if the French King were elected. In July, 1657, Gravel wrote to Mazarin that Mainz seemed " more inclined to the King of France than to any other." Mazarin then openly entered the field. He threatened to oppose the Habsburg election with a war of annihilation, and flooded Germany with pamphlets pointing out the dangerousness and incapacity of the Viennese dynasty. One script ended with a eulogy of the " noble, intelligent, and virtuous " Louis who would make Germany " powerful, victorious, and secure in the enjoyment of profound peace." Mazarin's agents backed their pamphlets with gold.

A veritable *danse des écus* now began. The French offered Brandenburg 100,000 écus. The Elector of Cologne was bought indirectly through his relatives, the two Counts Fürstenberg. William Fürstenberg received the bishopric of Metz with a revenue of 12,000 ; and Francis Fürstenberg was given the abbey of Saint-Arnould whose income was 4,000. The Elector of Mainz was offered 40,000 rixthalers.

The Elector of Palatine was more difficult to get ; negotiations with him lasted forty-eight hours. After the conference was over, the French agents, Gramont and de Lionne, reported to Mazarin : " He will cost the King presently only 60,000 écus . . . and 40,000 after the election. . . . His Electoral Highness has demanded from us, and with reason, that the secret . . . be guarded, and that only Their Majesties and Your Eminence and Count de Brienne be informed of it ; this we have promised him, and in consideration thereof we have not communicated it to any of our secretaries, and it was one of us who has put it in cipher." The money was deposited in Frankfort. Three months later the 60,000 were delivered to the Elector's agents in return for a receipt written by the Elector himself. " We do not believe," the French representatives reported to Paris, " that since the creation of the Electoral College such a receipt has ever been issued."

French money was wasted. When the Electors gathered in Frankfort, in March, 1658, the French emissaries spent a fortune in sumptuous entertainment. Nevertheless, the rapacious German princes were afraid of France ; perforce they favoured the weaker Leopold. They only wanted to curtail the Emperor's already reduced powers, for, like the Polish nobles, the German princes and ecclesiastics throve on anarchy. In the election settlement a clause was inserted whereby the Emperor was forbidden to furnish aid to Spain against France and her allies. This was definitely a French victory, the only thing Mazarin's money achieved. Penaranda, the Spanish ambassador, offered 100,000 crowns for the suppression of the two words *fœderatos Galliæ*. In vain. The Electors had taken money from France, and the least they could pay in return were two significant words. On July 18, 1658, Leopold was elected Emperor. Louis XIV was to remain a mere Sun King for the rest of his sumptuous days.

v

In England the government of Cromwell carried on a foreign policy worthy of Richelieu and Mazarin. Although the execution of Charles I had caused horror in monarchist countries on the Continent, the English parliament had the hardihood to send out ambassadors, indifferent as to whether they would be received or not. These Puritan English envoys abroad aroused a good deal of dread, for they made no secret of their hatred of monarchists. Cromwell, in fact, hoped to see republics established everywhere ; he wrote that it was necessary to help other nations to throw off the monarchical yoke. So zealous were these Roundheads that one of them, an admiral, upon landing at Cadiz, made a subversive speech in the public square.

" With the example afforded by London all king-

doms will annihilate tyranny and become republics.
England has done so already ; France is following in
her wake ; and as the natural gravity of the Spaniards
render them somewhat slower in their operations, it
will take Spain ten years to make the revolution."

And when a French diplomat arrived to see Cromwell, the Lord Protector mockingly remarked that he
would come to France in person " with 40,000 foot
and 12,000 horse " to help that country to be reduced
" to the state in which England now is." Cromwell,
so observed the Venetian ambassador, " desired only
the ruin of monarchies and the Catholic faith."

Nevertheless, Cromwell, though pious, was like
Richelieu in that he did not permit religion to influence
his foreign policy. Surrounded by enemies, especially
the followers of the Stuarts, Cromwell's Government
had to be constantly on the alert. Being a dictatorship,
the Protectorate needed an efficient machine to crush
all opposition. The French Revolutionists had their
Committee of Public Safety ; the Soviets their G.P.U. ;
Oliver Cromwell had his John Thurloe.

Thurloe became Secretary of State in 1652. He was
also Home Secretary, Foreign Secretary, War Secretary, and Councillor of State ; in short, Thurloe was
the Protector's protector. His intelligence system
became the most perfect in Europe. As Postmaster-
General, he intercepted an astonishing mass of letters,
especially Royalist mail. He had agents in every court
in Europe and his spies at home formed a network which covered every religious and political
activity.

According to Pepys, Cromwell spent £70,000
annually for intelligence ; " thereby Cromwell carried
the secrets of all the princes of Europe at his girdle."
The principle of the Protectorate in these matters was
to pay high for good information rather than little for
bad. Thomas Scot, for example, who held the office
of " Intelligencer " in 1649 and who succeeded Thurloe
as Number One Argus ten years later, was paid £800

a year " to manage the intelligence both at home and abroad for the State."

"Concerning a good correspondent at Rome," Thurloe instructed his agent in Leghorn, " I doubt not to effect it to content when I shall know your resolution what you intend to spend therein. These people cannot be gained but by money, but for money they will do anything, adventure body and soul too. . . . Such intelligence must be procured from a Monsignor, a secretary, or a Cardinal. . . . I should say 1,000 pounds a year were well-spent, with 500 pounds pension and now and then 100 pounds gratuity." No inconsiderable sum, this !

The " vigilancy of Thurloe " was more than a byword ; it was a grim fact. When Admiral Blake seized the Spanish plate-fleet at Teneriffe, it was due to Thurloe's secret service. A Jamaica agent had sent information about the fleet to London and the English squadrons waited for the Spanish ships for six months until the favourable moment occurred. Thurloe employed every possible kind of agent, including Puritan divines[1] and Jews.[2] He and Cromwell learned everything. A good illustration of their watchfulness is the amusing anecdote about the Englishman who, upon his return from the Continent, was asked grimly by Cromwell whether he had seen Charles II (which he did). When the Englishman denied it, Cromwell snapped : " Of course, you didn't ; you had turned out the lights."

---

[1] A fine description of Cromwell's religious-political policy is to be found in *Political Science Quarterly* (by G. L. Beer), XVII (1902), 46f. : " It was the commercial traveller who acted, and the Puritan Don Quixote who dreamt and spoke."

[2] A Jewish merchant, Antonio Fernandez Carvajal, who was given letters of denization for London, offered the Government the services of his correspondents on the Continent. Another wealthy Jew, Simon de Caceres, gave Thurloe plans for an expedition against Chile and for the fortification of Jamaica ; see S. R. Gardiner, *History of the Commonwealth and Protectorate*, III, 218.

Absolute secrecy was one of the characteristics of Cromwell's Government. Puritan agents abroad were required to correspond with London at least once a week, and to " labour industriously " to detect the secrets of foreign states. Thurloe, who intrigued with the Swiss and Dutch Protestants, warned his emissaries " to be careful lest our enemies become acquainted with our counsels." One agent, the Reverend John Pell who used Latin for diplomatic conversation, suggested in all seriousness that the British fleet under Blake should force the College of Cardinals, then in session, to " choose a Calvinist for this once, and call him Peter the Second." So inscrutable was Cromwell's administration that the Venetian ambassador, Sagredo, vowed that no " government on earth conducts its affairs with greater secrecy than this one, so much so that their decisions may be better judged by their acts and provisions than by what is learned from the statements of others." In the Puritan the Venetian had finally met his match.

" One of the best maxims of this government," to quote Sagredo again, " is to keep their secrets so closely that no effort can discover the true substance of their deliberations. The second is to maintain secret spies everywhere, to be informed of what is happening in the world. Certainly no government on earth discloses its own acts less and knows those of others more precisely than that of England. They meet in a room approached through others, without number, and countless doors are shut. That which favours their intent best is that very few persons, at most sixteen, meet to digest the gravest affairs and come to the most serious decisions. To keep them the more secret they pass through the head of a single secretary, who superintends political affairs and criminal as well. . . . To discover the affairs of others they do not employ ambassadors, but use spies, as less conspicuous, making use of men of spirit but without rank unlikely to be noticed. . . . Thus by their money and bribes they have found a way to use the forces of Rome (i.e. the use of Jesuits as spies) and draw profit from their enemies, as they call the priests in London. . . . In France, Spain, Germany, and at Venice they also have insignificant persons who from time to time send important advices, and being less under observation, penetrate everywhere."

Unlike the elaborate instructions given by contemporary governments to their ambassadors, Cromwell's " advices " were simple and direct. In 1656 William Lockhart, on a mission to Mazarin, was instructed by Cromwell to tell the Cardinal that he wished to " live in friendship " with France, but Lockhart must insinuate " that I have taken France for a friend, not out of necessitie, but choice." Lockhart was also to " take all opportunityes to penetrate into the counsells " of the French ministers, to " hold a good correspondence " with the friends of England, to " assist English merchants tradeing into France," and to " give frequent accounts of your negociations unto us."

CHAPTER VI

THE AGE OF LOUIS XIV

"Louis XIV and his despotisms and wars never did as much evil as resulted from the counsels of this good Fénélon, the apostle and martyr of virtue and the goodness of men."—J. B. SAY.

I

IMMEDIATELY upon Mazarin's death in 1661, the twenty-three-year-old Louis XIV, who had hitherto played the dandy, assembled the Royal Council. "I have assembled you . . . to inform you that until the present I have been pleased to leave the direction of my affairs to the cardinal; it is now time that I myself govern. You will aid me with your counsels, when I shall ask for them."

For the next half a century and more Louis XIV's foreign policy, following Richelieu and Mazarin, had one aim: to reach the Rhine and the Alps, the "natural limits" of ancient Gaul. This meant war with Spain, war with Austria, war with England, war with Holland, and war with whatever country happened to be allied to Louis XIV's enemy at the moment.

In Portugal the French King arranged for war against Spain and in Italy he allied with the local princes against the Habsburgs. In Germany he revived Mazarin's League of the Rhine, tying to him the German princes with chains of gold.

With the aid of able ministers—for the King himself, despite all the halo attached to his name, was a mediocrity—Louis XIV organized an efficient diplomatic service which became a model for all of Europe. The King read and corrected all the instructions given to his ambassadors. Prepared by the chief of the Foreign Office, the instructions were direct and lucid, containing elaborate analyses of the political conditions in France and abroad, and revealing the mechanism of European politics. Every ambassador was

given a Royal audience before his departure and was
impressed with the real aim and significance of his
mission.   Thus the envoy was made to feel that he
was part of the State, that his service had a lofty—
almost sacred—character.   A personal relation was
established between sovereign and servant, whose
reports came to be " amiable in tone, lively in style,
and often spiritual."

The diplomats were chosen from the ranks loyal to
the King, and rarely from churchmen ; they were
carefully directed and watched.   The ambassadors had
to report anything of a political, military, or commercial nature.   This made Louis the best-informed person
in Europe, familiar with all intrigues, parties, factions.
The envoys had to work hard and were expected to
know affairs in every European country ; for this
purpose they kept up a lively correspondence with
one another in cipher.   Louis' instructions always
insisted strongly that it was the duty of the ambassadors
to maintain " the rank and preeminence of the King
over all other kings, and consequently also his
ambassadors who have the honour of representing his
person, over all other ambassadors of other crowns."

The expenses of envoys were great ; the journeys
long and arduous.   Sometimes they had to follow the
sovereign to whom they were accredited to the field
of battle.   Charles X of Sweden was accompanied
across the Baltic ice by the French ambassador, and
later Colbert de Croissy had an interview with
Charles XII in the trenches while bullets were hissing
overhead.   Despite their exacting work, the ambassadors were poorly and infrequently paid.   Feuquières
had to maintain eighty persons and thirty horses on an
income of 36,000 livres.   Ambassadors were often
compelled to pawn their silver and to ruin their
private fortunes in the service of the *grand monarque ;*
yet they handled great sums for bribery of kings and
princes.   Their reward was a word of praise from
Louis, an honourable post, or the Order of St. Louis.

But they established French preponderance, and incidentally French culture, in Europe.

When a foreign ambassador arrived at Paris the monarch appointed an official to " introduce " him. Envoys were considered Royal guests and three days were usually consecrated to the solemn entry into the capital. Plenipotentiaries of distant lands, such as Morocco or Persia, were maintained at Government expense throughout their residence. In the seventeenth century the *Hôtel des ambassadeurs extraordinaires*, formerly the palace of Marshal d'Ancre, was devoted to these ambassadorial *grandeurs*.

Under Henry III there was created a special office, that of the *Grand Master of Ceremonies and Introducer of Ambassadors of Foreign Princes*. The first Grand Master was a henchman of Catherine de Medici, the Florentine Jerome de Gondi who died both rich and respected.

When a picturesque embassy arrived, the Grand Master became a bustling and important figure. In the middle of the seventeenth century Grand Master Nicolas printed programmes of the processions, with an engraving of the envoy, and sold them to the eager Parisians.

The glittering Mastership of Ceremonies finally deteriorated, for in the eighteenth century ambitious burgher upstarts found it easy to purchase the office and add lustre to their names. One of them, Nicolas Foucaut, was so ill-mannered and rascally that he had to be thrown into the Bastille. In 1752 Dufort de Cheverny bought the job for 400,000 livres and his first function was to introduce Maria Theresa's famous statesman, the later Prince Kaunitz. The present Ambassador Kaunitz, properly Cheverny had to acquire, at his own expense, laced liveries, festooned hats, and caparison for six horses, which cost the Master 10,000 livres. The expensive dinners and suppers finally ruined Cheverny, compelling him to sell his office. In the end, the French Revolution, to

Barras' great regret, wiped away the Mastership of Ceremonies.

II

Two years after Cromwell was buried in Westminster "with every token of royalty," Charles II was restored to the English throne. The "merrie monarch" and his women, known at Whitehall as "chanticleer and his wives," supported a lavish court, including seduced actresses who acquired the title of "His Majesty's servants." Charles' chief sources of revenue were the English Parliament and the French King. He played cleverly one against the other and succeeded in rifling the purses of both.

Since his restoration the needy Charles II was in the pay of Louis XIV, but the Stuart King found the subsidies insufficient and decided to sell Dunkirk to the French. Dunkirk, being incorporated in the realm of England, could not be alienated except by consent of Parliament. The French diplomat d'Estrades came to London, bribed the Duchess of York, who was the daughter of the influential Chancellor Clarendon, with "clock dials set with diamonds and other precious stones," and purchased Dunkirk for 5,000,000 francs in silver which Colbert paid in cash.

In 1667 Franz Paul von Lisola was sent by the Emperor to London to make an alliance with England against Louis XIV. Molina, the Spanish ambassador at London, helped Lisola to win over Members of Parliament. The ambassadors, however, met with two powerful obstacles. One was King Charles II, who was a pensioner of Louis XIV; the other was Edward Hyde, Earl of Clarendon, Chancellor of the Exchequer and Lord Chancellor, the most powerful minister in the State and the most hated man in England. Clarendon was anti-Habsburg and pro-French.

It was Clarendon whom Lisola feared most. "It is to be regretted," the ambassador wrote to his Emperor,

" that the King of England lets himself be guided by such bad principles, and his decisions are not in accord with the welfare of the State, but are made on private grounds, which undoubtedly will ruin him.

Parliament was hostile to both Charles and Clarendon. The King had bound himself to Louis XIV not to prevent French activities in the Netherlands for one year. Charles dismissed the protesting Parliament. From intercepted letters Lisola learned that the French King aimed to bring Charles in conflict with Parliament in order to make the English King more dependent upon himself; for this purpose Louis XIV sent Ruvigny to London with money to enable Charles to maintain himself against Parliament.

The dissolution of Parliament aroused excitement and bitter hostility against Clarendon, who was usually made the scapegoat for all the blunders of the Government. Lisola and Molina intrigued against the Chancellor. Finally Clarendon's enemies succeeded in bringing about his downfall. England rejoiced, and so did Lisola, although the latter was censured by the Emperor for interfering in the internal affairs of a foreign nation. Lisola and Molina had a great following in Parliament; hatred for the French increased, and Frenchmen were publicly insulted. But French money was more effective than public opinion; the English King decided not to act against his patron. " Ringing cash," Ruvigny wrote to Paris, " is more convincing here than all other arguments."

Despite the anti-French feelings of the nation, Charles concluded the Treaty of Dover (1670), promising the French King, in return for an annual subsidy of £230,000 sterling, to join him in the projected war against the Dutch and to become a Catholic. Louis XIV not only supplied Charles with funds, but also, and unnecessarily one should think, with a French mistress. The beautiful Louise de Kerouaille, a Breton girl whose charms the English King rewarded by making her Duchess of Portsmouth, served Charles amorously and Louis politically.

Up to 1675 the English King was more or less faithful to his French patron. But the pressure of home opinion, combined with the heroic defence of the Dutch under William III of Orange, compelled Charles to make peace with Holland. Louis continued to struggle, but was unsuccessful; his armies were defeated by Montecuccoli on the Rhine and the Swedes, allies of France, were expelled from Brandenburg. The astute William III did not wish to end the war, although Charles offered to mediate.

The plenipotentiaries arrived at Nymwegen, but the hostility of William of Orange remained an obstacle to peace. Isolated and discouraged, Louis XIV had to rely upon the friendship of Charles, even after England had abandoned the alliance, and continued to pay the English monarch an annual subsidy of £100,000. Louis offered to continue the pension, provided Charles gave him secret assistance. Charles agreed, but did not dare entrust the transaction to any outside person. On February 26, 1676, the English King personally wrote, signed, and sealed the secret treaty with France. "The King of Great Britain," Ambassador Ruvigny informed Louis, "has engaged not to conclude a treaty without the consent of the King of France, and to prorogue or dissolve Parliament, if that be necessary." Thus, "upon his honour as a King," Charles II put England's foreign policy into the hands of Louis XIV.

Two years later, however, the French King was forced to make peace with Holland at Nymwegen (1678).

The essentials of an efficient intelligence system being "a good purse," the needy Charles' service was deplorable. "We had Bristols and Cecils Secretaries," said the poet Andrew Marvell in the course of an attack in Parliament on Secretary of State Arlington, " and by them knew the King of Spain's Junto, and letters of the Pope's cabinet ; and now such a strange account of things ! The money allowed for intelligence so small, the intelligence was accordingly. A libidinous desire in men, for places, makes them think themselves fit for them. The place of Secretary ill-gotten when bought with 10,000 pounds and a Barony." Men still remembering Thurloe's marvellous system, declared in Parliament that the secret service had been better managed under Cromwell. Morice defended his office on the ground that he had never been given more than £750 a year for intelligence, while Cromwell had spent £70,000. In reality, between 1666 and 1667, the Exchequer paid £24,145 for secret service which, however, Secretary Arlington used for purposes known only to himself.

Although King Charles' secretary studied the secret service method of Cromwell, the Stuart monarch used his agents largely to watch malcontents and dissenters at home. English ambassadors abroad had no contact with the Government's secret agents. The secret service machinery was neglected to such an extent that in 1699 King William III, the Stuarts' successor, found it necessary to ask Dr. Wallis to train a young man in the " art of deciphering that it may not die with him." The Post Office, a Royal monopoly under the control of the Secretary of State, was likewise neglected as a means of detection, although the French Ambassador Comignes observed that the London Government had " tricks to open letters more skilfully than anywhere in the world." King Charles' easy-going administration took little advantage of its facilities ; only during political excitement was the Post Office searched.

The diplomatic inefficiency displayed by Charles II may have been due to a reaction both to his beheaded father's experiences and to the rigour of the preceding Cromwellian regime. Considering the King's personal and political experiences, such a reaction was natural, and it extended even to his diplomatic appointments. A case in point is Sir George Etherege, one of the blades of the Restoration Era. He was the author of *Love in a Tub* (1664), *She Would If She Could* (1668), and *Sir Fopling Flutter* (1675). A boon companion of Sedley, Dorset, and Rochester, he wrote obscene stuff, skirmished the watch at Epsom, tossed fiddlers in a blanket, had his head broken in a tennis court, and married a rich widow to pay off his debts. He was also reputed to be the laziest man of his time, and what was more scandalous, he could not hold his liquor like a gentleman.

The delightful Charles II chose this man as his envoy to Regensburg, seat of the German Imperial Diet, in 1685. An ambassador to Germany had to be supple, cautious, industrious, respectable, with a nice regard for punctilious etiquette and an ability to dissimulate. Hence, with perverse humour, Charles II chose George Etherege !

Etherege's appointment was due to his wit and amusing escapades. As ambassador he was expected to entertain his London employers with humorous accounts from Germany. " I hope," the Secretary of State wrote to Etherege, " in a little time we may hear something of your diversions as well as your business, which would be much pleasanter and perhaps as instructive." Sir George did not disappoint his masters. He amused London by describing the mistress of a certain German dignitary in ribald colours : " She wants not her little arts to secure her Sultan's affection, she can dissemble fondness and jealousy and can swoon at pleasure."

A few weeks after his arrival in Regensburg, Sir George became the most unpopular man in the city. The staid German nobles were offended by his free and easy manners. Etherege preferred to spend time in the house of the French envoy where he could play cards and drink in congenial company ; the Austrians

and Germans, therefore, began to suspect him of
French sympathies. Count Windischgrätz complained to the courts of England, France, Holland,
and Vienna ; he also bribed Etherege's secretary to
spy on his master. Finally, the fifty-year-old Etherege
scandalized the solid Germans by a flirtation with a
Regensburg actress.

The lady, Julia, was a " comedian no less handsome
and no less kind in Dutchland than Mrs. Johnson was
in England." To the gallant ambassador of Charles II
she was a dove among ravens. The Regensburgers
were outraged, not so much because Etherege may or
may not have had intimate relations with the woman,
but because a King's ambassador dared to flaunt an
actress in public. Etherege was enraged at the
snobbery. One evening he ostentatiously handed
Julia " into his coach before all the company, not-
withstanding all the giggling and hissing of the
Austrian ladies and of the ministers' wives and
daughters, himself walking humbly home on foot "—
reports Etherege's secretary who was in the pay of
Windischgrätz. Julia was not the only lady to con-
sole a lonely Restoration gentleman ; but the German
women did not satisfy him much. He regretted the
" kind nymphs of the Thames," although he did his
best with the available native material. " I have
only," he wrote, " a plain Bavarian with her sandy
locks, brawny limbs and a brick complexion, and yet I
find myself often very hearty."

III

After the siege of Vienna (1683) and the victory
over Spain in the Netherlands, Louis XIV looked for
more worlds to conquer. The old French ambassador
at Constantinople having died in March, 1685, Louis
sent the experienced Pierre Girardin to Turkey,
where he arrived in January, 1686. Girardin was
accompanied by a large suite and a number of vessels,
as well as by Captain Gravier d'Ortières. The group

also included naval engineers who were ordered to draw up exact maps of the Dardanelles, to chart the waterways and sketch the fortresses at the entrance. The draughtsmen were to make similar observations at the Archipelago, the coasts of Asia Minor, Syria, and Egypt. The ostensible purpose of the French delegation was to visit the French merchants in the Levantine seaports.

D'Ortières and his officers were given minute instructions by the French Government, which they carried out punctually. Their mission ended in 1687, after having visited Constantinople, Smyrna, Chios, Saloniki, Athens, Crete, the Islands, Cyprus, Aleppo, Tripoli, Said, Alexandria, Rosetta, and Cairo. D'Ortières's collected plans and maps filled three volumes, entitled: *The State of the Places which the Mohammedan Princes possess on the coasts of the Mediterranean Sea and which Plans have been made by the Order of the King under Cover of the Visit to the Levantine Seaports, which His Majesty has caused to be made in the Years 1685, 1686, and 1687, with the Project of making a Descent and becoming Masters of them.*

D'Ortières described Constantinople in great detail. He oscillated between the feasibility of a direct attack and bombardment. The French officer carefully studied the whole future campaign, the choice of vessels, pilots, munitions, rations. He concluded with plans for the disposal of the Turkish spoils. If Venice co-operated, she was to get Slavonia, Croatia, Bosnia, Dalmatia, and Epirus, in exchange for Morea, Achaia, and Negrepont to France. Poland was to receive Moldavia and Wallachia, Tekely, and Temesvar—to become a thorn in the Habsburg flank. Finally, France was to keep Morea, Achaia, Thessaly, Macedonia, Servia, Bulgaria, Romania, and the Archipelago Islands; this was to be consolidated in a new empire under a son of Louis XIV.

The enterprise, d'Ortières carefully pointed out, would necessitate the following expenses:

	Livres
20 vessels, including 5 or 6 light frigates .	4,803,340
Their maintenance for one year . .	4,051,080
Armament for 30 galleys . . .	1,800,000
Their maintenance for one year . .	2,135,520
12 fire-ships and maintenance . .	528,000
10 bombing galliots, and maintenance .	420,000
Reserves for ships and galleys . .	600,000
Freight for one year . . .	2,400,000
Biscuit, corn, flour, vegetables . .	800,000
30,000 bombs and 1,200 thousand-weight of powder	1,100,000
60,000 muskets	420,000
30,000 pairs of pistols for the cavalry .	180,000
60,000 sabres and swords for the cavalry .	180,000
30,000 saddles for the cavalry . . .	270,000
Grenades, spades, and digging instruments	600,000
Wages for 40,000 men for a year . .	3,500,000
Ready money	800,000
	31,787,940

This was too much money even to win an empire, and nothing came of the fantastic project.

Louis XIV's grandiose ambitions brought him in conflict with every power in Europe, including the Papacy, especially Innocent XI (1676–1689) who was a Habsburg supporter. As in the time of King Philip the Fair, the struggle was over the revenues from vacant benefices. A French clerical council under Bossuet drew up four articles opposing Papal supremacy and infallibility. Pope Innocent was angry and refused to confirm episcopal appointments in France, with the result that there were about thirty vacant dioceses. Louis XIV tried to win over the Holy Father by a persecution of the Protestants, but Innocent remained cool.

The Franco-Papal conflict sharpened over a new

issue, that of " extraterritoriality." Representatives of Catholic powers at Rome, as in modern China, had the right of immunity within the ambassadorial compound. The Pope resented this privilege as an infringement upon his sovereignty and negotiated for its abolition. Louis XIV alone of all the rulers refused to yield and the Pope decided to retaliate. When the French ambassador to Rome died in 1687, Innocent declared that unless the new envoy renounced the immunity he would not receive or recognize him. The negotiations, lasting for four months, remained fruitless and Ambassador de Lavardin marched on Rome with an armed force. The Pope ordered all religious services to be stopped and the French ambassador to be treated as an excommunicant. Louis XIV responded with a threat of war on the Papacy.

An unforeseen event suddenly changed the situation. The powerful Archbishop and Elector of Cologne— who also controlled Liège, Münster, and Hildesheim, was at the point of death. Strategically it was of vital importance for France that the see of Cologne be in friendly hands, for without Cologne Louis' Rhenish League would not be effective. The trouble was that the French King had antagonized the German national spirit, whatever there was of it. On the Rhine the Germans celebrated Emperor Leopold's victory against the Turks on the Danube ; this looked ominous. On August 13, 1687, thirteen days after the famous battle of Mohacz, Louvois wrote to Vauban, the military engineer : " The news which the King received of the defeat of the Turkish army has made him decide that it was time to furnish the last perfection on his German frontier."

With Emperor Leopold momentarily freed from Turkish pressure in the East, the succession to the archbishopric of Cologne became an affair of international importance. A pro-Imperial prelate in the Cologne see might be a danger to French expansion on the Rhine.

There were two candidates : the Bishop of Breslau, who was the son of the Empress ; and Prince Clement, brother of the Bavarian Elector and son-in-law of the Emperor. Louis now put up a candidate of his own : Cardinal Fürstenberg, Bishop of Strasbourg, and intimate friend of the sick Archbishop of Cologne. Fürstenberg, who had sold out to Louis long ago, was execrated throughout Germany.

The first skirmish took place over the election of a coadjutor. It was, of course, a money battle. Amsterdam merchants sent letters of exchange to Germany in favour of the Imperial candidate ; but the French louis were stronger than the Dutch florins, and in January, 1688, Fürstenberg was elected coadjutor, which put him in line for the archbishopric. Louis then realized his mistake in having alienated the Pope, who now refused to confirm Fürstenberg.

The real battle opened when the Archbishop-Elector died in June, 1688. Louvois sent an aggressive diplomat, Baron d'Asfeld, to " encourage Cardinal Fürstenberg in order that he be not lulled and to take all necessary measures for the success of his new election." D'Asfeld was to persuade Fürstenberg to consider the Pope " as his most dangerous enemy " as well as to convince the canons of Cologne of the danger of antagonizing Louis XIV. The canons could elect a candidate by majority vote, provided he held no other benefice ; if there was some irregularity, as in the case of Fürstenberg who held another benefice, the Holy Father had the right to choose whomever he pleased.

The German faction united behind Clement of Bavaria, a boy of twenty who, although not in orders, nominally held the bishoprics of Freising and Regensburg. This disqualified him for the Cologne archbishopric, but the Imperialists got around it by having the Pope grant the Bavarian prince a dispensation, while refusing the same to Fürstenberg who held the bishopric of Strasbourg. To be properly elected,

Fürstenberg needed two-thirds, or eighteen, of the twenty-four votes of the chapter; whereas a bare majority, or thirteen, was sufficient for the " dispensed " Clement. But all that Fürstenberg could muster was sixteen votes.

As everything depended upon the Pope, Louis XIV decided to make peace with him. He chose Marshal-General Chamlay to go to Rome disguised as a Flemish gentleman under the name of Count d'Orchamp. The instructions given to Chamlay, on July 6, were extraordinary. He was to quit Paris secretly, make his way to Venice, live there in hiding until further orders, and directly upon hearing of Fürstenberg's postulation to go quickly to Rome. There he should take all precautions in order not to be seen either by Ambassador Lavardin or by any other Frenchman; in case of discovery he should disclaim all secrets and say he came to get Papal absolution for some sin. As a Flemish gentleman he should demand a secret interview with the Pope; for this he should bribe the Papal mediator with a ring worth two or three hundred pistoles. Once in the Pope's presence, he should identify himself, and, after asking the Pontiff under the secret of the confessional never to mention it, hand him the King's letter; if the conference was unsuccessful, Chamlay should demand the missive back from the Pope. If Innocent accepted these conditions, Chamlay was to negotiate three things : peace of Europe, the question of episcopal bulls, and the regalian difficulties. First, however, the Pontiff must recognize Fürstenberg; the other mooted points could be settled ultimately. Chamlay was also authorized to grant the Pope, as a final concession, the French renunciation of the right of immunity in Rome. Before leaving the Holy Father, Chamlay should warn him that if he ever published the King's letter, both he and Louis would publicly give him the lie.

While Chamlay was at Venice studying his role, the

election was held at Cologne. Fürstenberg received only thirteen votes, and Clement only nine ; the former was five votes short, the latter four. Hence neither was elected. The decision was now in the hands of the Pope.

Upon hearing the news from Cologne, Louvois wrote to Louis that Chamlay must be ordered to see the Pontiff in a hurry, warning him about an inevitable war in Europe between Louis and the Emperor, for the French King could not very well abandon Fürstenberg. Louvois proposed a compromise : Fürstenberg was to be archbishop and Clement his coadjutor.

Chamlay hastened to Rome, but could gain no entrance to the Holy Father. Even when he tried to reach Innocent as a secret envoy of Louis XIV, he received a cold rebuff, for the Pope had the upper hand and knew it. Chamlay, in a fury, protested to the King, who bade him return to France.

Louis XIV sent a violent letter to the Pope, menacing him with dire consequences. The Holy Father's answer was prompt and to the point. He appointed Clement Elector of Cologne, and the French King's puppet Fürstenberg was left " holding the bag." This was too much for the pride and fury of His Majesty. Paris mobilized an army of more than 200,000 men and struck on two fronts. While the frightened Fürstenberg, who was after all a pawn in a ruthless international game, protested that he did not wish to be the cause of a European war, the French armies seized Avignon to punish the Pope and fell like a horde of savages on Germany, devastating the Palatinate. Germany, or rather the defenceless German people, paid a most terrible price for their own rulers' venality and the French King's vanity.

Louis XIV meted out a similar treatment to his other weak neighbours, particularly the little State of Savoy. The French King's method in dealing with international problems consisted of intimidation backed by military force. If diplomatic bullying failed, the King promptly resorted to armed pressure. Hence in the age of Louis XIV it is impossible to differentiate between diplomacy and war ; the two were the obverse and converse of the same coin and complemented each other at all times.

Savoy, located between France, the Empire, and Spanish Italy, had special grievances against Louis XIV. Not only did the French King treat the little duchy with contempt, but French merchants violated the Savoyard tariff regulations through the courier who passed regularly from Lyon to Turin on his way to Rome and fraudulently introduced foreign merchandise into Savoy. The abuse continued for ten years, for the courier's bags were protected by diplomatic immunity and Savoy was too weak to oppose powerful France. When the smuggling assumed dangerous proportions, the Chamber of Accounts at Turin, in July, 1689, decided to investigate the French courier's trunks. Hitherto the trunks had been taken to the customs house at Turin, where the goods were examined and then locked up, one key being held by the Savoyard officials and the other by the courier. Goods destined for Turinese were delivered upon payment of the required tax ; the other merchandise was returned to the courier upon his departure. Thus the smuggling did not take place in Turin, but outside the city. Now the Chamber of Accounts decided that the trunks should be sealed right at the frontier, at Suse and Asti.

Duke Victor Amadeus undoubtedly had the right to legislate on customs in his land ; but could he act so brusquely against Louis XIV without negotiating first ? If he thought he could, he was to be disappointed. Louvois informed D'Arcy, the French ambassador at Turin, that Louis would not suffer any change in the customs regulations. A conflict soon broke out. The French courier refused to have his trunk sealed at Asti ; the Turinese customs officers did it by force. A few days later the courier was stopped at the gates of Turin, and his trunk was seized despite the fact that he protested it contained nothing but despatches to the French ambassador.

Louis XIV promptly warned the Savoyard ambassador at Paris that if this occurred again he would order the governors of Pignerol and Casal to invade Savoy. Turin apologized, and for the moment the French King was satisfied. Victor Amadeus was compelled to suspend the new regulation, and the couriers passed unhindered. But the guileful Italians did make one change. Instead of, as formerly, the trunks being examined at the Turin post office, they were now taken to the French office. Savoy wanted to see how Louis XIV would take this innovation. The French King repeated: " The custom observed for twenty years must stay, and all innovations must stop."

Meanwhile smuggling continued, and the Turinese farmers of the revenue protested. Their lease was soon to be renewed, and they complained that the customs had decreased by about forty or fifty thousand livres annually, due to the fraud of the French couriers. The French post farmers, however, without denying the abuse, maintained, as did Ambassador D'Arcy, that the contraband amounted to no more than about 100 pistoles annually; a trifle not worth making an international issue over.

In December, 1688, Victor Amadeus sent Senator Gazelli to Paris to settle the affair. The haughty Louis XIV refused to receive Gazelli. At first Victor Amadeus protested gently against this injustice, as he called it; but a few months later he took different steps. In May, 1689, Paris was surprised not to receive the post from Rome in time. Soon the explanation came: the courier had been detained in Turin for four days. At Louvois' threat to break off all connection with Savoy, this reprisal ceased.

A great anti-French coalition was meanwhile being formed in Europe. The astute Victor Amadeus nego-

tiated on all sides ; he also armed. The ambitious
duke bargained with the Emperor and with Spain for
a Royal crown, for which he paid 120,000 pistoles.
When Louis heard of it, he considered such an
expenditure of money to his enemy as an " act of
hostility against me," and ordered Savoy to stop negotiating. Victor Amadeus apologized, in the words of the
French agent Rébénac, " with a torrent of marvellous
eloquence." But Duke Victor had his tongue in his
cheek. Despite French threats, he made an alliance
with the Emperor and Spain in June, 1690, to the
speechless surprise of Louis ; in October the bullied
Victor Amadeus joined the Grand Alliance against
France. Louis XIV now tried to win over Savoy by
offering her Casal and Pignerol, but it was too late ;
the King was beginning to find his Nemesis in the
Imperial general, Eugene of Savoy.

IV

The so-called Revolution of 1688 brought the
Prince of Orange to the English throne as William III.
With William began a new era in foreign affairs, for
the King, having devoted his life to fighting Louis XIV,
personally supervised all diplomatic matters.

The new King, who replaced the exiled Stuart
James II, reorganized the administration of foreign
affairs. He appointed two Secretaries of State, one in
charge of a Northern department and another of a
Southern ; but these men had little power. The King,
who remained also the sovereign of the Dutch, spent
from six to seven months of each year out of England,
and in his absence only William Blathwayte, the
Secretary of War, to whom the English ambassadors
addressed their despatches, knew what was going on.
The Secretaries of State were kept in ignorance.

King William reconstructed the diplomatic service.
He cared little for party attachments or national
affiliations, but insisted upon absolute personal
obedience. A diplomat's fortune depended entirely

upon convincing the King of his usefulness.   As a
rule, William had no permanent embassies abroad,
except when, as in the case of those accredited to
Turkey, they were subsidized by merchant companies.
Diplomats were appointed only when strictly necessary.
Even in The Hague, Vienna, and Copenhagen, an
agent of twenty shillings a day alternated with ambas-
sadors.   For years William had no representatives in
Regensburg, Florence, Turin, and in the smaller
German courts.

Ambassadors on special missions received a fixed
sum, as well as an allowance " for intelligence,
expresses, etc., payable by bills allowed by one of the
principal Secretaries of State."   Salaries were paid
quarterly in advance, from the day of departure to the
day of return, inclusive.   Often, however, it was
difficult to cash the warrants.

An ambassador's pay was £1,500 for equipment
and £100 a week ordinary allowance, besides a loan of
plate.   Envoys of lower rank (Turkey and Venice)
received £10 a day and £500 to £1,000 for equipment.
Envoys extraordinary were given £5 a day and £500
for equipment.   Emissaries of still lower rank ranged
from residents like Robinson in Sweden with £4 a
day and £300 for equipment, to lesser agents drawing
£2 and £3 a day, and even £1 daily.   Plenipotentiaries to a congress received £3 a day and £300 for
equipment.   A secretary of an embassy was paid from
£1 to £2 a day, with £300 for equipage.   The market
rate for private secretaries and chaplains was £60 and
£40 a year respectively, including board and room.

The King also paid for extraordinary expenses,
which included stationery, postage, Treasury fees,
special journeys, rents, secret service, loss by ship-
wreck, a boat to carry despatches to the English fleet
in the Mediterranean, and letters in vellum to the
Sultan and Vizier.

There were also English consuls in many cities.
Consuls, however, were not expensive to the Treasury,

for their salaries were paid out of merchants' fees. Consuls were usually merchants resident abroad, hence their extraordinary expenses were not high. English commercial consuls were to be found in Naples, Genoa, Locarno, Venice, Corunna, Cadiz, Seville, Barcelona, Alicante, Cartagena, Malaga, Smyrna, St. Sebastian, Lisbon, Nice, Oporto, Rotterdam, Amsterdam, Geneva, Flanders, Danzig.

From 1691 to 1700, the average annual cost of the diplomatic service was about £37,000.

Transportation and communication were slow and difficult. This was particularly true in the case of Turkey, whence some despatches never arrived. Post by water was cheapest and most reliable; by land it was expensive, slow, and dangerous. Twelve days was a record speed for a letter from London to Madrid. Travelling was costly. To transport Robinson and his family to Stockholm, the Government had to spend £215. It took Lexington from the middle of September to the end of November to go from Flanders to Vienna in 1694. A slow journey from Constantinople to England might take six months.

Apart from the regular diplomatic and intelligence service, the British Government also maintained spies in France to watch the exiled Stuart King, James II, who resided at St. Germain and whom Louis XIV used as a pawn against his implacable enemy, King William III of England. In 1698 the man in charge of the espionage system against James was the poet-diplomat Mathew Prior, secretary to Ambassador Portland at Paris.

Prior kept James' pitiful court under constant surveillance. He gloated over the former King's poverty. " I faced," Prior triumphantly wrote to a friend, " old James and all his Court the other day at St. Cloud. *Vive Guillaume !* You never saw such a strange figure as the old bully is, lean, worn and shriv'led, not unlike Neal the protector; the Queen looks very melancholy, but otherwise well enough; their equipages are all very ragged and contemptible."

Before Prior left Paris, in 1699, he wrote an account of his spies to Lord Jersey, to be used as information by his successor. Among the faithful he enumerated was Br(aconier) who spent four years in the Bastille; Brocard, an Irishman whose " pretended business is merchandise of English things," received " two and three hundred pounds a year"; Baily, whose real name was Johnston, " is a parson disguised, a cunning fellow and true debauchee," was paid two louis a week; and finally " my widow Langlois and her two daughters . . . , the old woman is a cunning jade as lives."

V

In the first years of the eighteenth century Louis XIV, despite interminable wars, was still in a formidable position, controlling the Rhine and the Alps, but in the face of a more or less united Europe the French King was slowly compelled to give way and by the time he died in 1715 France was so sick that it finally took a great revolution to revive her.

Among the ablest generals who inflicted constant defeats on the French were the Englishman Marlborough and the Austro-Italian Eugene of Savoy. Eugene, a grand-nephew of Mazarin, had, as a boy, offered his services to Louis XIV, who, disliking the lad's insignificant appearance, rejected the proposal— to his everlasting regret. A man of genius as soldier and statesman, Eugene attached himself to the Emperor and rose to the highest rank and power in the Empire, becoming a general, a prince, a councillor, a Mæcenas, a patron and collector of the arts, culminating as *Der Edle Ritter* in a huge equestrian statue on the *Heldenplatz* at Vienna.

Eugene's bluntness made him many enemies. When, after the battle of Turin in 1706, he learned that the supposedly neutral Pope had supported the

French with gold, he wrote a cutting letter to Vienna :

"If the Pope can send to the French 30,000 doubloons, the conqueror ought not be blamed when he asks 15,000 or 16,000 doubloons per month for defraying the necessary expenses. I know the tricks and evasions of the neutrals much better than the court does, where the wolf always wears sheep's clothing. The monarch has given me no instructions to execute the commands, or as it is delicately expressed, ' the wishes,' of a general of the Jesuits. Five letters which are in my possession, have proved to me how recklessly the Roman court is going on in its French partisanship. Langallerie will soon lay the evidence before the Emperor of how they in Rome will do anything for money."

The court of Vienna was under the influence of the Jesuits who were, of course, in the service of the Papacy. In his campaign against the French Eugene found himself constantly checked by the Jesuits who were the allies of Louis XIV. Aware that both his political and personal existence were in danger, Eugene fought his internal enemies, backed by the Papacy, as relentlessly as any other hostile power.

"As I am now on the list of the depredators of the Church," Eugene replied when the Pontiff accused him of sacrilege, "I will so much the more strictly fulfill my duty as a commander; and I think I shall be deserving of absolution on my deathbed, if I can prove that, with the property taken from the Church, I have but saved my soldiers from starving, at the very time when, by orders of the Holy Father, the French—the allies of the arch-enemy of Christendom (Turkey)—were supplied with all necessaries ; whilst everything was done to injure the Emperor, the protector of the Holy Roman Empire and of Christendom. On the same day on which I was honoured with the copy of the papal letter, I raised by execution part of the papal contribution ; and, as a priest never returns an offering, we soldiers can be even less expected to do so."

Eugene's sarcasms were duly reported to the Roman curia and the Jesuits decided to poison their enemy. After the battle of Oudenarde in 1708, while Eugene was besieging Lille, he received a letter inscribed *A Son Eminence le Prince Eugene*. The unusual form of address—Eminence is the title applied to Cardinals—aroused Eugene's suspicions. He opened the envelope and found inside a grey paper smeared with a greasy fluid, which he quickly dropped. Soon he felt dizzy. The general's aide-de-camp and his valet picked up the paper and, their heads swimming, crammed it down the throat of a dog. The animal died, despite a strong antidote.

" He who once and for all has to rely on God's protection," Eugene confided to his friend Adam Liechtenstein, " may laugh at such attempts. It is not the first of the kind which my *adversarii eminentissimi* have been pleased to make. They show that they have made good progress in the school of Marianism (named after the Jesuit Mariana who advocated political assassination). If the rules of their refined Christianity permit them to dispose of the life of a regent by poisoning his saddle or his clothes, an old general may be well prepared to be unhorsed by a dose of *ism*. Now only I may flatter myself that I am a good soldier ; the letter has given me courage to take Lille, whatever may be the consequences."

A few weeks later Eugene made good his promise and took Lille. He also lived to the ripe age of seventy-three.

" The secret negotiations between England and France that resulted in the Peace of Utrecht have always been associated in the world's mind with St. John, Lord Bolingbroke. . . . In fact, he had nothing to do with the affair until it had been going on for nine months. In the last week of April, 1711, the French

minister sent over to England the first official request
that the two countries should treat. . . . This document . . . purported to be the beginning of the whole
negotiation. But in reality it was in the end of the
first long stage. The French Foreign Office papers
have revealed to posterity that these proposals, while
appearing to emanate spontaneously from France, had
in fact been collusively arranged between Jersey,
Harley, and Shrewsbury on the one side and Louis's
minister Torcy on the other. . . . The French official
proposals in April, 1711, afterwards given to the world
as the beginning of the negotiations for peace, were
the outcome of this long preparation. . . . In the
last days of April, 1711, Shrewsbury insisted that
the Queen should lay before the whole Cabinet the
French official proposal for peace ' as a paper come to
her hands without saying how.' "[1]   Two months
later, on a certain July evening in 1711, the poet
Mathew Prior, who had participated in the Peace of
Ryswick in 1697 and was attached to Bolingbroke,
was smuggled into the gardens of Versailles where he
secretly met Madame de Maintenon and afterwards the
old King who was out walking. The result of the conversation was that Louis sent Mesnager as his secret
agent to London. Bolingbroke introduced Mesnager
by a private staircase to the Queen at Windsor. Thus
the preliminaries to the most important European
peace settlement of the eighteenth century started like
a stage comedy.

The plenipotentiaries met formally at Utrecht in
1712. England was so eager for peace that little by
little she gave ground and finally sacrificed her ally,
the Emperor, in the matter of Strasbourg and Alsace.
In November, 1712, Bolingbroke wrote that " we
may depend on everything reasonable . . . for all the
allys except the Emperor, at whose expense the peace
is likely to be made as the war has been at ours."

Peace was concluded in 1713. A grandson of

[1] G. M. Trevelyan, *England under Queen Anne*, III, 176 f.

Louis XIV, Philip V, was recognized as King of Spain. The Dutch were given a string of border fortresses, to protect them against France. England won certain French possessions in America, Newfoundland, Nova Scotia, and Hudson's Bay, as well as the Island of Minorca and the Rock of Gibraltar, two strongholds which made Britain master of the Mediterranean. The Emperor was given the Spanish possessions in Italy, as well as the Spanish (henceforth Austrian) Netherlands. But France retained Alsace. "Strassburg," a German historian has said, "paid for Saint Christophe and Newfoundland." The Imperialists considered the Netherlands poor compensation for the loss of Alsace. Eugene of Savoy told a British statesman, "that the Low Countries were of little value to the Emperor or empire, they were only a burthen to the former, and if he should consent to accept them, it would be more for the sake of his old allies than his own."

Two years after the Peace of Utrecht, Louis XIV died at the age of seventy-seven, leaving the throne to a five-years-old grandson, Louis XV. A new epoch, a "world of cyphers, periwigs, and mystery," began.

CHAPTER VII

THE PERFECT TECHNIQUE

"Without money one does not get far "—Bavarian diplomatic despatch, 1773.

THE age which was dominated by Voltaire in literature produced a number of diplomats and statesmen who were the apogée of Machiavelism. International law was a mockery and public ethics practically non-existent. Statesmen were systematically bought, diplomats regularly bribed, and letters intercepted and copied. Kings had so thorough a distrust of their servants that they spied upon them and negotiated behind the backs of their ministers. What had been mere expedients in the sixteenth century and necessity in the seventeenth, became institutions in the eighteenth.

It was, as may be expected, an epoch of diplomatic adventurers. A libertine like Casanova, a charlatan like Cagliostro, an hermaphrodite like d'Eon—all played the diplomatic-spy game. Even Voltaire, Diderot and Grimm at one time or another tried their hands at diplomacy. Every court of Europe swarmed with spies and secret agents who made a living from detailing high and low gossip. When the Jesuits were suppressed in the Catholic states and were made welcome by the Protestant-born Frederick the Great of Prussia, Cardinal Bernis, the French ambassador in Rome, wrote that in protecting the Jesuits, Prussia acquired in France and Austria " six to seven thousand spies who will serve better than if they were paid."

Undoubtedly European society, at the top, was rotten and ready to topple. How rotten the upper stratum was the French Revolution revealed. But throughout the eighteenth century the rulers—and their ministers and diplomats—acted as if there were no law and no ethical principle ; they were motivated solely by personal interests and monetary considerations. Diplomacy came to be played as a fascinating game in itself.

There was no pretence to "loyalty," "service," "honour." The prime consideration in almost every activity was financial. This was true even of writers like Voltaire. In politics the "cash nexus" was the motive force. Every Foreign Office set aside large funds for bribery. "I hazarded the compliment," wrote Cardinal Dubois about his negotiations with the English minister Stanhope in 1716, "and never did I have more pleasure than when he let me say all, up to the sum, which I fixed at . . . 600,000 livres, to which he listened graciously without being displeased."

"Without money," so reads a Bavarian diplomatic instruction of 1773, "one does not get far. *Vana est sine viribus ira.* Money achieves very much both in negotiations and embassies and in other things; therefore, in such matters, a grandee must not be parsimonious." A few examples will show the truth of the maxim that "without money one does not get far." Thugut, the famous Austrian minister, was a French pensioner from 1768 on. During the Imperial election of 1741, the Elector of Cologne received 100,000 florins from Austria. In 1773, while Poland was being partitioned, the Russian minister Panin proposed that Austria and Prussia "form a chest" for the bribery of Poles. Sir Robert Murray Keith, when he was English minister in Russia, was granted by his Government £100,000 sterling "only for such gratifications as I may judge it necessary to make, from time to time, to particular persons." When Benjamin Franklin returned to America from France, where he represented the American colonies, a committee was appointed to examine his accounts. The committee found a deficit of £100,000, and asked Franklin to explain. "I was taught when a boy," Franklin replied inscrutably, "to read the Scriptures and to attend to them, and it is there said: muzzle not the ox that treadeth out his master's grain."

Bribing was a fine art. The Austrian Chancellor Kaunitz, for example, accepted no direct bribes, but he thought it natural that friendly governments should send him expensive presents such as wines, horses, pictures. The *Livre Rouge*, which the French revolutionists published in 1793, shows that the French Government subsidized Austria to the extent of 82,652,479 livres between the years 1757 and 1769; in this Kaunitz is mentioned only once (January 8, 1759): " 100,000 livres subside à M. le Comte de Kanit."

Indirect bribing took various, and sometimes amusing, forms. Keith, the English ambassador at Vienna, relates how he lost " thirty bowing acquaintances, male and female," because he refused to play cards. Then he fell " upon an excellent way to please the public in the article of card-playing." Countess Clary—" a little, fat, round, tidy body, and extremely good-humoured "—who presided at Kaunitz's as hostess, was disconsolate when she had to give up cards on account of losses. This was an excellent chance for Ambassador Keith to come to the rescue of the fair lady and at the same time win a sturdy ally in the household of the Austrian Chancellor. " I immediately thought," Keith tells humorously, " I might strike an advantageous bargain with this dear creature, and satisfy all mankind. I therefore agreed to attack Dame Fortune with *my* money and *her* fingers ; and now she plays her three parties every day in my name, and at my risk ; and I am now one of the prettiest card-players in Vienna—*by proxy !* " The countess, needless to add, became a staunch friend of England. When a few years later an agent of the revolted American colonies was secretly introduced to Kaunitz by the French ambassador, the countess, ever loyal to the English, declared that she would boycott Kaunitz's card-parties if the Chancellor encouraged the American rebels.

In the middle of the eighteenth century the British foreign service cost, on an average, £67,000 annually,

LOUIS XIV
(1638–1715)

LOUIS XV
(1710–1774)

not including the pay of consuls. A large part of the expenses went for bribery. Lord Hyndford, the British ambassador to Russia, spent £1,500 on " gifts " between 1745 and 1749. Hyndford's presents included such items as a fiddle for the Chancellor, a " gold sponge box in the form of an egg at Easter " for Grand Duchess Catherine (later Catherine the Great), English hounds for the Grand Veneur, wines and liqueurs for General Apraxin and the Archbishop of Troitza, a " shaving equipage mounted with silver " for the Master of Ceremonies, and finally drinks and snuff for the " state dames of the court." Espionage was also costly. One spy, in offering his services to the English, wrote : " The least a gentleman can spend on such a business, and manage well too, will be a hundred pounds per quarter, and travelling charges."

The salaries of the diplomats varied. Ambassadors-extraordinary to Paris and Madrid received £100 weekly and £6,800 for expenses. Envoys-extraordinary to Berlin and The Hague were paid £8 daily and about £3,500 for expenses. The minister to Vienna was given £7 a day and £3,155 for " ordinaries." The remuneration of Residents in Tuscany and Venice was £3 daily and about £1,400 for expenses.

The running expenses of a Foreign Office did not include subsidies. During the American Revolution, for instance, the British Government bought mercenaries from the German princes at a cost of £5,126,620 sterling or 34,177,466 thalers ; by far the largest sum —£2,600,000—went to Hesse-Cassel, and £448,000 to King George's own Hanover.

The French Foreign Office had even more employees than the English ; certainly it was less efficient and more expensive. Aside from pensions, and these were vast, the total expenditures for the year 1787—on the eve of the Revolution—were 8,555,000 livres. The French ambassadors to Vienna, London, and Madrid cost 200,000 livres a year ; those to Rome and The Hague, 150,000 ; to Constantinople, 104,000 ; to

Turin, Naples, and Lisbon, 100,000; to Stockholm, 90,000; to Venice, 72,000. The minister to St. Petersburg received 100,000 livres; to New York, 72,000; to Berlin, 60,000; to Stuttgart, 18,000. The French diplomatic service in other capitals—Copenhagen, Parma, Dresden, Munich, Mainz, Trier, Bonn, Florence, Genoa, Brussels, Regensburg, Hamburg—consumed 760,000 livres. 52,000 livres were spent on the residents at Geneva, Danzig, and Frankfort. Eighteen ambassadorial secretaries were paid from 1,500 to 10,000 livres per person. There were four commissioners to Alsace and Lorraine who cost 32,400 livres. Agents, clerks, and surveyors consumed over 154,000 livres. The expenses for bureau employees and other services amounted to 333,000; while correspondence, couriers, gifts, and indemnities cost 550,000.

Besides the regular foreign service, the French Government spent 2,475,000 livres in 1787 on subsidies. Sweden received 1,500,000; the Duke of Deux Ponts, 500,000; Nassau-Saarbrück, 100,000; the infant Duke of Parma, 375,000. Many Swedish, German, and Polish nobles were paid pensions ranging from 6,000 to 14,000 yearly. The intelligence service alone cost 200,000. It is no wonder that France was bankrupt and that the Estates-General had to be called to save the State.

The Austrian diplomatic service in the same period was, relatively speaking, as burdensome as the French. In 1785 the cost amounted to about 2,025,000 florins; the couriers alone consumed 800,000 florins in that year. Austria was a much poorer country than either France or England, and it was only the drastic reforms of Emperor Joseph II that saved the Habsburg monarchy from the fate of the Bourbons.[1]

Bribery was one regular method of diplomatic procedure; subsidies another. But there was a

[1] See S. K. Padover, *The Revolutionary Emperor : Joseph II.* (London, 1937).

third, even more insidious, more systematic. It was
the interception and copying of letters and despatches.
Even the most complicated cipher was no proof
against the eighteenth-century experts. Thugut, the
Austrian minister at Naples in 1788, told the Queen
that he had ciphers of all the chief powers. Hence the
warning of the French statesman Montmorin to his
Neapolitan agent : " Cipher your despatches, even
those which are entrusted to Spanish couriers. Without mentioning other accident, the Spanish couriers
can be despoiled as certain examples show."

The most efficient system of interception was that
developed by Prince Kaunitz, Chancellor of Austria
from 1753 to 1794. Kaunitz continued and perfected
the custom, which started with Maximilian I, of opening all the letters sent through the post. In the German Empire the monopoly of posts was held by the
Princes of Thurn and Taxis who were loyal to the
Habsburgs. Post-lodges, secret offices for opening
letters, were established at all central points of the
Empire and at the crossing of high roads. The post-
masters were confidential persons, their families holding office sometimes for centuries by heredity. The
principal intercepting stations were Eisenach, Frankfort, Nuremberg, Augsburg, Regensburg, the Hanseatic cities, and the capitals of the ecclesiastical
Electors, especially Mainz.

Not only was the regular mail opened and copied,
but the private couriers were either waylaid or bribed.
All the Prussian couriers, except two, were in the
service of Kaunitz, and the Chancellor had also the
key to the Prussian cipher. At the Austrian frontier
the courier's bag was opened by the waiting Viennese
agents and the despatches copied. Thus Kaunitz
would read the Prussian correspondence at the same
time as the Foreign Office in Berlin.

Although Vienna had developed the system of
interception and deciphering to a fine art, Paris was
unaware of the practice until 1774, when Ambassador

Rohan made the exciting discovery and hastened to
warn his government. Rohan was startled when he
found out that " our ciphers of 1,200 held out for only
a short time against the cleverness of the Austrian
decipherers."

"All the despatches of Prince Kaunitz," Rohan
described the Austrian Black Cabinet, " all those of
the Imperial ministers at foreign courts, all those of
the courts and foreign ministers which are intercepted,
pass through what is called here the ' Cabinet.' It is
there that the bureaux of the decipherers are established." The director of the Black Cabinet made daily
five copies of each despatch and handed them to
Maria Theresa. The Empress sent one copy to her
son, Emperor Joseph II, one to her other son Leopold,
Grand Duke of Tuscany, one to Prince Starhemberg
at Brussels. " The copy left at the office is reserved for
Prince Kaunitz. . . . These five copies are transcribed
in half-margin. Every one sends back his copy
directly to the Empress with his observations, and it is
these combined comments and discussions which
form the projects and resolutions."

The amateurish Rohan may have been excited at
the discovery, but the practice of the Austrians
had long been known to experienced diplomats.
" I have lost my money at whist to Count Parr,
the Imperial Postmaster General," Ambassador Keith
complained in 1773 ; " I have made three bows
extraordinary, and given two pinches of snuff to
the Prince de la Tour Taxis, the Postmaster of
the Holy Roman Empire. It is not in the power
of man to form a more tender connexion with those
princely personages. Yet are our letters purloined in
part." When an English friend asked Keith to
describe him the notorious eccentricities of Prince
Kaunitz, the English ambassador replied he would be
happy to do so : " But I am afraid your lordship is
not the only person who dips into my letters, and there
may be people in the world who would rather forgive

a plot against the State, than the smallest and most harmless pleasantry in regard to personal foibles."

The copying of despatches sometimes had amusing results. Keith once humorously complained to Kaunitz that instead of receiving his original correspondence he was getting copies. "How clumsy these people are!" was the Chancellor's unabashed reply.

CHAPTER VIII

A CARDINAL AND A QUEEN

WITH the death of Louis XIV in 1714, Europe entered into a period of comparative peace which lasted until 1740. Not counting the so-called War of the Polish Succession, the period from 1714 to 1740 was the longest space of time in which European arms rusted in the arsenals. Though the equilibrium established at Utrecht was precarious, there was neither the will nor the resource to destroy the shaky balance of power, for Louis XIV had effectively exhausted the fighting efficiency of the Continental powers. Unable, or unready, to take recourse in violence, the states perfected their diplomatic technique to an extraordinary degree; the tortuous diplomacy of the period is still the despair of historians.

Louis XV was a child of five when his great-grand-father died. France, therefore, was ruled by a Regent, the Duke of Orleans, and the latter by an ecclesiastic, Abbé, later Cardinal, Dubois. He was the third Cardinal to govern France in the course of a century, and, on a somewhat lower level, he was a worthy successor to Mazarin. Diplomatically it was a difficult period for France, for the country was regarded with suspicion in Vienna, distrusted in Madrid, and detested in London. France had to win back her prestige. The Regent decided to reverse the traditional French hostility to England, and sent the sixty-years-old Dubois across the Channel. Disguised as a Dutch gentleman, sometimes posing as an invalid travelling for his health and sometimes as a book-lover searching for rare editions, Dubois joined the retinue accompanying King George I to Hanover, and secretly delivered to Stanhope, the Secretary of State, a letter from the Regent proposing an alliance between France and England. Dubois carried with him 10,000 livres in silver and 4,000 in gold to bribe the British ministers.

Dubois and Stanhope met at The Hague. The cultured Englishman, an admirer of French culture, was well-disposed to the Regent and Dubois. Encouraged by the friendly reception, the Frenchman offered the English statesman a bribe of 600,000 livres ; Stanhope refused politely, but expressed no surprise. The amazed Dubois considered such conduct " heroic and admirable." But although Stanhope was friendly, he acted with caution, for English public opinion was still hostile to France. Dubois complained to the Regent that all his " rhetoric was useless."

Unable to make any headway, Dubois decided to change his tactics. He sent to France for sixty cases of the finest wines, thirty of which he gave to Stanhope " with his regards," and thirty to King George with profuse compliments. Wine proving more effective than gold, Stanhope consented to the alliance, but had first to overcome the hostility of the King. Finally George I was won over by the argument that the French alliance would protect his cherished Hanover from both Prussia and Austria.

While these intrigues were going on, Dubois, who went under the pseudonym of St. Alban (ironically, one of the Regent's illegitimate sons), lived in Stanhope's residence at Hanover. The Frenchman's position was ludicrous. " We negotiated," he wrote, " in our dressing-gowns and in our nightcaps." When Stanhope gave a State dinner to thirteen diplomats accredited to the Hanoverian court, Dubois—who, of course, could not be invited—sat across the hall in his chambers with the door ajar and listened avidly to the indiscreet table talk. " The wine of the Secretary of State," Dubois informed the Regent, " was gay and talkative." It was more than gay ; it was stunning. For at the end of the dinner only Stanhope was sober—which proves that he was worthy of his office. The other thirteen had drunk seventy bottles of wine and six bottles of liqueurs. Seventy-six divided by fourteen (including Stanhope) makes about

five and a half bottles per person. Enough to make
even a diplomat drunk. While the intoxicated plenipotentiaries snored in their chairs and under the table,
Stanhope—what a constitution that man must have
had !—slipped across the hall to visit his " prisoner."
Dubois amused his host by showing him notes on the
snatches of conversation he had overheard.

Two months later—January 4, 1717—the Anglo-
French alliance was signed and in the next year
(August, 1718) it was enlarged into the Quadruple
Alliance by the entrance of Holland and Austria. The
aim was to maintain the terms of the Treaty of Utrecht,
especially against the designs of Spain upon Italy.

When the alliance was made public Dubois threw
off his disguise and appeared at the English court in
the full panoply of an accredited ambassador. The
Frenchman's wit and vivacity soon made him popular
in the London drawing-rooms. Dubois frankly
admits that he also served as a spy. His official residence was at Dukes Street, Westminster ; his other
address was at Trafalgar Square where he received
despatches and secret information, directed to him as
" M. Dubusson, maitre à danser, chez M. Hamton,
maitre charpentier à St. Martin, derrière l'église proche
Cherincross." Here he posed as a French dancing
master lodging with a carpenter residing back of the
church of St. Martin near Charing Cross.

Like Talleyrand, the clever abbé attached great
importance to good dinners as means by which diplomacy might achieve its designs. His nephew who
managed his property in France was constantly and
minutely instructed as to the wines, liqueurs, foods—
truffles, *paté de foie gras*, confectionery—which he
should send him to London. Dubois was also a careful distributor of silks among his English lady friends.
He knew precisely the effect an exquisite French
taffeta would have upon the mind of a cabinet minister's wife. Dress designs, patterns, and weaves he
studied as carefully as he did English politics.

CARDINAL DUBOIS

The Frenchman's espionage system in England enabled him to unravel a plot of the Spanish faction in Paris with the Spanish ambassador in France, the notorious Cellamare. He discovered the proofs in the Spanish embassy in London, to the discomfiture of Montelon, Philip V's ambassador. Cellamare thought he had corrupted Buvat, an attaché in the French King's library. Buvat revealed the correspondence to the Regent, but the attaché did not realize that for six months before this revelation both he and Cellamare had been carefully watched by Dubois' agents. Dubois had discovered the intrigue by securing copies of the letters which Cellamare had sent to his colleague, the Spanish ambassador at London. " The prince de Cellamare," Dubois wrote to the Abbé de Targny, " has sent hither a memoir which I have caught but a glimpse of, but in which I recognized at once the handwriting of your scrivener in the King's library. He is not to be blamed for having done this writing, but it is important to learn who made the deal of the Spanish ambassador with him, and then, to make as much use of him as possible in order to get copies of what is written for the ambassador, or at least to be apprized of everything he writes, both to know the subject of it and to intercept as much as we can. If scrivener is an honest man, since it concerns the service of the State, he ought not to scruple to give all the light he can. He will utterly fail in his duty of a faithful subject of the King if he does not divulge everything he can from his position." Buvat made a confession.

Before leaving England Dubois outlined to the Regent a typical programme of seduction and corruption. " Nothing must be neglected," he wrote, " in order to win the affection of the actors in this matter, both great and small ; not by direct proposals, which might make them think that we believed them capable of being suborned, but by practice of such noble manners as will seem to partake rather of generosity than of design to ensnare their infidelity. Your Royal Highness already knows the disinterestedness of Milord Stanhope. I would, however, approach him with a high compliment, and if Your Royal Highness would beg him to accept a portrait of the King embellished with diamonds to the value of 50,000 écus, or 200,000 francs, I do not doubt that he will accept it ; but whether he refuse or not, it will have a good effect." Furthermore, Dubois asked for 100,000 francs' worth of jewels for Lord Stair, the English ambassador at Paris, and a gold dinner service worth 40,000 livres for the Imperial ambassador, Penterrieder, who was notorious for his corruptibility. George I hinted to Dubois that a gift of plate worth from 20,000 to 30,000 livres from the French King would not be rejected.

The Treaty of Hanover, as the alliance with England was called, was ruinous to France, as it antagonized Russia in the Baltic, involved heavy financial outlays for subsidizing Sweden, and brought a costly war with Spain. In 1720, therefore, Dubois decided to ally with Spain and to conciliate Russia with Sweden in order to prepare for war with the Habsburgs. Paris began to negotiate for a marriage between the Orleanist Duke de Chartres and Elizabeth, the daughter of Peter the Great, with a prospect of the reversion of the Polish crown.

London was informed of Dubois' machinations. But the British Government was either hoodwinked or deliberately deceived Destouches, the French agent. " Mylord Stanhope," Destouches wrote home, " and M. Craggs believe us to be irreconcilably embroiled with Spain, and on this basis they do not apprehend any change on our part."

Stanhope, unwilling to break with France, proposed to Destouches that England, France, and Spain settle their difference at a congress ; he declared himself ready to surrender Gibraltar as " useless and dangerous." But Stanhope died in 1721 and Dubois made an alliance with Spain, promising secretly that France would help Spain to obtain Gibraltar.

Even after Stanhope's death, Dubois worked hard for a triple alliance of France, England, and Spain. But Gibraltar remained the stumbling block. In the end Spain joined the alliance (1721), but only after George I had written to the Spanish King that the question of Gibraltar would be submitted to Parliament. The Spaniards took this to be a promise that Gibraltar would be returned to them.

In 1723 Dubois died and was succeeded by another ecclesiastic, later Cardinal, Fleury. He soon got into trouble with Spain over a very ticklish matter. The question of marriage was involved, and this, in the *ancien régime*, was a matter of international importance. Young Louis XV was wifeless. It was necessary to perpetuate the dynasty. Moreover, the royal youth was a colossal glutton and always in danger of eating himself to death before he had given an heir to France. " It is prodigious," an English diplomat described one such gastronomical debauch, " the great quantity of melons, figs and unripe walnuts that are said to have been devoured, besides an omelet, in which they put no less . . . than fourscore eggs." Fleury was afraid that Louis XV would die before he had a chance to marry and have a son. Something had to be done quickly. The difficulty was that the young monarch was engaged to a Spanish princess, who was being groomed in Paris. This girl, however, was too young to consummate the marriage. An older bride had to be found, and the Infanta was ceremoniously shipped back to Spain.

Naturally, the Spanish royal family was outraged at this insult. Only war could atone for such a humiliation. The situation was already delicate enough, but it was aggravated by the vain Elizabeth Farnese, the " termagant Queen of Spain," whose chief aim in life was to provide, and provide well, for her brood. Uneducated, repressed, scorpion-tongued,

Elizabeth ruled her husband, her family, and her kingdom with an iron rod. Such a woman would not take an insult to her daughter lightly.

Alliance or no alliance with Paris, the Spanish Queen, too poor to go to war with France, decided to seek friends where she could. The best way to do so was to get in touch with the Austrian Habsburgs— against whom, incidentally, the Franco-Anglo-Spanish treaty was directed. For Elizabeth Farnese hoped to kill two birds at once : to marry her children into the Austrian family and, by allying herself with Vienna, to have her revenge on France. The plan was that her son Carlos should marry Maria Theresa, the daughter and heiress of Emperor Charles VI. Since the Emperor had no sons, and since Maria Theresa was to succeed him to all the Habsburg dominions, the Spanish Queen reasoned that by marrying the Austrian heiress her son Carlos would become Emperor. To make doubly sure, Elizabeth planned to marry her younger son, Philip, to Maria Anna, a younger daughter of Emperor Charles VI. The marriages consummated, Spain and Austria were to form an alliance in order to defend their family interests, win back Gibraltar and Minorca, secure recognition for the Pragmatic Sanction (by which Maria Theresa was recognized as Charles VI's legitimate successor), and give Austria commercial privileges in the Spanish colonies. The scheme was excellent, and, incidentally, the British secret service was aware of it. For the " termagant queen " could not keep her tongue.

The Spanish Queen's project required a very crafty diplomat to represent Her Majesty personally in Vienna. Without the knowledge of Grimaldo, the Spanish minister of Foreign Affairs, Elizabeth chose one Baron Ripperdà, a Spanish adventurer born in Holland, who had experiences as a spy. The Queen, her husband the King, and the confidential adviser Orendayn prepared secret instructions for Ripperdà.

If Vienna, the instructions read, regarded the proposed double marriage favourably, Maria Theresa should receive as a dowry, after Emperor Charles' death, all the hereditary Habsburg States in Germany ; Maria Anna was to get all the estates in Italy, to which Spain would add Parma, Piacenza, and Tuscany. The Austrian Netherlands were to be restored to Spain or be given to Elizabeth's younger son, Don Philip and his wife Maria Anna, on condition that the provinces be restored to Spain if the couple died without heirs. Emperor Charles was also to promise active aid in the recovery of Gibraltar and Minorca. The proposals amounted to a virtual partition of the Habsburg Empire.

Elizabeth, however, was not interested in politics as much as in the future of her children. Consequently she gave Ripperdà another set of instructions, kept secret from everybody. Ripperdà was orally informed that the chief aim of his mission was to secure the marriages at the expense of everything else.

Arrived at the gates of Vienna, in January, 1725, Ripperdà loudly announced that he was an emissary of Philip V to Peter the Great at Moscow. This gave him diplomatic access to the Vienna Chancery, and there he revealed his secret to Count Zinzendorf. The news was promptly passed on to the astonished Emperor, who opened negotiations. Ripperdà boasted that he had the complete confidence of the Spanish court and that he was slated to be foreign minister. To intimidate the Emperor, the Spaniard told him confidentially a fabulous story that the Duke of Bourbon had proposed to Philip V to conquer for him both Sicilies (which belonged to the Emperor), while the Czar and Sultan, with French aid, were to invade Silesia and Hungary. King Philip, Ripperdà gently assured the frightened Emperor, had indignantly rejected the proposal.

Emperor Charles VI believed the fairy tale. He also believed that Don Carlos would become King of

Spain, as Don Ferdinand, the heir to the throne, was too frail to live ; therefore Don Carlos, the proposed son-in-law of the Emperor, had a great future. The timid Charles, however, feared to arouse European jealousy. After wily negotiations on the part of Ripperdà, the Emperor signed two treaties, one of peace between Spain and Austria, and one of defensive alliance. As regards the marriages so eagerly desired by Elizabeth, the Emperor said that when his daughters were of age one or the other of them would marry a Spanish prince.

The treaty soon became known in Europe and produced the usual reaction. France, England, and Prussia formed an alliance mutually guaranteeing their possessions ; Sweden was bought with hard cash.

This Northern Alliance was a challenge to Austria and Spain, and Ripperdà took full advantage of the situation. While the English Admiral Hosier was sent to the West Indies to prevent the sailing of the Spanish treasure fleet and thus cripple Austria by depriving her of the supplies which Ripperdà had promised her, Ripperdà at Vienna was making costly presents to the Austrian ministers. By November the adventurous Spaniard had succeeded in getting Charles' secret promise for the double marriage. The Princess Maria Theresa was promised to Don Carlos " in case the Emperor should die before she became marriageable " ; but, it was stipulated, in no case were the crowns of Spain, Austria, and France, or any two of them, ever to be united.

In great triumph Ripperdà returned to Madrid and realized his ambitions by becoming chief minister. But unable to supply Vienna with the needed money and faced with the usual intrigues of power-politics, Ripperdà fell before he had time to consolidate his position. While congratulating Königsegg, the Austrian ambassador at Madrid, on Ripperdà's fall, the aged Prince Eugene of Savoy made some keen observations. " Yet one must confess," he wrote,

" that Ripperdà possessed very good qualities which, in a certain position, might have won him fame and distinction. I believe that, violent and desperate as he was, he might have been able to do the King services which were not to be expected of anyone else, certainly not of any born Spaniard. For the Spaniard will never venture to lay his hand on certain malpractices which have so long taken deep root, and are extremely injurious to the King's interests. On these subjects, at all events, Ripperdà has imparted ideas to me, which, if carried into execution, might have been of great value to the King's finances and the revival of trade."

Ripperdà's career was adventurous to the end. He was imprisoned in the castle of Segovia where he was fairly well treated and even received a small pension. In the castle, he won the sympathy of the governor's maid who helped him to escape. Madrid not unjustly suspected the Colonel Stanhope (later Lord Harrington), the British ambassador, of complicity. " All my endeavours have proved ineffectual," Stanhope wrote before Ripperdà's escape, " though I have omitted nothing. I have even met in private and in disguise with the governor of the castle, with whom I always used to lodge, and who is my particular friend, but found by him that the thing was impracticable, both from Ripperdà's indisposition (he had the gout), and from the governor's being watched by the Alcalde."

Ripperdà made his merry way to England, and then to Holland, but finding no scope for his gifts in Europe he sailed for Morocco where he took service. " The incredible news I sent you about Ripperdà is confirmed," wrote Keane, the British minister at Madrid, in 1732; " he is actually at Tetuan, and would have been a captain-general could his conscience have allowed him to turn Mussulman; but as yet they have only taken his presents, and as the country is cheap, they have granted him leave to spend the surplus of his income in the service of Muley Abdelah." Ripperdà soon overcame his religious scruples, fought in a war against Spain, and won the susceptible heart of the mother of the Moroccan ruler. He participated in every conceivable intrigue, and on his death-bed is said to have returned to the true faith.

Having failed to win effective Austrian support, and needing a strong ally against Britain, the Spanish Queen determined to cause a break between Paris and London. She called Fleury, the ecclesiastic who succeeded Dubois in the Foreign Office, a coward who cringed before that arch-heretic, Walpole. "If it please God," the Spanish King Philip V said of his ailing nephew, the young Louis XV, " that the King, my nephew, should die without male heirs, I, the nearest relative, or my descendants, ought to and will succeed to the crown of my ancestors." Madrid, therefore, sent the Abbé Montgon, an adventurer, to Paris with instructions to play the spy.

" I am quite aware," Queen Elizabeth wrote to Fleury in a conciliatory mood, " that it is not my business to give advice to so enlightened a person as yourself, but sometimes too some atom of reason may be found in the least reasonable people. What I say is solely by my wish to see the uncle (Philip V of Spain) and nephew (Louis XV) reconciled. That done, I most certainly have no further views than the good of the world at large. I am convinced that it is not fear of war that makes you speak as you do, but the welfare of the two crowns. It is just the same on my part, and so we two are playing on the same side. As to fear, we have none, and I have never seen anyone have less than the King ; he might be called with reason Philip the Fearless."

The Queen added as an afterthought that Fleury should destroy this letter.

Fleury did not fall for Elizabeth's compliments.

But the powers were deadlocked. There was bitter feeling between Spain and England. Queen

Elizabeth could not bear the sight of an Englishman, even of so amiable a man as Ambassador Benjamin Keane—"fat, easy and of universal knowledge." The Spaniards, Keane wrote whimsically, have given him "several hints that they should be glad to see M. Keane if I could contrive to leave the Englishman behind me." The Queen insisted that George I had promised the restitution of Gibraltar. To the French ambassador she said bitterly : "Is it not just that the English who are so rich should give the King a few millions. . . . You in France are nothing but English." She rummaged in a box and finally drew out George I's letter about Gibraltar. "Perhaps it is forged ?" she asked sarcastically. "Genuine," murmured the French diplomat. "I am glad," the Queen said, "to furnish you with such an excuse. . . . Let your allies fulfil their part, we will fulfil ours."

The climax was reached over an English ship which Spain had seized ; the English blockaded Spanish ports. War was imminent. But Spain, despite Elizabeth's fury, had no money for war. Emperor Charles mediated, and a congress was assembled at Soissons. The congress was a joke, for the envoys were rarely in town. In November, 1729, a settlement that was no settlement was reached. English trade privileges in the Spanish colonies were restored and Gibraltar was passed over in silence. The dynasts were precisely where they started.

While the Congress of Soissons was supposed to be settling the international problems of Europe, an unknown wit composed a satire on the diplomatic card game.

The Emperor : "All I need is a king to change."

The King of France : "I could play alone, but I prefer to be called."

The Queen of France : "If I had only one little king instead of my three dames I would gain more than the others."

Muscovy : "I am beginning to learn the game."

Spain : " All that prevents me from making a codille is a king."

England : " I cannot play, because I have only matadores and no king."

Poland : " I would prefer to let my son play in my place."

Denmark : " I am content to shuffle the cards without playing."

Portugal : " I play hearts and I call the colours."

Prussia : " I will go halves with him who has the best hand."

Sardinia : " I would like to play, but I do not know which king to call."

Duke of Lorraine : " I have no money to play."

Holland : " I would like to play, but I fear to have against me all the matadores."

Venice : " I never play, but I like to see others play."

The Pope : " I do not know how to play, but I pray that my friends win."

The Pretender : " I have no game, hence no one ever calls me."

Stanislaus Leszczynski : " I have lost, for they have cut my king."

Cardinal Alberoni : " I have been driven from the game because I have mixed up the cards."

Cardinal Fleury : " He who does not call my king will surely lose."

Ostend Company : " I fear to lose my capital at a double turn."

Switzerland : " Wherever one plays, I am always called."

Grand Turk : " I have lost too often to risk it again."

CHAPTER IX

THE BALANCE OF POWER

" The equilibrium of society depends at any given moment upon a tacit agreement that the whole truth shall not be openly proclaimed."—GEORGE BRANDES.

I

MID-EIGHTEENTH-CENTURY diplomacy is marked by a new development : the struggle for the maintenance of the balance of power. The two factors that necessitated this conflict were the emergence of Prussia and Russia as great powers. Peter the Great had brought Russia close to Europe, while the Hohenzollerns, especially the Great Elector, had made a powerful State out of the barren and sandy Brandenburg. The change is symbolized by two cities : Petersburg arose out of a swamp and Berlin was transformed from a Wendish fishermen's village to a European metropolis. Czar and Elector had given the first shock to the precarious European equilibrium, but it was Frederick the Great of Prussia who effectively destroyed it.

Frederick the Great's father, Frederick William I, was a despot with the mentality of a drill master. When he appointed an adventurer named Echard as Revenue Councillor, the Chamber dared to protest. " The high, praiseworthy Chamber," the Prussian King said roughly, " is entreated to let alone reasoning, and not to meddle with the honourable Echard, or We shall come and in our own person undertake the presidency of the Chamber with a good cudgel."

Cudgelling was Frederick William's favourite method of governing. He beat his subjects, he slapped his officers, he whipped his children (including the sensitive heir to the throne who later compensated his childhood humiliations by becoming a military conqueror). " I know from experience," Frederick William once said, " that people of position and merit are not fit for business. They entrench themselves behind their point of honour, when they do not choose to obey my commands. . . . This does not suit me, and for the future I prefer taking yelping dogs, whom one can order about without their being sulky, who must do whatever I wish."

Once this Hohenzollern was conversing with diplomats about the binding force of treaties. No sooner, he remarked realistically, was a treaty made when the parties were thinking of breaking it. " Count Manteuffel," he addressed the Saxon envoy, " you know what treaties are ; say honestly, is a single one ever made with the intention of keeeping it ? "

" Your Majesty is joking," Manteuffel replied suavely, " when you ask such a question. The prior question would be, whether great rulers are honest men, and are anxious to be esteemed as such. How could they pass for such, if they did not hold to truth and faith ? "

" That is all true enough," the King replied, " but what treaties are observed ? I know none."

" I know many," answered the diplomat ; " Your Majesty has made all your treaties with the intention of keeping them, and you do keep them in fact."

" Yes," Frederick William said, " I have always had the intention ; but I have not always abided by it. It pains me ; but I must admit as much." Then he added how he once solemnly promised Czar Peter the Great never to abandon him and never make a separate peace with Sweden, and yet he did both. " Was that right ? " the King asked ; " I do not think so ; but it was done. I held out a long time. I worked myself into a fever about it ; but what could I do ? My rogues "—pointing to the ministers who were present —" plagued me so. Kniphausen would not leave me a moment's peace ; I must sign. I might assent or dissent ; and I ended by signing. That was a downright fraud."

Candidness was one of Frederick William's virtues. But he was also eccentric. One of his queer habits was to abduct tall men for his guards. When some Hanoverians were thus abducted by the Prussians, King George II of England, who was also ruler of Hanover, retaliated by having the hay cut on a piece of land which adjoined Prussia. His Prussian Majesty decided that only blood could wipe out an insult of such magnitude, but added wisely : " Why should human blood, except George's and mine, be shed in such a quarrel ? " Wherefore he challenged George to a duel. His Britannic Majesty was eager to shed His Prussian Majesty's blood, but the diplomats on both sides hastily intervened and, characteristically, almost caused a European war.

The quarrel between Berlin and London was not ended so easily. Not permitted to slash at each other with sabres, the two monarchs resorted to calling names. " My brother the sergeant," George dubbed Frederick William. " My brother the dancing master," Frederick William sneered at George. " Must I," the Prussian King asked on his death-bed, " to go to paradise, forgive all my enemies ? " He was told that he must. " Eh, well, Dorothea," the dying King said to his wife, " write to your brother (George) and tell him that I forgive him all the harm he has done me. Yes, tell him that I forgive him, but wait until I am dead."

Such was Frederick the Great's Royal parent.

In 1740 Frederick succeeded his father to the throne of Prussia. He was slight in size and sensitive of face, just a boy despite his twenty-eight years. He was known to Europe as a friend of Voltaire and a clever prince who played the flute and wrote bad verses. No one realized that the young man, who had recently written a refutation of Machiavelli, entertained plans which would throw Europe into confusion for more than two decades and that he would turn out to be the most astute and unscrupulous diplomat in an age when diplomacy was an intricate game of subtle skill.

Frederick II (the title " Great " really belongs to a later period) took over a highly-centralized State ; he inherited an army which was perhaps the best disciplined in Europe—his father's most enduring achievement. Like his parent, Frederick employed ministers, but only as a species of clerks. He rarely consulted them and never permitted any expression of opinion or independence of action. Ministers and Councillors were there only to draft documents and obey orders. The only man who, in those early years, knew anything about Frederick's mind was his mysterious private secretary, August Wilhelm Eichel, who served his King loyally from 1741 until his death in 1768. Eichel, according to the report of a British diplomat (Hanbury-Williams), was " so carefully watched that a person may be at this court seven years without once seeing him." A memorandum in the French Foreign Office contains the same information : " M. Eichel is unknown and inaccessible to everybody ; he works every day with the King of Prussia and expedites all business. He has under him many secretaries as invisible as he is. He alone knows the business of His Prussian Majesty, to the exclusion of the other ministers."

Secrecy and swiftness were among Frederick's most effective techniques. Soon he had occasion to show his mettle—or his fangs. For in Vienna, too, there was a change on the throne. Five months before Frederick's accession in Berlin, Maria Theresa succeeded to the inheritance of the Habsburgs. Her father, Emperor Charles VI, had made sure of his daughter's succession by having virtually all the European powers sign the Pragmatic Sanction, guaranteeing Maria Theresa's right to the throne, as well as the indivisibility of the far-flung Austrian territories.

Frederick's father, the redoubtable Frederick William, had been one of the signers of the Pragmatic Sanction. But the son did not consider the father's

FREDERICK THE GREAT

signature as binding on him. He knew that Maria Theresa's vast heritage was poorly defended ; what was more, England and France, the two great Western powers, were in conflict over their colonial empires, and sooner or later one or the other would have to bid for Prussian support. Under these circumstances, a bold man, Frederick reasoned quickly, could seize whatever he wished ; he himself coveted Austrian Silesia in order to " round out " Prussian territory. He suspected, and rightly, that an inexperienced young girl like Maria Theresa would be in no position to defend herself. " There remains," Frederick wrote, " only Russia capable of giving us umbrage. . . . When the Empress (Czarina Anna) is dead, the Russians will be so occupied with their internal affairs that they will have no time to think of outsiders ; and in any case, to send a donkey loaded with gold to St. Petersburg is not impossible."

Frederick decided to seize Silesia in a sudden coup and then to offer Maria Theresa military aid against whatever enemy might show up—in other words, to offer his sharp sword at a huge price. The English Government, suspecting that something was in the wind, instructed its minister in Berlin (Guy Dickens) to urge the Prussian King to observe the Pragmatic Sanction which his father had signed. When Dickens pressed Frederick as to his plans, the King grew red— he was not yet an experienced liar—and said that the Englishman had no right to ask him that. Calming himself immediately, he added that Britain was too inclined " to bring other princes under her tuition." It was too late, anyhow, for Frederick promptly invaded Silesia and thereby started a European war which lasted, on and off, for about fifteen years.

Now, it was queer that London did not break openly with Berlin, despite the fact that England was Austria's ally. British diplomacy was badly bungled. Dickens was succeeded in Berlin by the (third) Earl of Hyndford, a novice and an incompetent. His Lordship's official documents were poorly written; his despatches were carelessly handled. In no time he succeeded, unwittingly, in giving away the English cipher to the Prussians. Finally he fell into a Frederician trap. He bribed one Schmettau, who was confidential Prussian agent, to sell him official intelligence, and Schmettau gave Hyndford precisely the news that Frederick wanted him to know. Ultimately His Lordship made his position untenable by giving refuge in his rooms, which had diplomatic immunity, to a disreputable woman fleeing from her creditors. The woman was arrested; Hyndford demanded an apology for the invasion of his quarters. Frederick wrote bitingly: " It seems to me, my lord, that you associate unseasonably the honour of a bankrupt with that of the King your master, the name of a prostituted person with the august name of a sovereign." Hyndford left Berlin and England remained unrepresented in Prussia except by one Laurence, or Lorentz, a German clerk who knew little English.

There was another little diplomatic comedy connected with Frederick's " rape " of Silesia. Fleury, the French Foreign Minister, was also worried about His Prussian Majesty's intentions, and he knew that only a very clever man could ferret out the King's secret.

There was such a man in France and his name was Voltaire. In the previous summer he had been invited by his Royal friend to visit Berlin, but could not make up his mind to do so. Now the famous writer was in Fleury's bad graces and to win back his favour he voluntarily offered his services as a scout in Prussia. In a letter replete with Voltairean flattery, the friend of Frederick appealed to Fleury to be permitted to visit Prussia; he included a copy of the *Anti-Machiavel*, Frederick's book which had just appeared without the august author's name, insinuating that the Prussian King's friendship for Voltaire might be of service to France. The cunning Fleury—Fleury, Voltaire, Frederick—what a wily trio!—did not wish to appear too eager to accept and wrote Voltaire an unctuous letter praising the writer's respect for religion. Fleury was a cardinal and he had an eighteenth-century French ecclesiastic's subtlety! On the following day the Cardinal wrote a more businesslike letter:

" Whoever may be the author of the work," Fleury wrote in reference to the *Anti-Machiavel,* " if he is not a prince, he ought to be one ; and the little I have read of it is so wise, so sensible, and contains principles so admirable, that if he has the courage to put them in practice he would be worthy to rule men. If he is born a prince, he has contracted a very solemn engagement with the public. . . . Corruption is so general, and sincerity so indecently banished from all men's minds in this unhappy age, that if we did not hold firmly to those high principles which bind us not to depart from them, we should be tempted to fail on certain occasions ; but the King, my master, at least makes it plain that he does not hold it allowable to use reprisals of such a kind, since no sooner had he heard the news about the Emperor, than he assured Prince Lichtenstein he would faithfully keep all his engagements. . . . I find myself unintentionally making political reflections. Let me conclude by assuring you that I shall endeavour to be worthy of his Prussian Majesty's good opinion of me. It is a pity he is a prince, for, were he only an ordinary mortal, it would be a pleasure to meet him in society. I envy you, and I congratulate you, all the more that you owe your good fortune solely to your talents and your sentiments."

The wily Voltaire saw the point. He was to go to Berlin and casually mention that Paris was ready to observe the Pragmatic Sanction ; so, by insinuation, should the very learned and very sincere Prussian King. When Voltaire reached Frederick's residence

at Rheinsberg he informed Fleury : " I have obeyed
the orders Your Eminence did not give me, and have
shown your letter to the King of Prussia."

More than cleverness, however, was necessary to
extract a secret from Frederick. The King joyously
entertained Voltaire, Algarotti, Jordan, and other
favourite guests in gay and Royal fashion. From
morning to evening there was witty conversation and
music and poetry ; Frederick himself versified and
played the flute. And all the time secret military
preparations were taking place.

Not only did Frederick keep his plans to himself,
but he took malicious pleasure in arousing the curiosity
of his brilliant guests. Once after finishing some
verses the King said : " That is all over ; the demon
of war is about to snatch me from the demon of
poetry." Algarotti, catching the meaning, flatteringly
suggested that His Majesty, now that there were no
male Habsburgs, should try for the Imperial crown.
" That," the cynical King retorted, " is the advice
which Antony gave to Cæsar."

Voltaire could find out nothing. Cajole and flatter
as he would, he could not pry open the King's mind.
Crestfallen and mortified, the vain and pampered
writer left the Royal residence. Fleury's little diplomatic agent was not a shining success. Voltaire had
failed in his mission ; he had quarrelled with the
King—over money matters, as usual. For the two
famous friends were parsimonious to a degree.
Voltaire had submitted to his crowned friend a bill
for the exorbitant sum of 1,300 crowns to cover his
travelling expenses. The tight-fisted King was furious.
" Your miser," he wrote to Jordan, " shall drink the
dregs of his desire to enrich himself ; he shall have his
1,300 crowns. His six days' visit will cost me 500
pounds. That is good pay for a fool. No court
jester ever had such wages."

And, one may add, no great writer was ever such a
poor diplomat.

Frederick fell on Silesia without the trouble of declaring war. European public opinion was universal in its condemnation. " All that a fickle and ignorant world is saying against me," the King of Prussia said coldly, " hardly embarrasses me. Only posterity judges kings."

Posterity judges kings, but allies help them ; and Frederick, though sure of posterity, had no friends. He found an ally in France, which was not of much help, for it was offset by England's joining Austria. Frederick's best ally should have been Russia, and how he lost Russia—or rather how England won her —makes a very strange story.

At the end of the seventeenth century Russia was not a member of the European " family of nations " ; it was a semi-civilized, semi-Asiatic, landlocked State, cut off from Europe by Sweden and Poland, and hemmed in south by the Turkish Empire. The interior of this vast land was full of forests and morasses, inhabited by wolves, and impassable. Moscow, the largest city, with a population of about 500,000, had wooden pigsty houses ; the streets were " paved " with faggots. Peter the Great had superficially galvanized Russia ; he introduced a number of European reforms, conquered the western provinces from Sweden, opened a " window on the Baltic," and cut off the beards of his subjects.

At the time when Frederick of Prussia was starting his little European war the ruler of Muscovy was Elizabeth, the handsome and lusty daughter of Peter the Great. She was, in the words of an English diplomat, " a selfish sybarite, a creature of moods and tempers," surrounded by the " basest sycophants and flatterers." Grand Duchess Catherine, the German girl who was destined to succeed Elizabeth on the throne as Catherine the Great, remembered her predecessor's court as a place where the " art of conversation was unknown, where hatred was mutual and sincere, and where the slightest serious word was a crime and treason." And where, she might have added, everyone had his or her price.

Imperial Chancellor Bestuchev was in the pay of Sir Charles Hanbury-Williams, the English minister. Not to be outdone, the Marquis de la Chétardie, who was the French ambassador, built up an anti-Bestuchev faction composed of Brümmer, the tutor of Grand Duke Peter, and Grand Duchess Catherine's mother (Catherine herself was Hanbury-Williams' friend). These factions were on the fringe of Royalty. Czarina Elizabeth herself remained aloof as between the English and French bribers, although Lestocq, a French adventurer, claimed that he had access to Her Imperial Majesty.

The Anglophile—or Anglo-paid—Bestuchev had the upper hand, for two reasons : Russia had an engagement with Austria and England, and the Empress was too indolent to intervene in foreign affairs. He was also in a key position to intercept the despatches sent to Paris by Chétardie (no less than fifty-seven of them). The Marquis knew that his letters were being opened by the Russian " Black Cabinet," but he could only vent his anger in impotent phrases. " It is without any shame or precaution," he said bitterly, " that they unseal letters here." He need not have been so indignant, for his government was doing the same thing in Paris. In any case, he thought himself fairly safe, believing that his cipher was impervious. The Russians, he thought with French vanity, were not clever enough to find a key to his cipher ; wherefore the Marquis expressed himself with great frankness. He may have been right about the Russians' cleverness, but he had not counted on the Muscovites employing three German officials in the post office ; these Germans easily found the key to the French cipher—and then " the fat was in the fire."

Chétardie's letters were really quite scandalous. Relying upon the indecipherability of his combination, he gave full expression to his opinions about the Czarina's character and her Chancellor's crookedness. When Bestuchev opened those letters he was one of the happiest men in Russia. At last he got that Frenchman! " If she knew better," one of Chétardie's deciphered letters read, " how to conciliate the duties of a Christian "—at this point Bestuchev made a marginal comment: " He expressed himself in so outrageous a fashion on a Majesty that it would be difficult to imagine anything worse "—" with those of her state the ill consequences of the instructions given to the Russian generals . . . would not have taken place, although such certainly was not the intention of the Czarina, but the work of the Vice-Chancellor who has more than once given similar orders without the knowledge of his mistress. The evil is without remedy, because the Czarina, given entirely to her pleasures and having a more and more decided aversion for business, will no longer have faithful ministers to whom she could entrust the care of government."

Imagine the reaction of a vain woman, who was also an autocrat, to such a slur on her character.

Bestuchev's marginal comment on this letter was : " Could one expect such ingratitude and that he would express himself so slanderously on a Majesty ? "

The wily Chancellor continued to pile up these intercepted despatches, to collect a respectable *dossier* against the French ambassador. Ignorant of what was taking place, Chétardie blithely continued to incriminate himself. " What can one expect," another one of his letters read, " of a . . . princess so frivolous and so dissipated ? " The gleeful Bestuchev wrote on the margin : " Her Imperial Majesty should demand the recall of de la Chétardie, as a man whom she believed honourable and grateful for the numerous marks of favour which she had accorded him, but not as a wicked person and a calumniator."

When Bestuchev submitted copies of the letters to

Her Majesty, the easy-going Elizabeth refused to believe the truth. " It is false," she cried, " it is an invention of his enemies of whom you are one." Bestuchev then showed her the originals in cipher and deciphered them in her presence. Here was full proof of conspiracy, of bribery given to her favourite Lestocq (2,000 roubles), to Brümmer, to Catherine's mother, Princess Dolgoruki (2,000 roubles plus an annual pension of 1,200), the ladies-in-waiting, and even the prelates of the Holy Synod. The ramifications of the intrigue, as they unfolded in the unlocked cipher before Elizabeth's eyes, stretched out to the representatives of Prussia, Sweden, Bavaria. Most bitterly of all, she, the Empress of all the Russias, she herself was ridiculed, despised, criticized in these despatches. And all this was done by the Frenchman whom she had liked so well, the Parisian who was so delightfully clever, so charmingly flattering, so genuinely amiable. Elizabeth flamed with rage.

The next day (June 17, 1744), as the unsuspecting Chétardie entered his home, he was accosted by the chief of the secret service, two members of the Foreign Office, and a number of officers. The Russians silently handed him a note. It was from the Czarina and was addressed, not to the French ambassador, but to the " Brigadier of the French armies." The letter, after briefly accusing the Frenchman of bribery and corruption, harshly ordered him " to leave, in twenty-four hours and without seeing a soul, this capital and to get out of the empire at once." The Marquis protested with voluble vehemence ; he was, he cried, a victim of base calumny. In answer, the Russians began to read some of his despatches. " That is enough," said de la Chétardie. And he immediately began to pack.

Such was the background of Russia's alliances with England and Austria against Prussia. The coalition came within a point of destroying Frederick the Great.

II

Seven years after Frederick's seizure of Silesia a temporary peace was concluded at Aix-la-Chapelle in 1748. The peace treaty settled practically nothing, for Silesia was left in Frederick's hands and the rivalry between England and France remained as acute as ever.

The next seven or eight years the Powers spent in laying the foundations for a new war. The imminent conflict revolved around two axes: the struggle between Austria and Prussia for the control of Germany, and the world-clash between England and France for the possession of colonies. Hitherto in every European conflict England could be found on the side of the enemy of France, that is, Austria, for Habsburg and Bourbon had been at dagger's point for the control of Europe for almost two centuries. In an unstable Europe one of the constants seemed to be Anglo-Austrian amity.

But Vienna had pathetically failed to meet the challenge of a powerful and aggressive military State such as Prussia. Even the easy-going Habsburg court realized that it was of vital importance now to meet military force with military force, and in this the British could not be relied on, for their aid had always consisted merely of subsidies. Hence Austria decided to win over France, potentially a great military power, and after five years of underground manœuvring the Diplomatic Revolution was a reality.

This Austro-French alliance, a prelude to a new war, meant the desertion of England by Maria Theresa. England was quite unprepared for peace or war. The Ministry was corrupt and incompetent. Newcastle, the Premier, was a fussy, dishonest, ignorant politician of whom George II said that he was unfit to be a chamberlain to a petty German prince. Newcastle thought that Jamaica was in the Mediterranean and that a squadron was composed of three ships. Foolishness, His Lordship once said, was an infirmity, not a fault. He left the country undefended.

The Foreign Office was easily hoodwinked by Austria. But in Russia British diplomacy was almost successful. This was Hanbury-Williams' handiwork. He arrived at St. Petersburg well supplied with cash, which made him a welcome guest. The Russians, Hanbury-Williams tells, thought that he had brought along " a large wagon loaded with nothing else but ducats." Not to disappoint them, the British minister lavishly distributed so much money that he soon had to appeal to London for " small additional helps " which were " absolutely necessary for carrying on His Majesty's business at this court with despatch as well as with success." Among his stipendiaries were Chancellor Bestuchev, who received £10,000 sterling, and Grand Duchess Catherine to whom Hanbury-Williams " loaned " an equal sum to be used in the " King's service." Czarina Elizabeth herself was tempted with £100,000 a year in the form of subsidies, as well as £50,000 for the army.

Hanbury-Williams' gold almost did the trick. Overjoyed with his £10,000, Chancellor Bestuchev eagerly promised to " accept and support " England's offer. For the same amount of money, Grand Duchess Catherine, though she had as yet no influence, became an important friend, " adherent and spy " of London. She not only procured valuable information for the British minister but she also helped him with translations ; on one occasion the future Empress of Russia " sat up all night to translate a despatch from Constantinople out of the Russian language."

Why, then, did Hanbury-Williams fail ? He was a meticulous diplomat ; he had distributed gold wisely and well : he had won the friendship even of Shuvalov, Elizabeth's current lover. The answer is that the Czarina acted out of personal spite—not against Hanbury-Williams, but against Frederick of Prussia. Just when the British minister was at the point of victory, news came to St. Petersburg that England had concluded an alliance with Prussia (1756). This made all the difference in the world. For Elizabeth loathed the scorpion-tongued King of Prussia whose malicious wit had often wounded this vain woman. Hence any friend of Prussia was *ipso facto* an enemy of Elizabeth. Hanbury-Williams, therefore, automatically found himself treated as a foe. Even Shuvalov, wishing to curry favour with Elizabeth, turned against his English friend, advising the Czarina to treat him as " a Prussian spy."

Hanbury-Williams asked London to recall him.

III

Elsewhere on the European stage, which was being prepared for war, the King of Prussia was busy with spies. His espionage system was excellent, although he underpaid his agents. He knew that Austria and France were making ready for war against him, but he wanted to have full information. In the first place, was Spain going to join the coalition against Prussia ? Secondly, what about Saxony and Russia ? Frederick sent his friend, the Scottish Earl Marischall, as Prussian ambassador to Spain with instructions to find out—" according to the penetration which I know you possess "—what Spain intended to do. The Earl Marischall did not disappoint his Royal friend. He had, it seems, an Irish friend named Wall who was Spanish Minister of Foreign Affairs, and Wall supplied the Earl Marischall with all necessary intelligence which the latter transmitted to Pitt in London ; Pitt, Frederick's ally, in turn sent his information to Berlin.

Another employee of Frederick's was Maximilian von Weingarten, the secretary of the Austrian embassy in Berlin. For his betrayal, Weingarten received 2,000 florins from the Prussians. Still another Prussian spy was one Menzel, a clerk in the Saxon archives, who submitted to Berlin a copy of the Austro-Russian alliance of 1746. Menzel, who was paid 500 thalers for his services to Prussia, also sent to Frederick the important despatches of the Saxon diplomats in Vienna and St. Petersburg. From all these sources Frederick acquired sufficient information to convince him that Austria and Saxony were planning to destroy him.

Frederick, therefore, acted with his wonted swiftness. As in the case of Silesia sixteen years back, so now he invaded Saxony without any declaration of war. Two Prussian officers broke into the chancery of Dresden, brushed aside Queen Maria Josepha who blocked their way, and carried off three sacks of carefully-chosen documents. The Prussian excuse for the violation of a neutral State was military necessity. Saxony, Austria, and Russia, according to Frederick, planned to partition Prussia. This was certainly untrue as regards Saxony. The fact was that Frederick had long coveted Saxony which he considered " an indispensable necessity in order to give the State (Prussia) the stability which it lacks." Saxony had no knowledge whatsoever of the secret plans of Austria. Nor, for that matter, did Austria have any immediate designs on Prussia. As for a possible Russian attack on Prussia, that was altogether out of the question ; even Frederick never believed it.

Frederick's invasion of Saxony caused a pan-European war—the second of his making in less than two decades. Prussia had to fight most of Europe ; her only ally was England. " Quires of paper," Hanbury-Williams wrote of Frederick in 1758, " would not suffice to do him justice . . . ; all I shall say of him at present is, that he is now waging war against six crowned heads, four electors, and four other considerable sovereigns, in all fourteen . . . , a double hydra, and that he is victorious."

IV

While France was engaged in a severe struggle for the balance of power on the Continent and for the retention of her colonial empire, Louis XV permitted himself to undermine his government by establishing a dual and contradictory foreign policy. Though fairly competent and comparatively intelligent, Louis XV was indolent and debauched. As a statesman he was a complete failure. Even against his better judgment, he always left the conduct of affairs to venal ministers and corrupt mistresses.

" The nation," Emperor Joseph II told his sister, Marie Antoinette, when she and her husband, Louis XVI, succeeded to the French throne in 1774," groaned under the burden which had been imposed upon it . . . by Louis XV . . . He placed at the helm of affairs men . . . who plundered and distracted the kingdom. I often pitied this prince from my heart, for having made himself so much the slave of his passions."

With no ability to be an autocrat—as he had a legal right to be—Louis XV permitted his favourites to rule him. " Do not," the Duke of Noailles had warned him as a youth, " allow yourself to be governed ; be the master. Never have a favourite nor a prime minister. Listen to and consult your Council, but decide for yourself. God, who has made you a king, will give you all the necessary light, so long as you have good intentions." But Louis' intentions were not always good. He was so intimidated that he did not have the courage openly to contradict his ministers. Thus he fell into the hands of a gang of unscrupulous adventurers, the leader of whom was Prince Conti, a friend of Louis XV's current mistress, Madame de Chateauroux.

Conti had a sparkling idea. He proposed to the King to form a secret cabinet which should function independently of and in opposition to the official ministry. This Secret Correspondence, as it came to be called, was to gather information, carry on a foreign policy, and keep check on the political events in Europe ; no one but the King and his secret agents were to be aware of the existence of this organization. Thus the feeble King would be able to rule mysteriously and independently of all hectoring ministers. The plan had a fascinating appeal to the timorous and inferiority-ridden Louis XV, a man so diffident that when his mistress, Madame du Barry, insisted that a certain minister be disgraced, he replied bitterly : "He deserves to fall, for there is no one but myself who supports him."

The Secret Correspondence began to function in 1748 ; in the meantime Conti was the King's chief adviser in foreign affairs. The Correspondence was destined to last for more than a quarter of a century ; it became the despair of the official French Foreign Office, whose ministers were hampered at every step by an invisible web. Conti's clever idea had a blighting effect on French foreign policy.

The members of the Secret Correspondence had their own Black Chamber in Paris to *perlustrer* all official despatches ; they also had their special cipher. Their doubly secret agents were to be found in every court of Europe, checkmating the official ambassadors. The Foreign Office was secretly at the mercy of the Correspondence. In fact, Tercier, the chief clerk of the Foreign Office, was the confidential secretary of the Secret Correspondence. Tercier received all the Correspondence's despatches and then handed them over to Lebel, Louis XV's valet. Tercier and his agents also made copies of the instructions and despatches of the official French diplomats.

Apart from Conti, Tercier, Lebel, and Broglie (who succeeded Conti as director), there were about two score other men in the dark secret—the " King's Secret," as another Broglie has since called it. Everyone who was admitted to the mysterious organization had to have the King's approval. There was, first of all, the famous Vergennes, who began his diplomatic career as French ambassador to Constantinople, in 1755, at a time when he was taken into the King's Secret.   Another member (since 1759) was Baron de Breteuil, who served as ambassador in Russia, Sweden, and Holland.   A third was the Chevalier de Saint-Priest, who succeeded Vergennes at Constantinople.   Durant, the minister to Poland, was also a member.   So was Hennin, the secretary to the envoy in Warsaw.   Des Rivaux, the secretary to the French ambassador in Holland, was likewise in the Correspondence.   Among the other members were Gérault, Broglie's secretary ;   the notorious Chevalier d'Eon ;   General Monnet and his wife ;   and Dubois-Martin (in charge of expenditures).   All these men, it will be noticed, occupied strategic positions.

Not all the members of the Secret Correspondence were connected with diplomacy.   There were two Polish " patriots," Generals Mokronsky and Jakubowky.   From the French army were recruited Baron de Bon, Brigadier de la Rozière, and his assistant Sieur de Nardin.

How did the Secret Correspondence work ?   The best illustration is the case of Poland.   For generations it had been France's policy to use the sprawling and inchoate Polish " republic " as an instrument against the Habsburg monarchy.   But since the Diplomatic Revolution had brought about a *rapprochement* between France and Austria, a new orientation was needed, because now, presumably, Austro-French interests in Poland were identical.   Hence Choiseul, the French Minister of Foreign Affairs, instructed Breteuil, the ambassador in Russia, not to interfere in Polish affairs.   Henceforth the official policy of France was to let Poland alone.

But the Secret Correspondence had different plans. Broglie, the director, sent private agents to Poland, supplied with large funds in order to bribe influential politicians " to oppose the Russians."   These agents were supported by Hennin, a member of the King's Secret.   On the other hand, Paulmy, the official ambassador, had instructions from Choiseul to do nothing in the forthcoming election of the Polish King. In other words, two sets of French agents pretended to represent France. The Poles were confused.

Meanwhile Catherine of Russia had made up her mind to force through the election of her ex-lover, Stanislaus August Poniatowski, to the Polish throne. She supplied her minions with money and sent an army into Poland. French diplomacy was at cross-purposes; no one knew what to do, or how to stop the Russians, or even whether the Russians should be stopped. Choiseul had virtually said : Hands off in Poland ! But Broglie's own secret agents were not given specific instructions. Hennin kept pleading for advice. He begged Tercier to let him know whether to " stir up the Poles or calm them." Tercier asked the King. The King was not sure ; he thought the " Russians were incapable of subjugating Poland." So why exert himself ? Tell Hennin, was Louis XV's instruction, to inform the Poles that His Majesty had an " interest in their welfare."

Poniatowski, who was not quite sure that he could be elected even with the aid of Russian bayonets, approached Hennin with an offer of alliance if France would exert herself on his behalf. This was, somehow, communicated to Choiseul, who thought Poniatowski's offer so important that he sent a special agent, General Monnet, to negotiate with the candidate. But Choiseul did not know that Monnet was a member of the Secret Correspondence ; Monnet apparently had contrary instructions from the Broglie group.

In Paris, the Russian ambassador proposed to Louis XV an entente concerning the Polish election. But here the same thing happened as in Warsaw. Louis hid from Choiseul the despatches from Poland, and did not inform him of the Russian offer.

French diplomacy in Poland bewildered everybody. Choiseul and his official diplomats carried on a policy of non-interference. Broglie, Monnet, Hennin and

CATHERINE THE GREAT

their agents interfered crudely and aimlessly. One
of the candidates to the throne, Prince Xavier, continued to appeal to Paris for help. Louis XV made a
half-hearted effort, but got nowhere. Finally he ended
by refusing to commit himself to any candidate.

Free from interference, the Russians overran Poland
and crushed all opposition. Hennin, the member of
the Secret Correspondence, was in despair. " I tell
you with equal frankness and regrets that if events
do not take a contrary course, before three months
have passed M. Poniatowski will be king, and we shall
not even have the satisfaction of having profited by
the opportunity to procure certain favours for our
friends."

Having conquered Warsaw, the Russian troops
forced the Polish nobles to elect Poniatowski (1764).
Louis XV recalled his ambassador and for over a
year refused to recognize the new King. But the stage
was set for the partition of Poland.

In France some people suspected the existence of the
Secret Correspondence ; Foreign Minister Choiseul,
for example, was sure of it, but had no proof. It
was reserved for the Austrian Chancellor, Prince
Kaunitz (a friend of Choiseul's), to make the astonishing discovery. What Kaunitz learned he kept to
himself and his chancery. But soon somebody
betrayed Kaunitz and the secret was out. It almost
killed Louis XV.

The story is pure melodrama. In 1772, when the
courts of Vienna, Berlin, and St. Petersburg were
negotiating the partition of Poland, Prince Louis
Rohan, a Cardinal of the Church, was sent as French
ambassador to Vienna. Rohan, a dissolute ecclesiastic
and a notorious *bon vivant*, was not versed in diplomatic
usage ; moreover, he was not in the secret of the
Correspondence. He knew little of the Austrian Black
Cabinet with its elaborate system of intercepting
correspondence, and he was of course unaware that
his own government carried on a dual foreign policy.

The Prince-Cardinal went to Vienna determined to enjoy himself, which he did, to the indignation of the pious Maria Theresa.

Rohan had a secretary who was a Jesuit named Georgel. One evening when Georgel entered his hotel the porter handed him a note. " Meet me to-night between eleven o'clock and midnight at such and such a place on the rampart ; things of the highest importance will be revealed to you." Georgel was suspicious, but decided not to " miss a perhaps unique chance to be of service to the king," and meet the stranger. At the appointed time a man in a cloak handed him a bundle of papers. " You have," the mysterious cloaked man said in a low, disguised voice, " inspired confidence in me ; consequently I wish to contribute to the success of the embassy of Prince Rohan. These papers will tell you the vital services which I can render you ; if you agree, come to-morrow at the same hour . . ., and bring me 1,000 ducats."

Georgel took the papers home and examined them ; they gave him an " agreeable surprise," for they contained an offer to deliver secret information from the Austrian Black Cabinet twice weekly ; there were also copies of some intercepted diplomatic correspondence. Apparently there was a " leak " in Kaunitz's guarded offices.

" I had proof of it there in our own deciphered despatches," Georgel relates, " even those which were written in the most complicated and most recent cipher ; I saw that this cabinet had found the means to procure the despatches of the various courts of Europe, of their envoys and their agents, through the infidelity and audacity of the directors and masters of the paid posts on the frontiers. In effect, I had before me copies of the despatches of Count Vergennes, our ambassador at Stockholm, of Marquis de Pont at Berlin, the secret instructions of the King of Prussia to his secret agents at Vienna and Paris,

agents to whom alone he confided the true course of
his policies and whose mission was entirely concealed
from his official envoys."

Georgel was excited. Here were diplomatic ramifications of which neither he nor his princely chief
had ever dreamt. But most important of all, among
the papers which the cloaked stranger—probably a
clerk in the Austrian chancery—had given him there
was the secret of Louis XV's pet creation. This was
a shock to the good abbé.

"This same cabinet," Georgel continues his revela-
tions, "had discovered the very secret correspondence
of Louis XV's private politics, a correspondence perfectly concealed from his Council and above all from
his Minister of Foreign Affairs. Count Broglie . . .
was the private and chiefly secret minister. . . . The
mystery of this private policy was not confided to any
of our ambassadors ; sometimes it was the secretary
of the embassy or some other Frenchman, travelling
under various pretexts, who was in the confidence.
Count Broglie confided the thread of this labyrinth
only to those persons whose attachment and discretion
he trusted. . . . Broglie, the enemy of the House of
Rohan, took good care not to initiate Prince Louis
(Rohan). . . . Among the number of papers which
the stranger had given me at midnight was the
deciphered correspondence of Count Broglie with
Count Vergennes."

Georgel hastened with the papers to Ambassador
Rohan who became as excited as his secretary. The
ambassador now had a chance to impress his King
that he was not merely "frivolous and occupied with
his pleasures," but that he was a devilishly clever
diplomat. He instructed Georgel not to fail to meet
the mysterious man again. "On the morrow," to
quote Georgel, "I repaired to the rendezvous with
the masked man. I gave him the thousand ducats ;
he handed me other papers whose interest kept on
increasing, and all the time I was in Vienna he kept

his word. The meetings took place twice weekly, and always about midnight."

Having accumulated this mass of information, Rohan sent the documents by swift courier to Paris. But it was a blunder on the part of Rohan. He had hoped to impress his King ; instead, the news of the discovery of his Secret Correspondence was a blow to Louis XV. The humiliation was too great for the vain King. He fell sick from aggravation, and five weeks later he died.

With the death of Louis XV in 1774 the Secret Correspondence was discontinued. But France had to bear the burden of its expense even under Louis XVI. Broglie asked the new King to pension the members of the Secret Correspondence, and Louis XVI, to save the monarchy from scandal, did so. The Ministry of Foreign Affairs set aside a special fund of over 100,000 livres annually to pay Louis XV's secret agents, the pensions ranging from 20,000 livres a year for General Mokronsky and 12,000 for the Chevalier d'Eon (who knew far too much), to 700 livres for an insignificant clerk (who also knew a good deal).

v

It was the boast of the elder Pitt that not a gun should be fired throughout the world without Britain knowing why. When the Seven Years War (1756–1763) was being fought on land and on sea, in Europe and in America, in the East as well as in the West Indies, and when Britain was exerting herself to the utmost to assert her imperial might, it was necessary to have hundreds of secret eyes the world over to observe and report events.

One of the methods of obtaining secret information was, of course, to intercept diplomatic correspondence. In the British Record Office, in the section entitled : " State Papers, Foreign, Confidential," there are no less than twenty-seven volumes of " Intercepted Despatches " for the years 1756 to 1763.

Another method was to employ spies. Here are some striking examples. At the outbreak of the war the strategy of France was to divide her fleet into several defensive squadrons, one for the Mediterranean, one for the English Channel, and one for the Atlantic Ocean. The plan was secretly drawn up, yet it was soon known in London. The information arrived in the British capital in a mysterious and roundabout fashion. A man named Bunge, it seems, was the Swedish representative in Paris. He was in close touch with the French Government, which was seeking a Swedish alliance. Bunge sent his information to a man named Höpken in Stockholm. Höpken communicated the news to someone (a British agent ?), who in turn transmitted the intelligence to London. In such a tortuous way important news continued to reach London throughout the war.

Take another example. Early in 1761 secret negotiations for peace were started. Prussia and France seemed willing to conclude the war, and England was asked to send a diplomatic agent to Calais to decide upon the preliminaries. Pitt agreed. Suddenly the British Government ordered the fleet to renew hostilities by attacking Mauritius. What had happened?

Pitt, it seems, had " smelled a rat." There was a change of ministry in Paris, headed by the belligerent Choiseul who was ambitious to form a Bourbon coalition against England. At the same time Choiseul advised Louis XV to " play two games together." One game, to quote Choiseul, was " to keep up negotiations with England in such a way that if it did not succeed this time it would serve from its simplicity as a base for the genuine negotiation which must take place if Pitt fell before the influence of Bute." The other, " and this was the second game which I thought essential," was to enter " into an exchange of views with Spain, so devised that if we were to make peace that crown would find it to its interest to support us in the negotiation, and guarantee the stability of the treaty. If, on the contrary, we failed in this, my plan was that Spain should be drawn into the war, and that France would be able to profit by the events which this new complication might produce and repair her losses. Finally, if the event proved unfortunate, I had in view that the losses of Spain would lighten those which France might suffer."

Choiseul was smart, but he outsmarted himself by communicating too openly with Grimaldi and Fuentes, the Spanish ambassadors in Paris and London respectively. Pitt, as was to be expected, intercepted this incriminating correspondence. If Pitt needed further proof of France's intrigues with Spain, he got it from his mysterious correspondent in Stockholm. A third source of information was the previously mentioned Earl Marischall, Prussian ambassador in Madrid. From all these sources the British Government learned that France was not sincere in her peace proposals. This explains the suddenness and swiftness with which the British fleet attacked the French possessions in the West Indies (Pitt had just given an order for the fleet to sail to India).

Clearly, the espionage system played no mean role in the building up of the British Empire.

In contrast to the efficient English secret service—especially under Pitt—the French system was poor indeed. How poor may be seen from the unsuccessful efforts of Paris to "plant" some reliable agents in England.

When the war broke out, the French Government sent Bonnac as ambassador to The Hague with instructions to take charge of the reports of the French spies in London. Louis XV offered Bonnac 180,000 livres annually to find a good "correspondent" in England. Bonnac was to make every attempt to do so.

Bonnac's first experiment was with a Sieur Maubert, an unfrocked priest and ex-convict. The French

diplomat offered this adventurer £200 sterling in
advance (as quarterly payment) to serve as a spy in
London. Maubert joyfully accepted. He went to
England and there assumed the name of Botteman.
His reports, under different names, were sent through
a Hague printer. Some of these letters were intercepted in The Hague, but since the cipher was difficult, Yorke, the British ambassador, could not discover
the contents.

Maubert-Botteman, living like a gentleman, succeeded in making many friends in the British capital.
Some of his information was, therefore, not without
value. In fact, Bonnac was so satisfied with his services that when Maubert asked for an additional £25
quarterly, the French envoy sent him thirty. What
Bonnac wanted from " Botteman " was that he should
bribe Selvins, a Member of Parliament, to get inside
information on the plans of the British Government.
The " deal " fell through, for Selvins' price was too
high.

To justify his salary—and, incidentally, to earn an
increase—" Botteman " hit upon a brilliant idea :
nothing less than the financial destruction of the Bank
of England. He submitted his plan to Bonnac. " In
England," so the spy wrote ingeniously, " there are
one hundred million pounds sterling in paper and
eighteen million in specie. If one were to make more
paper . . . , a greater number of claimants would appear
than the bank could satisfy. . . . There is a man here
who can imitate perfectly the different hands, making
them resemble the original ; furthermore, he is a good
engraver. I know him, he does not know me. He
is capable of everything and is discreet. Through a
man of whom I am sure, I have proposed to him to
counterfeit the handwriting of the powers (the directors
of the bank whose signatures appeared on the bills).
. . . The plan would be to buy a thousand bills and
make copies which one would abandon to the counter-
feiters on condition that they present them to the bank

for payment; the originals remain in our hands. Fifteen days later we present them at the bank; the bills are seized, perhaps together with the carrier, but the proof of legitimate possession ought to be easy. I will make the affair public and everybody will be alarmed. This is an abominable affair, but I regard it as a political matter. . . . Then the only obstacle is paper. It will be up to you to imitate it in France. . .; only a stationer has to be won over. . . . The secretary of the Russian embassy is with you, if you wish."

Bonnac submitted the plan to Louis XV, but the French King thought it too ungentlemanly. After all, he was a proud King and not a swindler. "The proposition which one of your correspondents in London has made to you," Louis XV wrote to Bonnac, "to counterfeit the bills of the Bank of England, could be considered here only with all the indignation and all the horror which it deserves "—a reply which was not unlike the one given by Emperor Francis II on a similar occasion some thirty years later.

Another spy whom Bonnac employed in London was named Robinson, whose pay was twenty guineas monthly. But the careless Robinson was soon thrown into the Tower. His place was taken by one Hensey, a practising physician in London. His only contact with the diplomatic world was his brother who was chaplain of the Spanish Ambassador Grimaldi. Dr. Hensey's salary was five guineas more than Robinson's. His reports to Bonnac were sent in the diplomatic bags of Colloredo, the Austrian ambassador in London. Except from a business point of view, the Hensey brothers were not a great success. They made some money by selling the same information sometimes to Bonnac, sometimes to Grimaldi, occasionally to Colloredo, and often to two of the ambassadors at the same time. But Hensey's letters to Bonnac were generally intercepted.

In October, 1756, Bonnac, who was not very successful, was replaced in Holland by Count d'Affry.

One day the inexperienced d'Affry was confronted by a Frenchman named Falconet who was a spy in the English service. " I come from England," Falconet told the count ; " I am dissatisfied, and I would like to serve the King, my master. I shall prove it to you." Falconet then proceeded to tell d'Affry that in the war of 1743–48 seventy-two Frenchmen had been in the secret service of England. All that the spy now asked was twenty louis a month. It sounded cheap, and d'Affry reported to Louis XV : " If that man would serve well, this would not be expensive." Pay Falconet the money, the King instructed d'Affry, on condition that he reveal the names of the seventy-two French traitors. Whereupon d'Affry gave the spy twelve louis and two letters of exchange for £20 sterling. Falconet promised to name the seventy-two, but, taking the money, he disappeared.

The sum thus lost was not large. Count d'Affry had other, and bigger, losses. Robinson, the spy who had been imprisoned in the Tower, made his escape to Holland and demanded money from the French ambassador. Upon d'Affry's refusal, Robinson drew two letters of exchange for 12,000 livres on the French diplomat—and succeeded in cashing them.

Numerous adventurers offered their services to the gold-dispensing French. Some were interesting types. There was Baron Hatzel, the Württemberg Resident in The Hague and a Chevalier of an Imperial Order, who wished to act as spy for France, saying that he had good contacts among the members of the English Parliament. The scrupulous Louis XV refused to employ him.

Then there was Count Ivan Golovskin, the elder son and secretary of the Russian ambassador in The Hague. Ivan was a dissolute gambler, deeply in debt. One day he appeared before Kauderbach, the Saxon minister in Holland, and told him that he had discovered a spy capable of giving important intelligence from England and Hanover, and even Cumberland's

correspondence; he asked for 600 ducats. Kauderbach could not pay the price himself and offered to
share the expense and information with the Austrian
ambassador, Reichach, and with d'Affry. Investigation soon revealed that the spy in question was no
other than Golovskin himself; his father was a
friend of the Duke of Cumberland and thus young
Ivan had access to State secrets. Overwhelmed by
gambling debts, he was willing to sell out his father.
Such infamous action shocked d'Affry, but as a matter
of duty he communicated the offer to Paris. Louis XV
was tempted to profit from this tainted source, but he
was afraid to commit himself, leaving the decision to
d'Affry. "It is, in general," the French King wrote,
"too dangerous to trust a man who betrays his most
sacred duties." Count d'Affry would not take it
upon his conscience, and he rejected Golovskin's offer.

Count d'Affry was not very lucky in his other ven-
tures. Once an Italian named Philipi offered himself to
go to England to observe "the state of the land and
sea forces . . . ; the true state of the kingdoms of
England, Scotland, and Ireland; the troops distributed in those kingdoms . . . ; the actual condition
of English America, the lands, their forces, their
inhabitants, their inclinations. . . ." He promised to
communicate all the "secrets of the London Cabinet,
all the projects proposed to the ministers, all the
intrigues in the foreign courts, all the campaign
plans . . . , and the agents which the English have in
France." It sounded very ambitious, and d'Affry
dutifully transmitted the offer to Paris, meanwhile
paying Philipi a ducat a day. Louis XV replied that
he would reward Philipi magnificently if he would
deliver a Frenchman named Pichon who was in Pitt's
service. Pichon was the man in charge of the English
secret service in France and who betrayed French naval
secrets. If Philipi would decoy Pichon to the Austrian
Netherlands, he would receive 500 louis as reward;
meantime he was given 100 gold pieces in advance.

Philipi took the money and sailed for England. Three years passed without news from him. Early in 1760 Philipi came to see d'Affry, offering voluble excuses for his failure and his silence. To show his good intentions, he proposed a project which, he said, would make England sue for peace. It was nothing less than the abduction of the English King and his family, the seizure of the Tower of London, and the capture of the artillery magazine at Woolwich. Philipi's intimate friend, the Corsican General Paoli who wanted revenge on England, offered from fifteen hundred to two thousand Corsicans for the expedition. D'Affry thought the project too romantic, but he sent Philipi to Paris to see Bernis, the French Minister of Foreign Affairs. "The Italian," Bernis replied to d'Affry's letter, "is at least a visionary if he is not a scoundrel. . . . Let me know the date of his departure from The Hague and send me his description so that I can have him under surveillance in Paris." Bernis simply treated Philipi as a scoundrel and an English spy, and gave him the alternative of either leaving France within twenty-four hours or to go to The Hague as a French spy. Philipi quickly made his get-away.

This left France without a reliable agent in England. for a long time Prince Galitzin, the Russian ambassador in London, was writing to Kauderbach, in a special cipher, about the important events in the English capital. Despite the state of war existing between Austria, Russia and Saxony against Prussia, these three States did not sever relations with England, the ally of Prussia. Strange as it may sound, diplomatic relations existed between Vienna, St. Petersburg, Dresden, and London. D'Affry, hoping to take advantage of the Russian ambassador's complaisance, asked him, through Kauderbach, for precise and prompt information concerning England's armaments. Prince Galitzin was glad to do it, although his government was at war with Prussia and consequently with France.

Nevertheless, Galitzin did not have much to say. Although Louis XV was pleased with the Russian's services, he asked d'Affry to procure " an informed and loyal correspondent " in London, adding that the Russian ambassador was not " sufficiently instructed." Either Galitzin was fooling the French, or he was really poorly informed.

D'Affry found a Swiss named Vautraves who, having been a tutor to some young English nobles, had good connections in London. Vautraves was promised a life annuity of 30,000 livres and the same sum in cash; his instructions were to discover the objective of the British naval expedition. He went to London, but failed to procure the intelligence. Instead, he advised France to make peace, and offered himself as mediator. The exasperated d'Affry told the impudent Swiss that he was a spy and not a diplomat. Louis XV, when informed of the affair, said that in his opinion Vautraves was " a double spy, with this difference, that he perhaps serves the English ministry with better faith than he serves us, and that he will end up by demanding a high sum from us."

After a few more costly adventures with various pretended spies, the French had to content themselves with what Galitzin, whose services were free, was pleased to send them. Unfortunately, Galitzin left London in 1762. His place as a French informant was to be taken by de Gross, the Russian ambassador in Holland, who was appointed to the London post. Louis XV wanted de Gross to perform the same services for France as had Galitzin, and ordered that 50,000 livres be put at his disposal and that he be paid 100,000 livres annually. De Gross was delighted with the gold, but while he was waiting to sail for England a courier arrived with an *ukaz* that he remain in Holland.

The change in de Gross' destination was due entirely to undiplomatic causes. Frederick the Great hated de Gross, a Württemberger who had spoken

disparagingly of him.   Gossip had travelled across
many lands.   It seems that de Gross had spoken to
Yorke, the British minister in The Hague ; Yorke
repeated the gossip in London ;   London in turn
passed on the words to Berlin.   And so when Frederick
heard that de Gross was to become ambassador to
London, he urged King George III to influence the
Russian Government to revoke de Gross' appointment.

Thus France lost a valuable spy, while Frederick
had his revenge.   The whole French secret service
was almost worthless.   " My brother of France," the
Prussian King mocked, " has twenty cooks and one
spy, where I have one cook and twenty spies."

VI

Only in Sweden was French diplomacy successful.
Sweden was the key-state in the northern balance of
power, and for more than a generation it had been
the battlefield of Franco-Russo-British ambitions.
The great powers spent millions in gold to corrupt
the Scandinavian land.   In the elections of 1746,
despite the heavy bribery on the part of the Russians
and the British, a majority of the deputies in the Diet
were pro-French.   Consequently the British envoy
left the country.   For the next twenty years Britain
and Sweden had no official relations.

In 1764 the situation changed.   Queen Louise
Ulrique, the sister of Frederick the Great, made a
personal appeal to King George III for money to
enable her " to break the insupportable dependence
in which Sweden had been held for twenty-six years."
London sent Sir John Goodricke as ambassador to
Stockholm and George III offered the Queen £10,000
in order to break the power of France which had
ruled Sweden, in the words of the Queen, " with the
same ease as if it were one of her own provinces."
Goodricke was instructed to co-operate with Ivan
Osterman, the Russian ambassador, but he realized
that much money would be necessary to bribe the

venal Diet. "The people in general," Goodricke
reported, "are well disposed to England, but as force
of money has hitherto kept them under the French
yoke, so it must be money on our side that delivers
them from it, and in case the King and the Empress
of Russia should be disposed to make the expense
jointly, there is the fairest appearance of success."

The chief obstacle to a Russo-British victory was
French gold. The French promised to pay the Queen
from 200,000 to 300,000 crowns; they also spread
rumours that Britain intended to ruin Swedish manu-
factures. "Neither calumny nor flattery nor offers of
money," to quote Goodricke, "nor any other artifices
are neglected at this moment by the French party in
order to detach the King and Queen of Sweden from
us, so that we have a hard game to play."

Goodricke estimated that both he and Osterman
would have to spend no less than £12,000 each. His
estimate was based on the following figures: To
bring 300 impoverished aristocratic deputies to
the capital would require £1,050; to maintain them
in Stockholm for six months would cost £6,300;
to bribe the bourgeois electors would amount to
£1,332. Moreover, he would have to spend £1,660
on the secret parliamentary committee; more than
£3,200 on clubs for the deputies; £2,000 to bribe the
speaker and other peasant deputies; £2,000 to pay
the forty pro-French nobles to absent themselves at
the opening of the Diet; and finally the same amount
to secure five or six important votes. Goodricke
thought "no moment since the commencement of
the French system so favourable for overturning it
as this." This critical moment, he said, will decide
whether England or France "should take the lead in
Sweden."

Goodricke had only £4,000. The French ambassador, on the other hand, was better provided. He was
authorized by his government to offer Sweden a new
subsidy of 1,500,000 livres annually for eight years—

an offer which the Swedish Senate accepted by a majority of one.

In the Diet, however, the anti-French faction (the " Caps ") won a victory. Of the fifty nobles on the secret committee, Goodricke counted only seven who were pro-French. But the struggle for supremacy was not yet over. " The French," in the words of Goodricke, " gave money, we had none to give. The whole court party . . . acted openly against us, and numbers of our people were absent. They must be assembled for the grand affair of the senators."

The " grand affair of the senators " was an attempt to unseat the seven pro-French senators. The secret committee, being in the pay of England and Russia, condemned four of the Francophiles as guilty of malpractice ; the verdict was vetoed by the nobles, but the other orders overrode the aristocratic veto. According to Goodricke, this vote of the nobles cost the French ambassador £7,000, while that of the burghers cost England only £2,000.

The Diet, seeing that much gold was forthcoming from the great powers, prolonged its session until October, 1766. By that time Goodricke had spent £17,000, and Osterman £98,000. "France and Russia," the Englishman complained, " make their pensions so large that they spoil the market." But Goodricke did succeed in concluding a treaty of friendship with Sweden.

In view of this sharp Anglo-Russian competition, France decided to change her tactics. In Sweden, as in Poland, a constitution favourable to the nobles and burghers served as a check on royal authority. France determined to undermine the constitution. Ambassador Breteuil was ordered to spend 1,400,000 livres for this purpose. In December, 1768, King Adolphus Frederick, incited by his ambitious Hohenzollern wife, attempted to strike at the Senate ; he appeared in person and demanded an extraordinary session. Humiliated by one vote cast in favour of his proposal, the King offered to resign. As the royal Senate could not very well function without monarchical authority, it was compelled to surrender and issue an order for the convocation of the Diet.

Promptly the foreign powers began their electioneering. Goodricke was supplied with £12,000 to bribe the voters. Osterman had even more money; and since Russia dominated Copenhagen, Danish money was also at work. But France was resolved to win at any cost. De Modène, the new French ambassador, spent money, in the words of Goodricke, " as if he had the mines of Peru at his command." An economic crisis also helped the French. There was much suffering in Sweden, and the burghers, nobles, and clergy returned heavy majorities against the incumbent pro-English government.

All that Goodricke could hope for was a schism in the ranks of the new deputies. The Anglo-Russo-Danish trio bribed Colonel Charles Frederick Pechlin, a deputy with a strong following in the Diet, with £2,000. Pechlin proposed three plans of action. At a cost of over £120,000 " to change both the secret committee and the Senate, and destroy the whole French system "; at a cost of £72,000, " to force the present ruling party to . . . take a part of our friends into the government, by which the actual system of alliance with their neighbours, as well as the constitution, may be preserved "; and, for £30,000 " to form such an opposition as shall preserve the constitution entire, and prevent other violent measures."

Though Goodricke favoured the second plan as " most reasonable and practical," the British Government preferred the last scheme, because it was the cheapest. England, Russia, and Denmark were to contribute £10,000 each. Upon this basis, Pechlin set to work and in a short while reported the constitution as saved. It was a costly process. Between 1769 and 1770 Goodricke himself spent £42,000. Unable to compete with such torrents of gold, the French Government ordered de Modène to stop wasting money.

The expensive Anglo-Russian victory did not endure. It was killed by an " act of God." Early in 1771 King Adolphus Frederick died suddenly. A new Diet was in prospect and neither Goodricke nor Osterman had the £40,000 necessary to bribe the deputies. A revolution in Denmark also cut off supplies in that direction. The Swedish Government was in difficulties : no money was forthcoming either from France or England.

The new Diet was deadlocked. King Gustavus III, who had promised to respect the old constitution, was secretly preparing a coup d'état with the aid of France. Apprized by its secret agents in Paris, the British Government warned its Swedish " friends " to protect themselves before the gathering storm. It was too late. Backed by France, Gustavus III forced the Senate to sign a new Form of Government which made the King absolute. Russia and Denmark protested ; but Catherine was busy fighting the Turks and dismembering Poland, and had no time to bother with Sweden. Alone, England was helpless. And so she lost a valuable ally, especially during the conflict with the American colonies, when American ships used Swedish ports to escape from British pursuers.

The Treaty of Paris (1763) which ended the Seven Years' War was a humiliation for the French ministry, especially the Duke of Choiseul, who refused to consider the settlement as final. Though hampered by the activities of the Secret Correspondence, Choiseul immediately began to prepare for a new war against Britain ; he started to organize the army, reconstruct the navy, encourage commerce, and finally to isolate England diplomatically. To tie Austria more securely to France, Choiseul arranged a marriage between the future Louis XVI and Marie Antoinette; to keep Britain out of the Baltic, he poured, as we have seen, a fortune into Sweden. Forty years later Napoleon was to duplicate Choiseul's programme, but on a grander scale.

At the end of the War half of the French Navy—forty-four ships of the line and ten frigates—was unseaworthy. Within two years Choiseul increased the fleet to sixty-three vessels and thirty-one frigates; forty more ships were to be added in four years. Choiseul also improved the artillery, restocked the arsenals, and rebuilt the forts of Brest, Toulon, and Valenciennes.

There was not the least doubt that France was energetically preparing for war. It was merely a question of time when the preparations would be completed. London was well aware of the French ministry's intentions. A report written in cipher by George Cressner, a British agent in Cologne, is most illuminating: " I am persuaded the King sincerely wishes, and that the plans formed by the Duc de Choiseul, and the steps taken in consequence, require his avoiding a war for a long time. Ships are built and building, to make a very formidable navy; but there are not sailors to man sixty ships of the line, and many of them are only boatmen. As commerce increases it will make sailors, but even that is a work of time; so that everything contributes to oblige and make desirable the continuance of peace, as necessary to France. . . . If Spain acts in concert with this Court, it is computed the combined fleets in a very few years will be stronger than the English fleet. . . . I have some reason to believe the present plan is to obtain a superiority at sea and to avoid a war till that is done."

The best plan of attack, Choiseul believed, was first to seize London. In 1767, therefore, he caused a survey to be made of the northern French ports and the southern English coast. But the English secret service was unusually efficient ; somehow the reports of the French surveyors were stolen from the Ministry of War in Paris and found their way into the hands of the first Lord Chatham.   These papers are now in the Public Record Office in London.

The reports of these surveyors are of unusual interest.   The first document was written by Colonel Grant de Blairfindy, a Scotsman in the service of France.   Colonel Grant opens his report with a description of Kent and Deal, eight miles from Dover, giving details to places, landings, fishing boats.   According to the Colonel, there were 150 boats at Dieppe, thirty (with room for 200 soldiers) at St. Valéry, and twenty at Fécamp.   Between Dunkirk and Honfleur the French could requisition enough boats to carry 80,000 men.   The Colonel's plan was for the French troops to assemble one day's march from the ports, and that a convoy of twenty ships, twelve frigates and forty corvettes should guard their crossing.   Light troops should embark with their horses, push into the country, and requisition cattle and food.   Grant was sure that there would be no resistance, for the English people were soft and ignorant in the use of arms.   The landing, by the way, was to be made without a preceding declaration of war ; but once landed, the French should issue a proclamation assuring the people that the invaders meant them no harm and that everything would be paid for in cash.

After landing at Deal, the French Army should march in two columns to London.   The roads were good though hilly.   Grant advised that the invaders establish three main provision depots.   One around Sandwich, with its 117 villages, which were rich enough to provide 750,000 rations of hay and oats, as well as 2,000 horses, 4,000 oxen, and 500 vehicles. Another in the neighbourhood of Canterbury and Rochester, with their combined total of 260 villages. A third in the region of Kent, which could furnish 3,890,000 rations of forage, 10,790 horses, 21,000 oxen, and 3,400 vehicles. One would like to know where the fanciful Colonel got his figures.

But would there be no defence on the part of the Government ? On this point Colonel Grant was an optimist. In the first place, the Colonel pointed out, the country could muster only 24,000 men, and these were mainly militia. The professional soldier had a profound contempt for these yokels. " I have seen them," Grant writes sneeringly, " an hour and a half before they could achieve (marching three deep) ; and no sooner did they try to advance than they were at once twelve or even more deep, like a sort of whirlwind round their standard ; so one can picture the confusion there would be, were a volley sent into their midst." Four thousand French grenadiers, the Scotsman boasted, could beat all the militia of England.

Choiseul, however, was not yet ready ; or perhaps he did not put too much faith in the Colonel's report. Next year, in the spring of 1768, Grant was again sent to England to investigate. He found the country excited about Wilkes and, with the fatuous facility of an amateur diplomat, was convinced that England was at the point of disintegration. The time was just ripe for an invasion.

" Everything there," the good Colonel wrote, " is in great confusion owing to the turbulence of the people, which is occasioned by one man in particular, named Wilkes. Both the King and all the leading men feel themselves in the greatest insecurity ; one hears nothing but cries of ' Long live Wilkes and Liberty ' in the streets. . . . They have even cried in the presence of the King : ' Wilkes' pardon or no King.' Moreover neither the Scotch nor English can tolerate each other at this moment ; in Scotland the populace goes about with a straw man stuck at the end of a long pole ; this represents Wilkes. . . . There is no leading man in the English ministry ; the King is timid and his cabinet weak. Nothing could be easier for a firm man than to instil order into this rabble, but no one dares show this firmness, the King least of all, because he is told it is contrary to the laws of Britain to coerce the people by arms."

Choiseul was partially convinced by Grant's report, and to make sure he sent another spy, Lieutenant·Colonel de Beville, to make a thorough investigation. In this case, Choiseul's instructions are more interesting than the reports of his agents. The Duke starts out with a history of the invasions of England, beginning with Julius Cæsar and Agricola. In 449 A.D., the French statesman continues his learned paper, the Saxons descended close to the mouth of the Thames. In 1066 William the Conqueror landed on the Sussex coast. In 1588 the Spanish Armada was to sail for the Thames, while a century later William III (was this a subtle Gallic touch, that William III was an invader?) debarked at Torbay. In short, Choiseul concludes his historical dissertation, invaders of England had the choice of landing either at the Thames (Tilbury) or on the Sussex coast. With this in view, de Beville was to determine which of the two was the most favourable for debarkation and also to select a bay where the whole French fleet might anchor in safety. The Lieutenant-Colonel was instructed carefully to observe the roads, the strategic places, the rivers, and the encampment sites; he was to verify the extent of the fortifications at Plymouth, Portsmouth, Chatham, and Dover. Finally the French officer was warned that " in view of the great attention paid in England to the movements of all strangers and particularly Frenchmen," he should never permit himself to be caught with plans and drawings.

During his two months' stay in England de Beville made accurate observations of Dover, Canterbury, Rochester, Windsor, Maidenhead, Oxford, Gloucester, Bristol, Bath, Wells, Bridgwater, Taunton, Tiverton, Barnstaple, Okehampton, and Plymouth. The last-named, he found, was inaccessible by sea on account of the forts and a squadron of thirty-five ships inside the port. Beville also visited most of the cities and ports in the east and south. From London he made excursions into Surrey, Sussex, and Essex ; he looked over the roads, banks, bridges, and arsenals. He paid special attention to Woolwich docks and arsenal ; the place was inaccessible to strangers, but he found that " from the churchyard, which is a little raised, one can see over the wall of the enclosure." From this point of observation he noticed " on the stocks a ship of ninety cannon, and one of sixty, on which it looked as if no work had been done for some time."

Beville succeeded in reaching France with twenty carefully drawn plans and a map of England. His chief suggestion to the French Government was that the " object of the expedition " should be " to destroy their navy."

Choiseul had so high an opinion of de Beville that he submitted Grant's reports to him for comment. In a sixty-page answer, the Lieutenant-Colonel criticized the conclusions of his Scottish confrère. But Choiseul would not act hastily. His main fear was that the invading army would be attacked at the moment of landing ; hence he had to make sure of a powerful navy and a large army. Upon de Beville's return the French Government began to fit out ships and to assemble troops. Rumours of the preparations reached London and Horace Walpole, the British ambassador in Paris, was instructed to get an interview with Choiseul.

" He received my question and representations in good humour," Walpole tells, " and assured me upon the word of a man of honour that no orders were given to arm. I cannot, from any good authority and in contradiction to the assurances the Duc de Choiseul has given me, assert that any number of extraordinary ships are put into commission, or that any positive orders are yet given to prepare an armament."

Walpole took Choiseul at his word and so he reported to London. But the British Government had better information.

" I am sorry to find," Lord Weymouth wrote to Walpole, " that our intelligence does not agree with that which you have transmitted. We are informed that carpenters, seamen, and fishermen have been sent from other parts of the coast to Brest, to fit out several ships of war. I cannot be too earnest in recommending vigilance on this head."

Choiseul, on his part, pretended that England was preparing for war against France. To deceive the British, he instructed Francès, the French ambassador in London, to find out the intentions of His Majesty's Government. Ambassador Francès made an appointment with Lord North, the Prime Minister, after dinner. But let Francès tell the little story himself :

" I found Lord North at nine o'clock at night as drunk as a cabman, and I presume that all the members of the British cabinet were in as good condition as their chief. This circumstance in a little affair in which only the fate of three kingdoms (England, France, and Spain : concerning the Falkland island), was involved, was in itself sufficiently interesting."

Francès sounded the drunken lord and found that he repeated the same peaceful intentions as he did when sober ; so the Frenchman wisely concluded that England really meant peace.

So, one may conclude, did Louis XV. The French King knew that his ambitious minister was preparing for war against Britain, and for a long time he did nothing about it. But when Choiseul actually began to mobilize, Louis XV bestirred himself. " My minister," he wrote to his ally, Charles III of Spain, " would have war, but I will not." The morning after this letter was written, on December 24, 1770, a *lettre de cachet* sent Choiseul into exile and ended his political career. The invasion of England was postponed indefinitely.

VII

" What ! " exclaimed a Russian colonel, " this
Elliot, this amiable, sociable, light, gay, gallant, fine
gentleman, consents to be immured in cabinets !
Why, it is larceny perpetrated against society ! . . .
After such a phenomenon I do not despair of seeing
some day or another the Pope in the uniform of an
hussar ! "

Such was the opinion among friends when the
mordant and reckless Hugh Elliot became British
ambassador to Berlin at the age of twenty-five.

Frederick the Great was not pleased with the new
ambassador accredited to his court. The Prussian
King could bear no rivals, and in Elliot he found a
man as impudent and witty as himself.

" What," Frederick asked maliciously, " is this
Hyder Ali who knows so well how to settle your
affairs in India ? "

" That," came Elliot's swift retort, " is an old
despot who has pillaged his neighbours but who,
thank God, is beginning to dote."

The young ambassador's biting wit cost him dear,
for he not only alienated the touchy Prussian King
but also antagonized the Prussian ministers. As a
result he had but few important contacts. His chief
sources of information were a few army officers, an
erudite friend of the King, and a few royal servants.
Elliot despised the Prussians, whom he considered
barbarians, and scorned the German women, whom he
called grenadiers. For the King, Elliot had a deep-
rooted hatred which Frederick repaid in kind. Whenever the two met they lashed out at each other with
poisoned tongues.

" What," Frederick asked Elliot about a much disliked Prussian diplomat, " do they think of my new
ambassador in England ? "

" A worthy representative of Your Majesty," Elliot
shot back.

Elliot's diplomatic methods were no less remarkable than his tongue.   One of his adventures deserves telling.   In the summer of 1777 Arthur Lee, the Virginian who represented the American colonies in Europe, arrived in Berlin.   Prussia was then on hostile terms with England, and the American agent hoped to win Frederick's support for the American revolutionary cause.   The British Government, warned by its spies about Lee's movements, instructed Elliot to keep a wary eye on the American.

Elliot acted in characteristic fashion.   He bribed the servant of the inn where Lee was staying and obtained false keys both to Lee's room and to the bureau where he kept his intimate journal.   When Lee was out for dinner, Elliot entered the room, took the Virginian's papers, and hastened to the embassy where four English friends were waiting to make copies of the documents.   In the meantime the bold Elliot went back to the inn and waited for Lee.   When the latter arrived, Elliot, pretending to be a friendly stranger interested in the American cause, engaged the Virginian in a two-hours' conversation.   About ten o'clock in the evening the tired Lee excused himself, saying that he must go up to his room and do some writing. Elliot left ; but when he was only a few paces away from the inn he heard sudden shouts of : " Robbers ! " He ran to the embassy, found that most of the papers had already been copied, and, disguising himself, returned the originals to the inn.   He told the inn-keeper to say that the papers were brought by a stranger who had " left them and ran off."

Liston, Elliot's attaché, took the copies and on the same night he hurried away from Berlin to London. Elliot knew that a storm would break about his head, but he stayed in Berlin to be " subjected," as he said, " to considerable trouble and perhaps lose my situation."

While Liston was galloping with the copied documents to Hamburg, Lee reported the theft to the

Prussian authorities. Suspicion immediately fell on Elliot who was known to be capable of anything. But he was also equal to the emergency. Instead of denying, he offered profuse apologies to the Prussian Government, saying that a servant of his " from over-officiousness committed this unwarrantable action," and that as soon as he, Elliot, discovered the theft he had immediately returned the papers. Elliot insisted that his government had absolutely nothing to do with the affair. " I alone," he informed Frederick, " was in fault, and if His Prussian Majesty chose, I am ready to ask for my recall."

Frederick, as may be imagined, was furious. Not that he was morally indignant at a breach of inter-national law—he himself was a champion law-breaker —but that he really hated this man Elliot. " Oh," the King shouted, " this worthy scholar of Bute, this incomparable man : your goddam Elliot. In truth, Englishmen ought to blush for shame that they sent such ambassadors to a foreign court." Officially, however, the King wisely said that he did not wish " to make an issue " of the affair.

Nevertheless, the British Government was per-turbed. However useful, Elliot's escapade was not quite cricket. " I applaud his zeal," Lord Suffolk said, " but I don't mightily affect a dasher." King George III called a special meeting of the Cabinet and officially expressed his " dissatisfaction with the conduct of a minister whose zeal in the public service is as little doubted as his ability, and who, by an excess of the former quality, has been induced to swerve from that discreet regard to his own situation and the dignified principles of his court." The information which Elliot had procured, however, was valuable enough for the British Government not only to forgive the ambassador but also to grant him a handsome gift of £500.

Twenty-three years later John Quincy Adams met Elliot and asked him frankly about the truth of the matter. " Elliot," Adams writes, " solemnly declared that the seizure of Mr. Lee's papers was not made by his orders ; that it was entirely the act of an officious servant, who thought to do him a service by it." Which merely shows that Elliot always remained a diplomat. Anyhow, Adams was convinced that Elliot was telling the truth.

Elliot always remained an irrepressible figure. One year after the Lee affair, a French officer in Berlin engaged the irascible ambassador in a conversation about the French fleet which Admiral d'Estaing took to help the American colonies. " There at least," the Frenchman boasted, " France will deliver a stout blow to England."

" And here," Elliot burst out, " is the blow which England delivers to France through my hand." And he boxed the Frenchman's ears.

A few years later Elliot was in Paris and went to see *The Battle of Ivry* at the Comédie français. In one scene the victorious Henry IV tries to stop the bloodshed with the words : " Spare my subjects ! Save the French ! " At this point Elliot rose from his seat and cried in a loud voice : " Don't give yourself any trouble ! They will save themselves ! "

CHAPTER X

THE FRENCH REVOLUTION

I

THE French Revolution and the Napoleonic epoch caused no essential change in diplomatic technique. There was, however, an acceleration of tempo. The Revolution having shaken the European equilibrium, the consequent adjustment took a violent form. Spectacular events succeeded each other like films on a screen, dazzling to the eye and startling to the senses.

The diplomats of the Revolutionary era had less brutality and more finesse than those of the preceding centuries; they were, if possible, even more unscrupulous and amoral. Napoleon himself, for example, had all the diplomatic subtlety of a Renaissance despot. His assistant and later enemy Talleyrand had no peer as a diplomat, and Metternich was a close runner-up to both.

Revolutionary France set the tempo for the rest of Europe. But in England there was little change. British statesmen of the Revolutionary period—Pitt and Fox and Castlereagh—still lived in the eighteenth-century tradition of righteous conservatism, cautious, dogged, and hypocritical. There was, however, an exception. This was George Canning who was definitely a product of the Revolutionary era, and, free of scruples, he was able to compete easily with his Continental rivals. A distinct, and odd, type was Alexander II, Czar of all the Russias, who had sentimental dreams about a Europe made permanently safe for autocratic monarchs.

In February, 1792, Prime Minister William Pitt of Great Britain said solemnly : " Unquestionably there never was a time in the history of this country when, from the situation of Europe, we might more reasonably expect fifteen years of peace than we may at the present moment."

Twelve days after this strange prophecy the pacific Emperor. Leopold II died in Vienna and was succeeded by the more reactionary Francis II. The new Emperor immediately complained of the subversive activities of the French revolutionists ; the latter, in their missionary ardour, decided to forestall their enemies by taking the offensive.

It was done in this way :

Louis XVI, who was still a king, though only in name, entered the hall of the Legislative Assembly. The deputies rose and took off their hats. The King sat down; the deputies did the same. General Dumouriez read a report, detailing the grievances against Austria. Louis XVI followed the General with a speech for war. " The Assembly," replied the president of that body, " will take into consideration the proposition which you have made." Louis XVI gravely left the hall; the deputies shouted : *Vive le Roi !* In the same evening the Assembly declared war against Austria " as a just defence of a free people against the unjust aggression of a king."

So ended, within a few weeks, Pitt's prophecy of fifteen years of peace.

This happened on April 20, 1792. Mark the date. It was the beginning of a world war that lasted, with rare interruptions, for twenty-three years.

The war shook the precarious throne of Louis XVI who, frightened, began to spend money to buy supporters for the tottering monarchy. Danton, according to Lafayette, received 50,000 écus. " We are at ease," the King's sister wrote ; " we can count upon M. Danton."

Nevertheless, Louis XVI was not saved. The first act of the Convention, when it opened its session in September, was to abolish the monarchy and proclaim a republic. The Royal Family was accused of " perfidious machinations." On this occasion Lebrun, the future Consul, gave an interesting account of the fund of 6,000,000 livres which had been put aside for propaganda. But now that France was at war there was no longer any need, so Lebrun said, for "vile means of corruption."

" To-day when our policy is to be frank and uncomplicated ; to-day when all we. have to offer to the peoples is justice and liberty, when we have to demand for ourselves only peace and justice, the National Convention has decided that this wealth could be employed more usefully in exchanging it for iron, the metal of liberty."

The revolutionists had spent only some 2,000,000 out of the 6,000,000. How· those 2,000,000 were distributed is illuminating. Five hundred thousand went to Belgium. Fifty thousand was spent by Gorani, the French secret agent in England. Large sums were consumed by the commissioners whom the Paris Commune sent to the provinces to preach massacres. Most of the money, however, was used up by Danton who, as Minister of Justice, was the virtual head of the Revolutionary Government.

Toward the end of 1792 Louis XVI was on trial for his life and Baron Louis de Breteuil, the King's accredited agent abroad, conceived the idea of counterfeiting French assignats in order to ruin the Republic. Breteuil's justification was that the British Government had done the same in the American Revolutionary War. He proposed that 150,000,000 livres be printed : 40,000,000 to be given to Austria and Prussia each ; the same amount to Louis XVI ; 14,000,000 to the Russian army ; and the rest to be distributed among the *émigrés* and their friends. Breteuil demanded an initial outlay of 1,500,000 livres and a safe place in which to work, preferably some Prussian or Austrian town. The engraver was all ready for the job, waiting for the matrix to arrive from London. " When the English," Breteuil explained, " had counterfeited American paper money, they kept the artist prisoner all the time and then made his fortune."

Breteuil submitted the plan to the Prussian Govern-

WILLIAM PITT THE YOUNGER
(After Hoppner.)

ment and the latter in turn consulted Vienna. " Such an infamous project," was Emperor Francis II's curt reply, " is not to be accepted."

But money was needed to save Louis XVI. A few days before the King's execution, Danton was asked to save him. "I am willing to try," he replied, " but I must have a million of money to buy up the necessary votes, and the money must be on hand in eight days."

The money was not forthcoming.

II

After the King was guillotined, the Revolutionary Government organized a comprehensive intelligence service, not unlike the later Russian Cheka. Epionage and propaganda, in fact, were among the costliest efforts of the French Revolution. In January, 1793, for example, the Convention spent no less that 1,300,000 livres, and in the following months more than 1,400,000 livres on agitation and spying.

The central espionage bureau was located in the Ministry of Foreign Affairs. Here daily reports were received and submitted to the various ministers. Every week there was a ministerial conference and each chief gave a résumé of the reports. Some of the information thus sifted was sent to the Committee of Public Safety and to the Paris Commune.

There was only a small number of agents, but these were " well selected, instructed, discreet, and above all revolutionists." Twelve of them kept the city of Paris under surveillance ; they watched the clubs, kept an eye on the cafés, checked on the dance halls, observed the hotels. Gamblers and adventurers were daily reported upon. Special attention was paid to foreigners, "notably Gouverneur Morris, of the United States, the greatest enemy of liberty."

Two kinds of agents were busy in the provinces, local spies and Deputies on Mission. They were instructed to stimulate public enthusiasm, to crush conspiracies, to preach respect for law, and " above all,

respect for the Convention, our only palladium." The
agents were required to denounce those " who betray
by action or omission."

Another set of spies was in the army. These were to
report to Paris all that happened, to keep a close eye
on the officers, to check up on the provisions and
equipment, to listen to the complaints of the soldiers,
and to ferret out abuses.

Finally there were the foreign agents. True, the
Convention was not optimistic as to the possible
achievements of the agents in foreign countries, for
" the peoples have the veil of despotism on their eyes."
But, on the other hand, the emissaries abroad could
" do harm to our enemies." Once and for all, the
Convention resolved that it was necessary " to abandon
for a time the principles of scrupulousness in dealing
with enemies who are as unscrupulous, or rather, as
ferocious, as ours are : all means are good against an
ungodly race."

As a result, the foreign agents were instructed to
neglect no means to ruin the enemies of France. It
was to be a war without rules. Everything was to be
attacked : " Their ports, their arsenals, their factories,
their ships." Even " their guiding heads " might be
felled. " Their," of course, meant monarchical European. " We have the Curtiuses, let us employ them,
plot with them the most disastrous projects against
the English, the Spanish, etc. ; let us choose intrepid
but honest men."

The official French diplomats abroad were not asked
to indulge in any overt activities. They were merely
to send home detailed reports, under two headings.
Despatches containing accounts of negotiations were
to be labelled *Politiques*. General news, gossip, and
" useful and interesting discoveries made in the
sciences and arts " should come under the heading
Bulletins. Every ambassador was instructed to keep a
full diary and make notes of all his observations and
conversations. Special accounts and financial reports

were to be sent separately and registered in a journal.
To facilitate the home ministry in the reading of the
despatches, the envoys were asked to make a brief
summary of the contents on the margin. At the end of
each year the diplomat was required to send an account
of his mission to the Ministry of Foreign Affairs in
Paris. This report was to include the following items :
    The condition of the people, " their virtues, vices,
        progress in civilization."
    Agriculture and industry, imports and exports.
    Revenues, expenses, public debts, credits, and
        financial resources.
    Military and naval forces, militia, ports and forti-
        fications.
    General reflections on the Government, its faults
        and virtues.
    Character of the principal personages of the State.
    Contacts with foreign countries, negotiations and
        alliances.
    Summary of all the negotiations during the year.
    State of French commerce in each particular country.
    Ways and means of spreading French political and
        commercial influence.
    Where the diplomatic agent had no information to
give, he was asked to leave a blank in his report.

III

After the Convention declared war against Holland
and England, the latter formed a European coalition
against France. Britain was to pay the money and the
European powers, especially Prussia, were to do the
fighting. Lord Malmesbury went to Berlin—a
capital which shocked him with its venality and corruption—and concluded a subsidy treaty, promising to
pay £2,500,000 sterling provided that 62,000 Prussian
soldiers joined the allies on the Rhine. In asking the
House of Commons to vote the subsidy, William Pitt
publicly admitted that only bribery could keep the
Prussians in the field. The Prussians were paid

£1,200,000, but they sent no army. Instead, King
Frederick William used the British gold for an
invasion of Poland and despoiling that country of an
important slice of territory.

For more than a year the disgusted Malmesbury
hoped that the insatiable Prussians would fight the
French. He urged his government not to spare any
money. "The main difficulty," Lord Grenville
replied grimly, "is where sums to that amount can
be found. German princes think England a pretty
good milch cow, but, surely, hardly to the extent
supposed in the account you have transmitted."

The money was wasted, and the First Coalition
against Revolutionary France was a failure.

Nevertheless, Britain pursued her relentless war
against France. Military action having failed, Britain
changed her tactics. If the French could carry on
insidious propaganda against the established regimes
of Europe, why could not the latter plot revolts
against the revolutionists ?

The British Government established in Switzerland
an espionage centre and appointed the thirty-three-
years'-old William Wickham as director. Wickham
was instructed to co-ordinate the activities of the
French *émigrés* and to combine them with the British
agents on the Continent ; the object was to organize
a Royalist uprising in France. "His Majesty," Lord
Grenville piously assured Wickham, "desires only to
see such a government established there, as may lead
to the permanent establishment of general tranquillity."

Wickham made contacts with the Royalists and
"expended a very considerable sum in gaining the
leading persons in some of the lesser cantons" in
Switzerland. Like the Nazi propagandists in Europe
to-day, Wickham was authorized to spend large sums
of money. Together with the disgruntled Royalists,
he drew up a plan for the invasion of France through
Lyons ; at the same time there was to be a co-ordinated
attack by the Austrians through Piedmont. Without

such an armed assault, Wickham explained to his government, "the Lyonnese will not take up arms against the Convention—that if they do not, the Jura will remain quiet also, and . . . all hope of any effective and general co-operation with the Royalists in the interior must be at an end." A third element in this project was a simultaneous diversion of the British fleet in Brittany.

The scheme failed, and Wickham devised a new one. Plentifully supplied with the " gold of Pitt " (£29,214 in November, 1795), the British agent made overtures to the Republican general, Pichegru, to betray his country. Pichegru assured Wickham of his " full determination to attempt something whenever a favourable opportunity shall offer." Meanwhile, Pichegru inspired his officers with a " disgust for the Convention " and got in touch with the Royalists.

But the French secret service was not asleep. Soon deliberate rumours were circulated throughout the Revolutionary army that the British had betrayed Pichegru to the Paris Government; the result was that when French officers were approached by British agents, they refused to place the " smallest confidence in the English." Wickham tried hard to discover the " leak " and finally concluded that it had come in a roundabout way " from Verona from some traitor to the King of France, and that the Directory obtained a copy of the letter written from Hamburg by the Bishop of Arras, who had a conference on that subject with M. Barthélemy's brother, who was sent to Hamburg by Carnot." Such were the tortuous paths of espionage.

Although the French Directory was suspicious, Pichegru continued his confidential correspondence with Wickham under the pseudonym Baptiste. " My confidence," Wickham informed the fatuous general, " is . . . without limits. . . . *My means* are always at his disposal. . . . It is for him alone to indicate how they should be employed. For the rest, I admonish him to have courage . . . , but at the same time not to trust his enemies who are sharp, clever, united, and . . . audacious." Pichegru was sure he could take care of himself; all he asked of the British agent was that his "pecuniary supplies" should be continued.

Four times the vacillating Pichegru attempted to betray his country and four times he failed. The fault, he apologized to Wickham, his paymaster, was not his. He had given, he said, the Austrian army four opportunities to defeat him and they had not taken advantage of the favourable openings. "First," Pichegru made a remarkable explanation, "in not passing the Rhine either so soon, or with so sufficient a force as he might have done; the second in composing the garrison of Mannheim of 10,000 of the best and at the same time the most desperate troops of the whole army, under the orders of a man who was quite incapable of commanding them; the third and fourth, in twice committing his *whole* army . . . in a fair field of battle, in such a way as no republican general had ever done before or since, and so that if the Austrian generals had had the spirit to have done the same, the *whole* might and probably would have been utterly destroyed." The Austrians were simply stupid and had not taken advantage of the favourable opportunities Pichegru had offered them; nevertheless, he repeated his "firm intention" of serving "the cause of the allies" to the best of his abilities.

Pichegru failed in his treason, for which, incidentally, he was in the end strangled in prison. Wickham likewise failed in all his attempts to overthrow the French Government. The French secret service intercepted important documents which piled up a mass of evidence against Wickham's machinations in Switzerland. Paris protested vigorously and the Swiss Government was compelled to expel the British agent.

IV

For another five years England and Austria remained in the coalition against France. Britain bore the financial burden, which was heavy, and Austria the military, such as it was. At this time the " sovereign of Vienna " was not Francis II but his chancellor, Francis Thugut, the only plebeian ever to occupy the chancellorship in aristocratic Austria.

Thugut played a great role in these years and a short portrait of him—particularly as he is almost unknown in the English-speaking world—may be permitted. He was the son of a Linz boatman whose surname derived from his nickname Thuniggut—Good for Nothing—which was changed to the more respectable Thugut, or Do Well. A gifted linguist, the young Thugut became interpreter to the Austrian ambassador in Constantinople and finally, at the age of thirty, plenipotentiary to Turkey. Maria Theresa rewarded Thugut's excellent services with a Privy Councillorship and a baronage. In 1780 Emperor Joseph II sent him to Warsaw as Austrian minister. On his first presentation at court Thugut, or rather von Thugut, made a blunder in mistaking the all-powerful Russian ambassador Stackelberg, who actually ruled Poland, for the Polish King ; but that same evening the adroit Austrian made up for his error. While playing cards with King Stanislaus, Stackelberg, and the Prussian minister Lucchesini, Thugut played a knave (valet) instead of the king and took a trick over the queen. When Lucchesini pointed it out to him, Thugut, smiling innocently, remarked : " Behold, twice in the same day I have taken a valet for a king."

During the French Revolution Thugut went to Paris and negotiated with Robespierre to save Marie Antoinette ; the failure of his mission and the excesses of the Revolutionists embittered the Austrian diplomat. He returned to Vienna, consumed with hatred for the republicans, and devoted the next seven years of his life to crushing the Revolutionists abroad and radicals at home.

None of the allies could get along with the unscrupulous and dour Austrian chancellor who knew only two passions, contempt and hatred. " The mind of Baron Thugut," Lord Minto said, " is not open to any reasoning." The Russian diplomat Vorontzov called the chancellor " false and ambitious," without " faith or law." Admiral Nelson was equally uncomplimentary. " For the sake of the civilized world," he urged Ambassador Minto, " let us work together, and as the best act of our lives manage to hang Thugut. . . . As you are with Thugut, your penetrating mind will discover the villain in all his actions. . . . Pray keep an eye upon the rascal."

Thugut trusted no one, loved no one, feared no one ; his contempt for mankind was almost maniacal. He had little contact with, and even less confidence in, his chief assistants, Barons Collenbach and Sylbach, to whom he handed State papers in silence and from whom he received replies in silence. Qualities which society considered evil, Thugut joyously condoned, for they proved the depravity of man. His private secretary Hüschle was rarely sober.

To prevent the spread of revolutionary ideas Thugut organized a dreaded espionage system and used agents-provocateurs to destroy opponents. Persons suspected of democratic activities, as were the Viennese Town-Major Hebenstreit and the Hungarian Bishop Martinowitz, were beheaded. In his foreign policy the chancellor was no less arbitrary. He rarely bothered to read despatches ; when he left his position in 1801 there were found in his office 170 unopened reports and over 2,000 unread letters. His hatred for the French republic was so violent that anyone who dared speak of peace was treated as an outlaw. His " mad and ruinous policy " finally brought Austria to complete and crushing defeat.

Thugut may or may not have been involved in an extraordinary murder mystery, known as the Rastadt affair.

At the end of 1797 a congress opened at Rastadt to settle German territorial questions; the diplomats squabbled for fifteen months and then a queer tragedy took place.

Archduke Charles, who commanded the Austrian Army in Germany, was informed that the French plenipotentiaries in Rastadt were taking advantage of their diplomatic immunity by plotting and spying. The archduke, now on the march against the French, expelled the French representatives from various German capitals (Regensburg, Munich, Stuttgart), and ordered the conference in Rastadt to be broken up. The French and Prussian envoys ignored the command. Then Barbaczy, an Austrian colonel, entered Rastadt and announced that the city was no longer considered neutral territory. Barbaczy solemnly promised to respect the persons of the French plenipotentiaries, but ordered them to leave the city within twenty-four hours.

The three French representatives, Bonner, Roberjot, and de Bry, asked the Austrian colonel for a formal assurance that their journey home would be unmolested. Barbaczy sent them an officer and two soldiers as escort. At the same time—it was eight o'clock in the evening—the city gates were suddenly occupied by a troop of Austrian hussars under an officer named Burckhard. Who had given them the command to occupy the gates? This was a vital question, but the three Frenchmen seemed to pay no attention to it as they rode through the gates into the night. When the three men reached a bridge they were suddenly attacked and two of them were killed; only de Bry escaped heavily wounded.

This brutal murder—presumably on the part of Austrian soldiers—of accredited diplomats caused a European sensation. Paris immediately accused Thugut and his master, Emperor Francis II, on the ground that both men were capable of anything. Others considered the French Royalist *émigrés* as the murderers, because Auguste Danican, a Royalist general, had recently written a pamphlet *Cassandra*, in which he openly advocated the murder of the French Directory; this pamphlet was distributed around Rastadt.

The assassination produced a bad impression in Vienna also. Thugut, suspecting or pretending to suspect his rival Archduke Charles, said that the murder was " disastrous " because it would give the " Directory and all the evil-minded persons a fine excuse to declaim against us and to impute to us the most extravagant horrors." He then appointed a military commission of inquiry, urging that the investigation be " carried out with publicity and in an authentic manner, in order to justify us in the eyes of all Europe by a striking punishment of those who will be found guilty."

The investigating commission must have made some startling discoveries; for six months it carried on a secret inquiry, but the results were never given to the world. Barbaczy, Burckhard, and the thirty hussars who had been imprisoned after the murder, were all set free; both officers were retired, however, the former with the rank of general and the latter with the rank of major. Was this a reward of assassination ?

The murderers have never been discovered; later investigations have tended to the conclusion that neither Thugut nor Archduke Charles had anything to do with the murder. Who committed the deed will always remain a mystery.

v

The murder at Rastadt has remained an impenetrable secret, but there is nothing mysterious about the assassination of Czar Paul I of Russia. Although this royal murder does not belong in the realm of high diplomacy, it had an effect on international policy.

Paul was the son of Catherine II who had overshadowed his life and who had kept him, throughout his youth and adulthood, in well-deserved obscurity ; for, if the truth must be told, the offspring and heir of the " Great " Catherine was not quite in his right senses. He had become Czar, upon his mother's death, in 1796, and in his dim mind there flickered the sparks of an ambition to play a manly role in Europe. He had inherited from his domineering mother an Austro-British alliance against France, and the fact that it was the work of his unlamented parent was enough to make Paul hostile to his allies. In any case, the Czar did not like to be reminded of his mother's friends. Consequently Paul got rid of the Austrian ambassador, Ludwig Cobenzl, and then he proceeded to annoy Whitworth, the British envoy. Whitworth's life became so unbearable that, " to avoid scandal," he decided to leave Russia voluntarily.

" The Emperor," Whitworth confided to London (in cipher, of course), " is literally not in his senses. This truth has been for many years known to those nearest to him, and I have myself had frequent opportunities of observing it. But since he has come to the throne his disorder has gradually increased."

This letter, it seems, was intercepted by the Czar's Black Cabinet and the furious Emperor ordered the recall of Ambassador Vorontzov from London. He, the Czar, who incidentally developed a queer liking for Bonaparte, would have nothing to do with the British. Vorontzov, who loved England, commented angrily —to friends—that Paul was " a demented sovereign who had ended up by becoming a cruel tyrant."

Everybody was agreed that Paul was crazy ; his own son, the future Alexander I, seems to have shared this opinion. The Czar was unable to follow any policy or pursue any straight line. His ministers were at each other's throat. Rostopchin, the chancellor, was pro-French; Panin, who had been Paul's tutor and was now his vice-chancellor, was pro-Austrian. Chancellor and vice-chancellor fought each other cruelly and openly, and the Czar alternately fought both. " You call me a minister," Rostopchin wrote bitterly to a friend, " and I am nothing but a secretary." Panin, an experienced intrigant (from the halcyon days of Catherine), made the chancellor's life miserable; but he too complained that he had " no means to do good and rarely the means to prevent evil."

And all this time Bonaparte was furiously flirting with Paul. The First Consul flattered the unbalanced Czar by sending him a sword which Pope Leo X had once given to the Grand Master of the Order of Malta. Then Bonaparte amazed the Russians by returning their prisoners of war without ransom or exchange. Chancellor Rostopchin pressed the Czar to join the French. He spoke vehemently of the " insatiable house of Austria" and the " arrogant despotism of England." Panin, on the other hand, was very bitter at Russia's desertion of Austria and England. " In a few months," he groaned, " Russia will be the laughing-stock of Europe." Finally Paul screwed up enough energy to exile Panin and to send a general to Paris to inform Bonaparte that Russia wanted "good harmony" with France.

But before Paul was able to come to an agreement with France he was efficiently murdered with the tacit consent of his son, now Alexander I. The assassination was carried out by ten army officers, headed by General Bennigsen and Platon Zubov; these names should be remembered, for they continued to play a considerable role in Russian history. The murder took place in bed, where the Czar lay ill. Drunken officers invaded the Imperial chambers, stunned a faithful valet, struck the Czar a blow on the temple, and then strangled him with a sash.

This cold-blooded murder aroused no indignation anywhere. Secretary Ross of the British Embassy reports that when the news of the strangling was announced, "the people were seen embracing, and giving each other joy in the streets."

Czar Alexander I handsomely rewarded the murderers of his father. Chief Assassin Bennigsen was made Governor of Lithuania and Assistant-Chief Assassin Zubov, whom one contemporary called "naturally a beast," became the new Czar's favourite. Thereby, it must be remembered, Alexander I acted in the family tradition, for his grandmother, Catherine II, had also befriended the murderers of her husband, Peter III. Europe forgave Alexander—or rather never remembered anything—as it had forgiven Catherine. "I know," Voltaire had said cynically of Catherine, "that she is reproached with some trifles on account of her husband; but these are family affairs in which I do not mix."

CHAPTER XI

THE CONSULATE

I

IN this period a deadly duel was being fought between industrial-aristocratic England and revolutionary-democratic France. It was a conflict of opposing ideologies and social-economic systems, and no compromise seemed possible. The Revolutionary-Napoleonic wars, in fact, ended only with the complete victory of the British, which meant the victory of commerce, industry, and technology. England, and not Napoleon, destroyed the principles of the French Revolution.

Bonaparte, it is interesting to notice, was acutely aware of the capitalistic undertones of the struggle. Although, as Consul and Emperor, he encouraged industry and fostered agriculture, he hated the financial classes and the new industrial capitalism of which Britain was the classic, the only, example. Bonaparte considered capitalistic contractors " the scourge and scab of the nations." Commerce to him was legalized thievery. " I do not love merchants," he once crudely told a deputation of Antwerp businessmen ; " a merchant is ready to sell his country for a thaler." From this point of view it is quite significant that Napoleon's gigantic effort to break the power of Britain took the form of a commercial war—the Continental System—designed to ruin British trade and industry.

Nor, to pursue this argument a few steps further, was the British governing class any less conscious of what was involved. Rationalize as the British statesmen might about " balance of power," " law and order," " rights of nations," they knew full well that they were fighting for markets, for trade, for colonies, for commercial supremacy ; in short, for the wealth upon which depended their privileges and position. The contemporary diplomatic correspondence is full of references to trade routes, commerce, control of India and Egypt, colonies, et cetera. The ruling class, one is bound to admit, acted more or less instinctively. The idea of *Empire* came later, clarified by economists and sung by historians. Which may help to explain why, in the Revolutionary epoch, there was so much bungling and fumbling in London, as well as personal feuds and jealousies.

A few examples of British carelessness and incompetence at this period will suffice. Pitt, the Premier, and Grenville, the Foreign Secretary, constantly pulled in opposite directions and, like Louis XV's Secret Correspondence, brought confusion into policy. Ambassadors, such as Malmesbury, were compelled to write two kinds of despatches, one (vague and general) to Pitt and another (specific and important) to Grenville. In Home affairs there was like chaos. Ambassador Vorontzov once informed Lord Hawkesbury that he had discovered a notorious French spy in London. When sometime later the Russian envoy asked Hawkesbury whether the spy's paper contained anything important, his lordship replied that he was sure he did not know, that it was the affair of the Alien Office, and the Alien Office, be it remembered, was in charge of a clerk who was himself a foreigner.

The same planlessness and leisureliness pervaded the Foreign Office. Letters sometimes went unanswered for years. Lord Broughton relates that when the Whigs came to power in 1806 they found several American despatches unopened. "I had heard," Broughton says, "a similar story of a closet full of American despatches in the Duke of Newcastle's time, and I recollected a remark made on that anecdote by ——. 'Yes, that is very true, and those who succeeded Newcastle took to reading despatches; and what was the consequence? The American War.'" Once a secretary in the Foreign Office gave orders to the commander of the British naval forces on the African coast to punish one of the Barbary

powers for some insult which he read about in a
despatch on his piled-up desk. A short time later it
was found that the secretary had not noticed the date
of that despatch, nor the nature of the insult; the
one was three years back, and the other had been
apologized for and forgiven.

The diplomats abroad were worthy of their superiors
at home. Drunkenness among them was universal.
"Drunk as a lord" is a byword dating from those
days. It was the practice to ply the candidates for
diplomatic posts with liquor and then to notice who
divulged fewest secrets under the table. Presumably
the theory was that the hardest drinker made the best
diplomat. There were, of course, exceptions. One
need only mention such a fastidious, and able, gentleman as Lord Malmesbury. Malmesbury needed no
liquor to be a successful diplomat. He was a past
master in all the tricks of this international trade.
When the young John Hookham Frere entered the
diplomatic service, the veteran Malmesbury gave
him "some excellent advice." Among other essentials, he recommended warmly the "use of rascals in
doing any dirty piece of work." It was of the utmost
importance, Malmesbury told Frere, "never to mix
yourself in any such business," but to leave all diplomatic dirty work to "foreign adventurers ready for
anything of the kind." Malmesbury then quoted the
Greek proverb:

> " Not with rascals altogether
> Nor without rascals either."

II

One day in June, 1800, while the French cannon
was mercilessly slaughtering the Austrians at Marengo,
British and Austrian diplomats in Vienna concluded
a treaty binding each other not to make separate
peace with that monster Bonaparte.

A week after the battle the victorious Bonaparte

met an Austrian officer, Count Joseph Saint-Julien, in Milan and gave him a letter to Emperor Francis II. Saint-Julien hurried to Vienna and handed the letter to his monarch, who was disconcerted to read that Bonaparte proposed an armistice in order to begin negotiations for peace. Francis II was in a predicament. He could not afford to reject Bonaparte's proposal and he was in no position to desert his British allies who had just paid him a subsidy of £2,500,000. Chancellor Thugut advised his sovereign to temporize and, to gain time, the Austrian chancery sent Saint-Julien back to Bonaparte with a letter which was a masterpiece of ambiguity—an art in which the Austrians excelled. This particular diplomatic epistle was so phrased that the First Consul could read it either to mean that Austria was ready to make a separate peace—since England was nowhere mentioned by name—upon favourable terms, or that Vienna would not make peace except " in accord " with her other engagements, meaning the British alliance.

Both the vagueness of the letter and the choice of the messenger were intentional. For if Thugut had really meant peace he would have chosen a professional diplomat and not a scatter-brained army officer. Furthermore, the letter, intentionally or not, was addressed to *General* Bonaparte—presumably a commander on the field of battle—and not to the First Consul, that is, the chief of the French republic. Saint-Julien hastened to Milan with his letter, but he found that Bonaparte had already departed for Paris, whither the Austrian messenger now made his way.

The trip to Paris took two weeks. Arrived in the French capital, Saint-Julien handed the letter to Talleyrand, the Minister of Foreign Affairs. Talleyrand asked him blandly whether he had " other powers " besides the Imperial letter. Either out of vanity or, what was more likely, out of stupidity, Saint-Julien replied that having been in Vienna only a few days he had " neglected to provide himself with a document which was diplomatically necessary to sign preliminary or definitive conventions." Talleyrand, the shrewdest diplomat of his time, assuming that Thugut had deliberately chosen this young fool in order to deceive the French Government, laid a neat trap for the luckless officer and his employer. " Monsieur Saint-Julien," the Foreign Minister said suavely, " would appear sufficiently qualified and accredited.

Talleyrand decided to treat Saint-Julien, a mere courier, as a fully accredited plenipotentiary of the Imperial Government in Vienna. The trick was worthy of the best European diplomatic tradition.

For a moment Saint-Julien hesitated ; he had a vague feeling that he was beyond his depths, that the foxy ex-bishop was playing him for a sucker, and murmured something about his return to Vienna for further instructions. Very well, Talleyrand said coolly, but the moment you leave, the " First Consul will find himself obliged to renew hostilities."

" *Eh bien*," Saint-Julien replied quickly, " I will sign."

And Saint-Julien signed. He signed away the Rhineland, Salzburg, and Bavaria, and a promise to close Austrian ports to England.

Poor Saint-Julien ! He did not know that it took a Napoleon or a Metternich to treat with Talleyrand without losing his possessions.

When Saint-Julien returned to Vienna with the amazing document which he had signed in the name of the Austrian Government, Chancellor Thugut became raving mad. Apart from its being disgraceful, the treaty was highly dangerous, for if Britain ever found out about it, Austria would lose her only ally and be completely at Bonaparte's mercy. " I have not closed an eye all night," the sick Thugut groaned ; " in all world history there is no example compared to the insane conduct of Saint-Julien, who, without the slightest authority, signed preliminaries which must necessarily compromise us before the whole world." There was only one thing to do, and that was immediately to inform the British of what had happened and to write to Paris a rejection of the convention which Saint-Julien had not been authorized to sign. To the British, Thugut explained that Saint-Julien's action was the " work of inexperience and of a moment of complete confusion." Talleyrand was informed that the treaty was " null and void."

As for the luckless Saint-Julien, he was imprisoned in a fortress and ordered by the Emperor to keep his mouth shut—*dass er sich allen Gesprächs über Geschäfte enthalte.* The would-be doplomat was set free after one year's confinement and advised never to mention the subject.

The sequel to Saint-Julien's little adventure was not tragic. Furious at the " big chatterer," as Bonaparte called that officer, the First Consul took the offensive against the Austrians, defeated them as usual, and forced them to make peace at Lunéville. This led to Thugut's resignation.

The peace of Lunéville left Britain isolated ; she was also beginning to feel drained after almost a decade of war. " There is hardly an inch of ground," Paget, a British diplomat, said bitterly, " or a bit of silver or gold in all the south of Europe which is not at his (Bonaparte's) disposition." Britain was too exhausted to fight and too proud to yield, after so much effort. How, indeed, could Britain make peace with France when the latter controlled the Rhine, held Switzerland, and dominated the Low Countries ? " Is all this to last eternally ? " Paget asked.

But there was no way out for Britain. Moreover, her fleet was not in a good condition ; the famous mutiny of the Nore frightened the Government. And so, after a full year of haggling, England and France temporarily ended the war (Amiens, 1802). " The state of the fleet," Lord Liverpool admitted frankly, "had been one of the motives for concluding peace."

Paris celebrated gaily. Cannon boomed, fireworks crackled, public buildings were illuminated. Then the proud and victorious First Consul, already dreaming of world empire, invited the diplomatic corps to the Tuileries. In glittering uniforms the diplomats first bowed to the " exquisitely dressed " Josephine, and then they were conducted to the audience-chamber of Bonaparte who, surrounded by resplendent dignitaries, smiled graciously. The dictator of France was proud to have ended a ten years' war.

" We are at present," he addressed the assembled diplomats, " good friends and I hope that the union will be indissoluble. When the powers are united the rest of Europe cannot help but be at peace. When they are disunited it is a calamity for science, art, humanity." And smiling affably, the First Consul turned to the British ambassador and told him that it was desirable for France and England to " remain friends in order to civilize the world."

The Russian ambassador resented the implication.

III

The First Consul, like all dictators, was in daily danger of assassination. Paris swarmed with *déracinés*, Royalist soldiers and adventurers, who were organized by one Hyde de Neufville to kill Bonaparte. At this time the First Consul was poorly guarded. The Royalists thought they could easily dispose of the two or three officers who usually accompanied Bonaparte on the streets. The first plot, in which our old friend William Wickham (then at Augsburg) had a hand to the extent of £50,000, failed ; but it brought on the scene a very remarkable individual : Fouché.

To protect the life of Bonaparte, Fouché—" the *bête noire* of the nation," as a Russian statesman called him—organized the most efficient secret service in

NAPOLEON IN 1812

Europe. It was Fouché who made Napoleonic France a perfect police-*cum*-spy State. France, the mother of Liberty, Equality, and Fraternity, now harboured no less than six fully-organized police systems. The chief one was the regular ministry of police, under Fouché himself, which employed a corps of un-uniformed agents, justices, magistrates, and inspectors, as well as hundreds of spies. Then there was the independent gendarmerie, in uniform. The city of Paris had its own police agents under a Prefect of Police, and so had the commander of the guard. A fifth police system was attached to Napoleon's personal household. Finally, the Ministry of Foreign Affairs possessed a separate espionage department.

This complicated network of spies and agents produced and poured a steady stream of denunciations into Napoleon's cabinet. "One hardly knew to whom to listen," Prefect of Police Pasquier recalls ; "it was nothing but a continual series of complaints and denunciations. . . . The Emperor was suspicious to an extraordinary degree." Moreover, Napoleon, as Emperor, was in the habit of employing society women, like Mme de Genlis, as spies. The dictator carefully sifted all this mass of information. "Daily," Fouché tells, "he received four bulletins from the separate police, coming from different sources, and which enabled him to compare them, without counting the reports of his confidential agents. This was what he called *feeling the pulse* of the nation."

The insatiable curiosity of Napoleon throve on this torrent of reports. He found them such pleasant reading that he devoted daily a few precious hours to them. He knew everything. If he did not, he soon learned. No one was safe from his prying. He made everybody's business his business.

"The good old code, like Argus, had a hundred watchful eyes."

In Napoleon's *Lettres Inédites* one finds characteristic examples of his meddling.

" They tell me," he writes to the police, " that very seditious talk goes on at a wine-shop, Rue St. Honoré. . . . Pay a little attention to these small taverns."

" A man named Curti, uncle of the *podestá* of Venice, is a dangerous man. Let him know that if he mixes himself up with the carrying of letters for the Roman court he will find himself arrested and will pass some years of his life in prison."

" I am informed," this to his stepson Prince Eugene Beauharnais, " that you wrote to a woman named D——. I do not know if you are aware that she is only a meddlesome girl, who has been often used by the police. A woman of this kind ought never to get a letter from you."

Generally the Napoleonic police-spy system functioned superbly, but it sometimes met with clever opposition. The British secret service, for one, often eluded the vigilance of the French, for England never trusted Napoleon's post office, but used Continental banking houses for transmitting letters. Diplomatic despatches from Paris were sent to London by special courier twice weekly. Others likewise frequently got around Napoleon's spies. For example, Louis XVIII, an exile often in need of money, duped Fouché by having one of his confidential agents join the French secret service ; the pay of the supposed spy became a regular source of income to the exiled Bourbon King.

There was also some smart counter-espionage. Count d'Antraigues, a French adventurer living in London, established a regular diplomatic information agency in Paris and sold valuable news to Austria, Russia, and Britain in turn. D'Antraigues' sources were usually good. Among his agents were two brothers Simon who were employed in the French Ministries of War and Foreign Affairs. The greatest *coup* was that of a spy named Michel. He had access to Napoleon's private book-case marked *États de Situation*, which contained confidential materials on military and financial affairs. For ten years Michel sent information from this book-case to Russia—a discovery not made until 1812.

But the chief weakness of the Napoleonic administration was venality.   Talleyrand and Fouché—ministers both—were notorious for their corruption. During the conferences between the Germanic princes and the French ministers for the settlement of German territorial questions—*Reichsdeputationshauptschluss*, to give it its concise German name—most of the responsible French officials accepted heavy bribes.   Prussia gave Talleyrand a snuffbox worth 1,000 louis, and 100,000 francs in cash ; Hesse spent 1,000,000 crowns ; Baden, 500,000 livres.

IV

Talleyrand, whom we have already met and whom we shall meet again, deserves a section by himself. First a portrait of the man.

A noon visitor to the chambers of Napoleon's Minister of Foreign Affairs would see a man with a lip like a cat's, drawn up and clinging to the gums, rise from bed and limp to the dressing room where his valet held a water bowl and sponge.   The lame man was swathed from head to foot in flannel and his head crowned with a funny nightcap.   The visitor would observe other visitors—ladies and gentlemen, mainly diplomats—standing in respectful silence, while the man in flannel washed his mouth and had his clawlike feet cleansed.

Such was Maurice Talleyrand de Périgord, whom Lord Acton called " one of the wonders of modern politics."[1]

[1] Acton, " Talleyrand's Memoirs," *Nineteenth Century*, XXIX (1891), 67–84, thus described Talleyrand : " The unscrupulous priest, the money-getting sybarite, the patient auxiliary of the conqueror and tyrant, the royalist who defended the tenth of August, the republican minister who brought on the Empire, the imperial dignitary who restored the Bourbons, the apostle of Legitimacy who hailed its fall."

He was born in 1754, fifteen years before Napoleon. At the age of nineteen this scion of an ancient family became an abbé. At thirty-four he was a bishop; at thirty-five a revolutionist; at forty-two a minister; and in the end a duke. He served many masters, wrecked a number of governments, accumulated and squandered a fortune, and when he died at the ripe age of eighty-four he left for posterity a legacy of wisdom in eight words: " The only good principle is to have none."

Napoleon found Talleyrand indispensable, for the aristocratic ex-bishop possessed *ce parfum d'ancienne noblesse* which the upstart Corsican was conscious of lacking. " He has," Napoleon said of him, " much that is necessary for conducting negotiations: the experience of a man of the world, knowledge of European courts, finesse, or something more, immobility of countenance, which nothing can alter, and finally a great name." This is a well-nigh perfect recipe for a model diplomat. But a time was to come when Napoleon regretted that he had not hanged his accomplished minister.

One year after the Emperor made Talleyrand a duke, in 1807, the ex-bishop left the Foreign Office. With uncanny political sense he realized that his master was beginning to overreach himself. " I do not wish," Talleyrand commented on the Emperor's grandiose schemes, " to be the executioner of Europe." He was, however, willing to be the executioner of Napoleon whom he promptly betrayed to Czar Alexander I. Napoleon discovered the treason and splashed his ex-minister with a shower of abuse. " You are a miserable fellow," the Emperor shouted; " you have betrayed all the governments you have professed to serve; and will betray again whom now you vow you regard. But I will not give you the leisure. . . . I will punish you as you deserve." The duke remained silent.

" Talleyrand," the Emperor thundered, " you are a traitor and I ought to have you hanged."

" I don't agree with you, Sire," was the duke's calm answer.

Talleyrand, as Napoleon said, not only " betrayed religion, Louis XVI, the Constituent Assembly, the Directorate," but he was, as we have observed elsewhere, notorious for his venality. Within three months after he entered the Ministry of Foreign Affairs, he had accumulated 12,000,000 francs. Gold continued to pour into his cabinet. He received 6,000,000 francs from the King of Saxony, about 1,000,000 from Murat, no less than 1,000,000 from the Margrave of Baden, some 3,700,000 from King Ferdinand IV of the Two Sicilies. Suppliants even played with his poodle to win his favour. When Livingston, the representative of the United States, went to see Talleyrand, the first question the French minister asked was : " Have you any money ? " " I do not understand," the shocked Livingston stammered. " In this country," Talleyrand explained affably, " matters are difficult to manage without it. With the aid of an abundance of money all difficulties are surmounted. Reflect well on this."

Talleyrand then introduced Livingston to Bonaparte. " Sir," the First Consul said significantly, " you have come from another world into a very corrupt one." The American diplomat understood little French and Bonaparte turned to his minister for aid.

" Monsieur Talleyrand," the First Consul said ironically, " you understand English very well ; have the goodness to explain to the gentleman what I am trying to tell him." The one man whom Talleyrand never fooled was Bonaparte.

For all his cynicism Talleyrand wished to be remembered as a constructive statesman. He denied ever having committed crimes. " Did you ever know crime of use to a sensible man ? " he once asked Lamartine. " It is the recourse of political fools, and is like the breaker which returns to overwhelm you. I had my failings, some say vices—but crimes, never ! "

As Talleyrand well knew, crime was a matter of definition. He would never sacrifice anything for ideas, " not even," he added cynically, " if they were my own."

In politics he was a moderate, an admirer of limited monarchy and a foe of democracy. " A democracy," he sneered, " what is it but an aristocracy of black-guards ? " During the period of the Directory, the noble Bishop showed contempt for his low-born colleagues who, he said, " had never walked on the parquet." Proud of his aristocratic origin, he said of himself that he " dressed like a coxcomb, thought like a deist, and preached like a saint."

" He is," the plebeian Director Reubell remarked cruelly, " the powdered lackey of the ancient regime ; at most he could be used as a servant for purposes of parade, were he only provided with a decent pair of legs, but he has no more legs than heart."

As a diplomat Talleyrand was the flower of perfection. A good diplomat, he said, must be endowed with an instinct for the job, must seem open yet remain impenetrable, reserved yet with a mask of frankness, adroit yet simple and even ingenuous. " Diplomacy is not a science of craft and duplicity. If good faith is necessary anywhere, it is necessary in political transactions, for it alone can render them solid and durable. The world has been pleased to confuse reserve with cunning. Good faith authorizes cunning, though it admits reserve." All these characteristics Talleyrand possessed, withal a total lack of scruples. " Why," Napoleon groaned at St. Helena, " did I not have him shot ? "

Talleyrand so divested himself of passion that hostile opinion never penetrated his armour. A master of cutting repartee, he could outsneer anyone. At the first restoration of Louis XVIII—who, incidentally, rewarded Napoleon's ex-minister with a chamberlainship worth 100,000 francs annually— Talleyrand, leaning on Fouché's arm, went to see the

TALLEYRAND

new King, and Chateaubriand commented grimly that it was a picture of vice supported by crime. Louis XVIII asked Talleyrand how he had managed to ruin so many governments, including Napoleon's. " There is something about me," was the sardonic answer, " which brings ill-luck on governments that neglect me." An ominous statement ! The Bourbons did not precisely neglect him, but fifteen years after their restoration he helped to put the Orleanist Louis Philippe on the French throne. His life-work was done, and at the age of eighty he said that he was a great composer whose masterpiece was a trilogy. Act I : the Empire and Napoleon. Act II : the Reign of the House of Bourbon. Act III : the Reign of the House of Orleans.

V

The peace which Napoleon concluded in 1802 did not last. The chief reason for the removal of hostilities was commercial, for the British, whose trade with the Continent had increased tremendously during the first years of the Revolution, were disappointed when they discovered that Napoleon had no intention of permitting them to control the European market. Bonaparte, in fact, was taking advantage of the breathing spell to build a powerful navy and to dominate the Mediterranean, for which purpose he wanted the island of Malta which the British had promised to cede. " Malta," the First Consul admitted, " dominates the Mediterranean ; and I do not wish them to have two Gibraltars in this sea."

Britain knew the danger. To maintain the peace meant to observe the Treaty of Amiens, and to observe the treaty involved giving up Malta. Hence France had everything to gain from peace, and Britain everything to lose.

"Inform your Court," Napoleon said to Ambassador Whitworth at the end of 1802, " that if, on the receipt of your despatches, orders are not issued for the immediate surrender of Malta, then war is declared."

"But, General, the negotiation is not yet broken, and there is every reason to believe——"

At this Bonaparte lost his temper and raised his arm as if to strike ; Lord Whitworth gripped his sword.

"Is it necessary," the First Consul cried, "to negotiate what is conceded by treaty—to negotiate the fulfilment of engagement and the duties of good faith ? "

Bonaparte did not strike the ambassador and war did not break out immediately. The British should have acted swiftly, but the incompetent Addington-Hawkesbury ministry was afraid of war. Vorontzov, the Russian ambassador in London, in fact accused Hawkesbury of feeble-mindedness. "There is an actual imbecility in His Lordship."

War broke out in May, 1803. Bonaparte's first act was to order the arrest of all British male subjects between the ages of eighteen and sixty who were to be found in France, a total of about 10,000. Among these hostages was the Earl of Yarmouth, better known as the Marquis of Steyne in Thackeray's *Vanity Fair*.

Britain now renewed her old technique of fomenting insurrection in France. Georges Cadoudal, the Vendéan, was supplied with English money and went to France, where he organized a "very wide and deep-laid plot," together with General Moreau and our old friend Pichegru. But Fouché's secret service was far superior. to that of the Directory. Within a month the three chief conspirators were arrested and forty others, including the Duke of Enghien, were implicated. Cadoudal was executed, Pichegru was found strangled in prison (by whose orders is not known), Moreau escaped only to die in the campaign of 1813. Arbuthnot, the British Under-Secretary of State, bewailed the unfortunate "result of all our fine Projects."

This famous conspiracy had wide ramifications. Count Ludwig Cobenzl, the Austrian Foreign Minister, was " strongly suspected" of having betrayed the plotters, particularly Pichegru, to the French ambassador in Vienna—and this rumour ultimately ruined Cobenzl's career. Bonaparte himself cleverly took advantage of the public sympathy which the discovery of the plot brought him and crowned himself Emperor. But the most ludicrous consequence of the conspiracy was *l'affaire Drake*.

Drake, the British minister in Munich, was entrapped by the French secret service into correspondence with a Napoleonic spy. Now Paris published these letters, and Drake, accused of conspiring under the cloak of diplomatic immunity, was expelled from Munich. German newspapers, inspired by Paris, printed " most outrageous and indecent attacks on the British Government," so that Drake's life was actually in danger. He escaped to Berlin in disguise, but the Prussian Government, dreading the wrath of Bonaparte, ordered the hunted diplomat to get out of the country. There was nowhere to go, for the Continent swarmed with French agents. " In a great fright," lest he fall into the " claws of the French"—who would have made short work of him—Drake swallowed his dignity and disguised himself as a handsome woman. But even a " handsome woman " met with difficulties and it took Drake many anxious weeks before he finally reached England.

Europe roared with laughter at the spectacle of a British diplomat fleeing from the French in female guise. A cartoon showing Drake in woman's dress, and heavily loaded with bottles and books, was widely circulated. Underneath was the motto : *Aquila non capit muscas*. Napoleon's eagle was undoubtedly soaring, while British prestige was no larger than a fly.

But twelve years later the *aquila* was himself in a cage.

CHAPTER XII

THE EMPIRE

I

THE Anglo-French war which started in 1803 finally developed into a world conflict which ended only with the complete defeat of Napoleon at Waterloo. For the next twelve years Napoleon was to have no rest from his implacable British enemy. The Emperor won almost every battle, but lost the war. Every weapon was pressed into service. There were military fronts, economic fronts, propaganda fronts. Couriers were waylaid, despatches seized, mail intercepted, and agents abducted. The most notorious case of abduction was that of Sir George Rumbold, the British minister to the Hanseatic cities residing in the neutral territory of Hamburg, who was seized by French soldiers and sent to Paris. When the timid King of Prussia, the protector of Hamburg, was asked by Russia to protest, he replied that he would not " go to war for a box of papers."

Britain's military allies—Austria and Russia—were badly defeated, and the failure of the coalition broke the spirit of Pitt. The British Prime Minister folded up the map of Europe and died ; he was succeeded by the more pacific Fox who, having failed to secure peace, soon died, but not before he had, perhaps unwittingly, entangled Prussia in war with Napoleon over the question of Hanover. Napoleon moved swiftly. He cut off the Prussian forces from their capital, annihilated them at Jena, and entered Berlin. In Charlottenburg the Emperor discovered the secret Russo-Prussian correspondence which showed that the two powers had closer connections than he had realized. One letter in particular, " slipped behind a sofa cushion," made Napoleon " quite furious " against the Prussians. From Berlin Napoleon moved east and fought a desperate battle at Eylau ; there was no victory. Sheer exhaustion brought the fight to an end. When the battle was over, 18,000 Prussians, 18,000 Russians, and 30,000 Frenchmen lay dead on the snow.

Such battles were too costly, but Napoleon burned with revenge. He recovered, swooped down on East Prussia, seized Danzig and Königsberg, and at last destroyed the Russo-Prussian armies at Friedland.

Now the invincible Corsican was master of Europe, and he was ready to make peace.

"All the great people" gathered for the peace conference at Tilsit, in East Prussia. At the head of the table sat the Czar, worried about the wretched state of his empire; beside him was the melancholy King of Prussia, an exile from his capital, brooding over the French invasion of his realm. The handsome British diplomat, Lord Granville Leveson Gower had his private worries; he knew that his "Little Barbarian," Princess Galitzin, was paying more attention to the Czar than to him, her lover.

At this preliminary gathering the dominant figure was the impressionable Alexander I who was torn between friendship for Prussia and need for peace with France. Napoleon spared no effort to detach him from his allies, and the Czar yielded in the end, mainly because his vast empire was in a wretched state. "With the granite in the quarries," as Minister Tchitchegov said, "the iron in the mines, and the fields sown and scattered over a surface of a thousand million square versts, and the roads frightful, one can hardly hope to give the law to Europe."

And so, while the Prussians and the British passed the time in playing Blind Man's Buff and Hunt the Slipper, the rulers of France and Russia got together secretly to remake the map of Europe.

Hereby hangs an extraordinary mystery.

It was June 25, 1807, when Alexander and Napoleon met on a raft moored in the Niemen River. The raft —" a little house beautifully furnished "—contained two apartments, one for each Emperor. Here the two rulers held long conversations, protected from prying eyes and eavesdroppers. The result of the intimate talks was a treaty which was to agitate Europe and to remain a deep secret for eighty-four years.[1]

The secret articles of the Treaty of Tilsit remained impenetrable to the devouring curiosity of all the diplomats, especially the British who, it happened, were most affected by them. Besides Alexander and Napoleon, only the King of Prussia knew—the Czar told him—what was in the articles. Alopeus, the Russian ambassador in England, was not taken into the secret. Ambassador Gower was in complete ignorance, as was every other diplomat in Tilsit.

Some Russian friends of England, especially General Budberg, advised the Czar to communicate the whole treaty to London. "It is more than probable," Budberg argued, "that England will get to know . . . sooner or later, and we shall have gratuitously thrown away an opportunity of showing confidence to an old ally who may still be useful in the future." Alexander refused.

A word as to the documents. Napoleon's copy of the Treaty was deposited in the Ministry of Foreign Affairs in Paris, whence, incidentally, it disappeared in 1815. Alexander's copy was preserved in St. Petersburg (it was this text that was published in 1891).

At this point, before we go on with this strange story, the reader should be informed what was in the secret articles—a privilege for which many a European government a century and a quarter back would have paid a king's ransom. In these secret articles France and Russia promised to support each other "in every war" which they might engage "against any European power," meaning Britain. Should the latter refuse mediation, Russia was to make "common cause

---

[1] The text was not published until 1891.

with France." Most important of all, Denmark, Sweden, and Spain were to be compelled to close their ports to British ships ; Austria likewise was to be induced " with force " to make common cause against England. In short, Napoleon and Alexander were to dominate Europe and destroy the British Empire.

The first act was to close the Baltic to Britain. " If England," Napoleon informed Bernadotte, his commander-in-chief in the Baltic provinces, " refuses to accept Russian mediation, Denmark must declare war against her or I declare war against Denmark, and you will seize the whole Danish fleet." The Danish Navy was to be the instrument with which to beat England in the Baltic.

Had Napoleon succeeded in a swift seizure of the Danish fleet, he would have closed the Sound and made the Baltic a Franco-Russian lake. One may well imagine what a fatal blow this would have been to Britain, especially her commerce on which her life depended. But now something extraordinary happened, something that had remained a diplomatic mystery for more than a century. The British Government suddenly forestalled Napoleon !

What exactly happened in London no one knows. One must go back to Tilsit and pick up a few threads. The day after the fateful interview between the two emperors at Tilsit, a letter was written from nearby Memel to the British minister at Copenhagen ; this mysterious letter was immediately forwarded to London, where it arrived on July 16. Mark this date. The letter was read by George Canning, the brilliant Foreign Secretary, who had the rare ability to put two and two together and make it four. Whatever the letter contained, Canning concluded that if France and Russia were plotting against Britain it meant that the control of the Baltic was in question, and if the Baltic was involved, the Danish fleet was the main object. Acting upon this logical reasoning—if it was mere reasoning—Canning hastily instructed the

British fleet in the Sound to demand securities from Denmark.

The source and extent of Canning's information, whatever it was, has long been a subject of speculation. Almost every person of any importance—Talleyrand, General Bennigsen, Ambassador Gower—has been, at one time or another, given the credit or discredit. Canning himself never divulged the secret, but a recent biographer, Temperley, believes it was a secret agent whose information was supplemented by Talleyrand. Lady Lyttleton, in a contemporary letter, stated that Lord Gower had got possession of the original treaty for £20,000.[1] But all these statements are unsubstantiated.

To return to Canning. On July 16, the date of the first mysterious letter, Canning received another letter, this time from Garlike, the British minister in Copenhagen, which contained the information that French troops were assembling near Holstein. Thereupon Canning sent Brooke Taylor to Copenhagen to demand an explicit statement from Denmark, backed by " sufficient security "—meaning the Danish fleet. One day *after* these instructions were given to Taylor, Mackenzie, a British agent at Tilsit who has sometimes been given the credit for informing Canning, reached London. Whatever the news that Mackenzie brought with him, it had no effect on the policies of the Foreign Minister, whose arrangements were already made.

[1] See Temperley, *Life of Canning*, 91–3 ; H. Windham, *Correspondence of Sarah Spencer Lady Lyttleton* (1912), 4–5. The historians Oscar Browning and J. H. Rose ascribe the information to the British agent Mackenzie who was present in Tilsit ; later evidence, however, made Rose change his mind ; see Rose, *Napoleonic Studies*, 153–65 ; O. Browning, " A British Agent at Tilsit," *English Historical Review*, XVII (1902), 110. For a criticism of Rose, see J. Hall, " The Mystery of Tilsit," in his *Four Famous Mysteries* (1922), 9–33 ; cf. " The Mystery of Tilsit," *Athenæum*, Sept. 27, 1902, 414–15, and June 17, 1905, 752–54.

GEORGE CANNING
(After Lawrence.)

The next act took place in Denmark. Admiral Gambier with a fleet of twenty-four ships sailed to the Sound, where he was joined by the Baltic fleet, making a total of over one hundred vessels—" perhaps the most powerful fleet which had ever left our shores."[1]

Canning's zeal, one should add in parenthesis, was due to misinformation regarding the strength of the Danish Navy. Just before the orders from London reached the fleet in the Baltic, a British sea captain made a secret visit to Copenhagen and discovered there only eighteen " sail of the line, eleven frigates, ten sloops, four floating batteries, and several small gunboats "—not enough to menace the British Empire.

While the navy was threateningly manœuvring outside the Sound, Francis Jackson, the British plenipotentiary, entered Copenhagen with an ultimatum that Denmark hand over her fleet. Jackson, however, was instructed to present the drastic demand of His Britannic Majesty in such a way as " to spare the feelings as well as the interests of Denmark."

" The delivery of the Danish fleet," Canning's instructions read, " must be stipulated to take place forthwith, and without waiting for the formality of the ratifications of the treaty."

Jackson presented the ultimatum to the Danish minister Bernstorff. In return for their handing over the fleet to Britain, the Danes were to get a subsidy of £100,000, a relaxation of the blockade, and a defensive alliance. The government was to make up its minds in eight days. " If a sword is drawn, or a shot fired, it will be a matter of sincere and painful regret to His Majesty."

The proposal was galling enough to a sovereign state —*not* at war with England—but Jackson aggravated matters by an insufferable arrogance (with a fleet of

---

[1] Rose, *Napoleonic Studies*, 135n.

one hundred ships supporting him). The indignant Bernstorff denied passionately, and truthfully, that his country had any relations with Napoleon. Jackson who, to quote his own words, knew that the " Danes have not entered into any coalition against us," replied ironically that Denmark's past conduct " would have alone been sufficient justification for action."

" What then," Bernstorff exclaimed, " because you know that France has the intention of wounding us in the tenderest spot, would you struggle with her for the guilty priority and be the first to commit the deed ? "

Jackson's contemptuous answer was that the Danish minister should " lay aside figures of speech which it was so unfit for me to hear as for you to utter."

The proud and outraged Danes rejected the ultimatum and Admiral Gambier began a four days' bombardment of Copenhagen, killing 2,000 civilians and burning part of the city. Denmark capitulated and the British towed away her wretched fleet.

This brutal attack on Denmark aroused indignation throughout Europe. Even Englishmen were outraged at Canning's high-handed procedure. Lord Malmesbury, then Under Secretary of State, resigned in protest. Lord Grenville, admitting that " it is time for us to fight our enemy with his own poisoned weapons," thought the action put England in " a most horrible position." Czar Alexander, in protest, expelled Ambassador Gower from Russia.

King George III expressed his protest in a solemn joke. When Jackson returned from Denmark the King wanted to know whether the Danish Crown Prince had been upstairs during the interview.

" He was on the ground floor," replied the puzzled Jackson.

" I am glad of that for your sake," was the King's answer, " for if he had half my spirit he would certainly have kicked you downstairs."

Such was the result of the secret Treaty of Tilsit. Canning's swift action undoubtedly " stole a march " on Napoleon and prevented the French and the Russians from dominating the Baltic. But the question still remains : Who informed Canning ?

Did Count d'Antraigues, the French *émigré* who had an espionage bureau in London, reveal the secret to Canning, as Sir John Hall believes ? Hall bases his theory upon the fact that a few weeks after Tilsit d'Antraigues was suddenly dismissed from the Russian secret service without compensation, while Canning granted him an annual pension of £400. This is merely begging the question, for one would like to know who informed d'Antraigues. Obviously the Tilsit Treaty was known only to those close to either Napoleon or Alexander, and certainly an adventurer-spy like d'Antraigues was not in the confidence of either Talleyrand—who, despite rumours, probably had nothing to do with the case, as Napoleon distrusted him—or Alexander. As for other secret service agents besides Mackenzie—who, as we have seen, could not have given the information to Canning —the British records show no evidence of any awards granted in this period.

Where, then, did Canning get his information ? Despite the uncertainty among historians, there seems little doubt that the Foreign Minister had some knowledge of the secret articles of the Treaty. There is proof that Canning did not act solely upon guesses. Immediately after the conclusion of peace between France and Russia, Canning ordered Arthur Paget to go to Constantinople and make peace with Turkey. " You will further state," the Foreign Minister's letter to Paget read, " . . . that His Majesty's Government have received the *most positive Information of Secret Articles being annexed to the Treaty*, from the tenor of which . . . it is in the contemplation both of Russia and of France to expel (Turkey) from all the Territories which it at present possesses in Europe." The full Tilsit Treaty, published eighty-four years later, proved Canning to be correct.

If Canning really knew what was in the secret articles there was only one person who could possibly have given him the information. Strangely enough, this person has never, until this writing, been so much as suspected by those who wrote about the " mystery of Tilsit." This informant could have been no other than Vorontzov, until recently Russian ambassador to England, and a man who loved that country so much that, when he was supplanted by another envoy, he refused to leave it.

The proof that Vorontzov was the man is as follows. On July 14—note the date—he seems to have known what had happened in Tilsit, for on that day he wrote to his son Michael : " My spirit is disquieted by the news which arrives from all sides, announcing that the Emperor was going to make peace with Bonaparte, that he had an interview with that monster. I hope to God that this is false."[1]

Canning received the first intimation of the Tilsit meeting on July 16, two days *after* Vorontzov knew about it. Is it not reasonable to assume that Vorontzov informed his friend Canning, especially as they both shared a violent hatred for Bonaparte ? Three days later, on July 17, Vorontzov wrote to young Michael about " a certain Captain Hervey, just arrived from Memel," with whom he had a conversation. Who was Hervey ?

We must remember that Vorontzov was in touch not only with British diplomats and agents like Lord Gower, Sir Robert Wilson, and Colonel Bathurst— about whom, by the way, we shall have to tell an amazing and tragic story—who were in the vicinity of Memel and Tilsit, but also on close terms with the intimates of the Czar, especially Prince Czartoryski. Alexander I's friends bitterly opposed any alliance

[1] *Arkhiv Kniazia Vorontzova* (Moscow, 1880), XVII, 159; *cf.* 165.

with the detested Napoleon. What more natural than for some confidant of the Czar, possibly Czartoryski, to inform Vorontzov in London of what had taken place? The supposition becomes almost a certainty when one learns that the son of the ex-ambassador, Michael Vorontzov, who was an officer in the Russian Army, was *on the raft during the interview*.[1] It is possible that Michael, who was brought up in England and shared his father's feelings about that country, hastened to Sir Robert Wilson, the English adventurer then in the service of Russia, with the news of the interview. Wilson may have consulted Czartoryski and together these three Napoleon-haters probably disclosed the secret to Vorontzov in London. Or any one of these men may have done it by himself.

A letter of Czartoryski to Vorontzov will show the state of mind of the Czar's intimate friend. It was written on September 2, 1807, and carried to London by Wilson.

" I am profiting from the departure of Chevalier Wilson to write to you these lines. . . . I did not have the heart to do it sooner. Knowing your attachment to the glory and prosperity of your country, I imagine all that you must have suffered at learning of the fatal events which have terminated the Prussian campaign. . . . The sole consolation which remains to your friends to-day is in having been sufficiently fortunate to maintain their character without blemish in the midst of these unfortunate circumstances, in not having had any part whatever in the disastrous transactions of Tilsit, and before things have reached such an extremity, in not having ceased to warn and enlighten the Emperor by their strongest representations—which he never heeded—on the abyss which he prepared for himself. It is useless to revert to the past, in which a series of unpardonable errors had necessarily caused an accumulation of evils and carried them to a frightful degree.

[1] *Arkhiv Kniazia Vorontzova*, XVII, 159n.

" Wilson, who carries this letter, is already known to you ; he is an excellent young man, beloved by our whole army ; he has conducted himself perfectly. The Emperor wishes him well and has distinguished him. Wilson is filled with zeal for the good cause. He will inform you of a thousand details which would take too long for me to write ; he has a quantity of anecdotes relating to affairs of the moment. God give that we avoid a rupture between Russia and England."[1]

It only remains to be added that if Vorontzov was really Canning's informant, the Foreign Minister acted with understandable tact in refusing his whole life long to divulge the source. Obviously a statesman of Vorontzov's position could not be incriminated ; whereas Canning need not have been so scrupulous where ordinary agents like Mackenzie or spies like d'Antraigues were involved. Since all records on the subject have been destroyed—a significant fact in itself—the circumstantial evidence points strongly to Vorontzov.

III

Confident in his star, Napoleon proceeded to conquer the Iberian peninsula. He invaded Spain, robbed the Bourbons of their crown, and made his brother Joseph king. Joseph got little out of his kingship ; the few valuable paintings which he stole he had to leave behind when Wellington subsequently defeated the French.

The French invasion having aroused a fierce outburst of patriotic fury in Spain, Napoleon himself went there to direct the campaign in person. But no sooner had he left Paris than Fouché and Talleyrand, men with a vulture-like instinct for the disastrous, conspired against him. Informed of the intrigue by his watchful mother, the Emperor hurried back to Paris,

[1] *Ibid.*, XV, 422.

leaving the conduct of the war to his best marshals, Masséna, Ney, Soult, Junot, Augereau, Suchet.

They were an interesting lot of buccaneers, these marshals. Masséna, according to Napoleon, had only two passions, money and women. During the Spanish campaign he was accompanied by a beautiful young girl dressed as a dragoon. When Napoleon offered Masséna a huge sum to stop grafting, the marshal replied that he could not afford to do it. Soult was an art collector. He developed a taste for Murillo, bought or confiscated paintings from the Spanish churches and monasteries, and took good care to export his works of art to his château in France. One of his pictures, Raphael's " Ascension of the Virgin," was bought with two human lives; two monks had been condemned to hanging for espionage and the townsfolk purchased their freedom with the Raphael. Another Soult favourite was Murillo's " Conception of the Virgin "—he had a predilection for virgins—which, however acquired, was sold after his death for 563,000 francs.

Marshal Augereau, on the other hand, had no taste for beauty—feminine, martial, or plastic—but he prided himself upon his red-blooded literary style. His chief joy in life was to draw up thunderous proclamations. Marshal Lannes had a taste for architecture and town planning. When he besieged Saragossa he decided that the best way to take the city was to blow it up systematically, house by house. His colleague, Marshal Suchet, who had similar tastes, took over the ruins and rebuilt the whole city, squares, plazas, bath-houses, and a bull ring.

They were gallant men, the marshals, but Spanish hatred and British doggedness were too much for them. Moreover, the French neglected to establish an efficient intelligence system and in some of the most important battles, as in that of Lisbon for instance, the French were literally in the dark. The British had been fortifying the neighbourhood of Lisbon for

eighteen months, but, to quote General Marbot:
"Neither Ney . . . nor Masséna . . . had the least
inkling of these gigantic works."

In contrast to the French, Wellington had an excel-
lent espionage service. He possessed the key to the
French cipher, but could never puzzle out that of
Joseph Bonaparte, the temporary King of Spain.
Years later when Napier, the historian of the Peninsula
War, found the key to Joseph's cipher Wellington
declared that he would have given £20,000 for such a
key at headquarters.

The British commander was aided by Spanish
peasants, who, out of their hatred for the French, not only
brought voluntary intelligence but frequently also intercepted French despatches and killed the messengers.
"There was no beggar so poor," to quote Frere, the
British minister in Lisbon, "that bribery could
induce him to carry French despatches. These were
brought to our officers to an extent incredible to those
who have no experience of a war carried on against
the national feeling." Frere relates how a peasant
came to him with an account of how he had knocked
down a French courier with a rock. "I brought him
to the ground," the peasant said simply, "and killed
him with my knife." Then the peasant rummaged in
his pockets and pulled out some papers, saying:
"Here is what I found upon him."

Wellington paid a round sum for every French
despatch that the peasants brought him. The reward
attracted many spies and adventurers. Once an agent
in Portugal offered to carry off Marshal Soult and
bring him dead or alive to British headquarters.

Apart from this type of casual information, Wellington got intelligence from his own well-organized
service. The best of these agents were four British
officers, Grant, Waters, Hay, and Cocks; all excellent
horsemen, good linguists, and, needless to say, cool
heads.

THE DUKE OF WELLINGTON

Take, for example, Major Colqhoun Grant, an officer with a Robin-Hood-like reputation for adventures in espionage. In 1812 Marshal Marmont invaded Portugal, and Wellington chose Grant to discover the French position. The major, however, fell into Marmont's hands, and the French commander, who knew of Grant's reputation, asked his parole that he would not escape. Grant gave his parole. " I wish he had not," Wellington commented when he heard of it ; " if he had not done so, I should have offered a high reward to the guerilla chiefs for his rescue."

But even though he was closely watched, Grant succeeded in sending information to British headquarters. " Grant," said Wellington, showing some twisted scraps of paper which a peasant had brought, " is really an extraordinary fellow. What think you of him, at this moment, when a prisoner, sending me information ? "

Marmont then sent Grant to France under escort. The major had a chance to escape, but chose to enter Paris in order to gather intelligence for his chief. In the French capital he procured an American passport and as a citizen of the United States he was able to send much useful information to Wellington about Napoleon's preparations for the Russian campaign. When the French police grew suspicious, Grant escaped to London in a fishing boat, and three months later he joined his grateful commander. Wellington made him a colonel and appointed him chief of his intelligence service.

Other British agents were no less bold. One officer entered the French lines and said that he was a deserter from the British Army. Masséna, though disgusted at the man's treason, was fooled and accepted the officer's promise to reveal intelligence about Wellington's forces. While the two were conversing, Marshal Junot came to headquarters and recognized the Englishman as a faithful British agent. The French generals decided to have him shot, but the agent escaped that night from a third floor window and swam across the Tagus River. Before he escaped, however, he took care to break into Masséna's office and carry off the marshal's notebook containing a list of the French regiments. Next morning Masséna roared with wrath.

Years after the Peninsular War, Wellington was asked whether his agents in Spain had supplied him with really valuable information. " Oh, yes," the duke replied, " I knew *everything*."

IV

After Napoleon seized the Spanish crown he regarded himself also as master of the Spanish colonies in America. But Spanish America would have nothing to do with the Bonapartist usurpers. " Our old King," the Mexicans said, " or none." Napoleon, therefore, resolved to incite Latin America against Spain (and, of course, Spain's ally, Britain). And how well and systematically this was carried out will be seen from the following account.

At the end of 1809 José Desmolard, the chief of the Napoleonic agents in America, came to Norfolk with letters from Joseph Bonaparte and proclamations presumably from the deposed Spanish king, Ferdinand VII. This propaganda material was to be distributed in Central America, where French agents were to preach independence.

Desmolard's instructions contained interesting advice regarding propaganda technique. In the first instance the French were to appeal to the hatred of the natives for their Spanish rulers, to play upon the friction existing between the creoles and peninsulars, to stir up the pride of race and the desire for self-government on the model of the United States. On the constructive, " symbol-creating," side, French propaganda was to represent Napoleon as an heroic fighter against tyrants. After the passions have thus been stirred up, the French were to organize a simultaneous revolution in all the Spanish colonies. Napoleon added the suggestion that before the outbreak of the revolt, hostile government leaders should be poisoned.

The carefully-prepared French campaign met with obdurate opposition from Luis de Onis, the unofficial representative of the Spanish Junta in America. No sooner had Desmolard landed, than Onis purchased a vessel and despatched it to Central American ports with warnings that French propagandists were coming; Onis advised the Spanish authorities to check all passports and to hang all spies.

In the meantime Onis' agents kept close watch on the French in the United States. In a few months the French, who had taken out American citizenship and travelled as merchants and sailors and cooks, built up a great organization. They established contacts in California, Mexico, and New Orleans, and purchased three or four ships. In New Orleans there were one hundred and fifty French agents, commanded by a general, equipped with money and proclamations. One such proclamation, issued by " King " Joseph Bonaparte and addressed to the Hispanic-American priests, informed the *padres* that " they commit a mortal sin, without hope of pardon, if they oppose the will of God who has sent Napoleon and his brother to regenerate the Spanish nation." The appeal—in which England was represented as " the most Machiavellian government which has ever existed "—concluded that it was a " grave offence against God not to submit willingly to the obedience of a sovereign, one whom that same adored God has destined for them."

But, warned by Onis, the Spanish authorities were on their guard. Guatemala, for example, checked up on every foreigner in the country and then sent out a list of the French agents to all the provinces for surveillance. The Viceroy of Mexico ordered burned in the public square the proclamations of " José Napo-

leon I, by the grace of God, King of Spain and the
Indies." Another Mexican official offered a reward of
20,000,000 pesos for Napoleon's head.

In the summer of 1810, Desmolard, who had so far
been a failure, left the United States and was replaced
by Jacques Athanase D'Amblimont who had submitted
to Napoleon a plan for a combined attack on the
British in Portugal and a simultaneous revolution in
Central America, the latter organized by himself.

Onis knew about that too, but he found it difficult
to counteract the French espionage in the United
States, mainly because President Jefferson seemed to
support the Napoleonic intrigues in the hopes of
acquiring Florida. Onis, suspecting that Napoleon
planned to force the United States into war with
England, was convinced that Jefferson had assured
the French Emperor his indirect co-operation in the
movement of independence in the Spanish colonies.

Nor was Onis far wrong. Before D'Amblimont had
put his plans through, revolution broke out in Mexico
under the leadership of Hidalgo, a priest of Dolores.
Hidalgo acted independently, but it seems certain that
there was a close relationship between his revolutionary
forces and French money. Mexico was only a beginning. The revolutionary conflagration spread throughout Spanish America and continued to flare even after
Napoleon's defeat at Waterloo. Thus, although it
did him no good, Napoleon was successful in America.
He failed to destroy the British Empire, but he put a
match to that of Spain.

V

While Napoleon's agents were busy in America, the
British kept a vigilant eye on Europe. As an illustration of British cleverness and success one should tell
the amusing story of Brother James.

" Mr. Robertson," the Earl of Wellesley, Wellington's brother in the Foreign Office, addressed a short,
stout monk with a merry face, " you are a man of

resource and you say you are a man of courage. Would you go to Germany at a day's notice on a secret mission ? "

James Robertson had been brought up in the Scottish Benedictine monastery in Regensburg and he knew German like a native.

" That," Brother James replied to His Lordship, " would I with the utmost alacrity ; I should be working for the cause of my religion, and the cause of every people in Europe against the most unjust of oppressors." Which shows that Brother James read the (censored) English newspapers.

Wellesley explained that he needed a reliable man for service in north Germany, as his last two agents were " missing." Then His Lordship introduced the monk to Canning, who, however, was not impressed by the rotund and voluble little cleric. Robertson certainly did not look like a secret service man, but perforce Canning had to use him, since few Englishmen knew German.

Robertson was carefully informed that his mission had to do with the Spanish Army under La Romana, then marooned in Denmark. How the Spaniards got that far north is a long story which cannot be told here except in a few words. When Napoleon was making plans to attack Spain he wisely decided to get rid of the pick of the Spanish troops and persuaded Godoy, the Spanish minister, to send 15,000 of the best soldiers under Marquis de La Romana to Denmark which, as a French ally, was threatened by Britain and Sweden. London knew that this Spanish Army was somewhere in or around Denmark, but did not know that the Spaniards were scattered on the Danish islands and mixed with Bernadotte's French troops. Since La Romana was known to be anti-French, Canning decided to help him and his army to escape by sea. It was for this purpose that James Robertson was chosen.

Robertson's password was a line of poetry about which La Romana and Bartholomew Frere, the secretary of the British Legation in Madrid, had once argued. This obscure poetic quotation was to serve as a key to the confidence of La Romana, since London did not wish to endanger Robertson's life with any formal credentials. Having won the Spaniard's confidence, Robertson was to give him a verbal message about the disposal of his troops for sailing away on the British ships that should be waiting at a pre-arranged point.

The first stage of the journey—which took three days—was the newly-acquired island of Heligoland, where Mackenzie was in charge of the British secret service operations in Holland and north Germany. Mackenzie arranged with smugglers to land Robertson in Germany. This short trip almost cost the monk his life. At the mouth of the Weser the boat was pursued by a French revenue cutter, but escaped at dusk. Even then Robertson was not out of danger, for the ruffianly smugglers threatened to throw him overboard to meet " the fate of Jonah " if a French boat should approach them upon landing. Fortunately no French vessel appeared.

The real danger began on German territory, which was completely under French domination. Robertson's life now depended entirely upon his wits, which, fortunately for him, he knew how to use. He walked on foot to Bremen, where he equipped himself with a new outfit and, what was more important, a set of papers making him out to be one Adam Rohrauer, a native of Bremen who made his living as a commercial traveller. Wearing a long snuff-coloured coat, " Adam Rohrauer " reached Hamburg. It was here that he first learned that La Romana's army was not in Denmark proper, but dispersed on the isles. This made Robertson's mission even more dangerous. Moreover, he knew no Danish.

Brother James now bethought himself of ways and means of getting in touch with La Romana. The first step was to find out the Spanish commander's where-

abouts. This proved to be easy for a man with brains.
Robertson heard that there were sick Spaniards in the
hospital at Altona. So he went to Altona, which was
within walking distance from Hamburg, and made the
acquaintance of the Spanish chaplain. The two
brothers conversed in Latin and after Robertson had
sounded out the Spanish priest's political convictions
(they were strongly anti-Napoleonic), he confessed
that he, too, was a priest and that he was the bearer of
an important message to La Romana. At this the
Spaniard embraced the Scotchman and introduced
him to the sick Spanish captain. The two Spaniards
told Robertson all he wanted to know about La
Romana.

Now the problem was to reach the Spanish general.
Brother James, or rather Adam Rohrauer, bought
several boxes of chocolate and cigars, to look his part
as a commercial traveller, and started on his perilous
journey northward. He reached Copenhagen by
devious routes and then crossed the Great Belt to the
isle of Fünen where La Romana was virtually a prisoner.
The Spanish general had long been cut off from the
outside world; he could neither receive nor forward
letters, and all he knew about the events in Spain
was that King Ferdinand had abdicated.

On the island Robertson-Rohrauer took lodgings
in the best inn, unpacked his wares, and went out to
sell his cigars and chocolates to the Spanish soldiers.
Having made friends with the men, the genial vendor
finally got a chance to meet the general. When the
two men were alone Robertson confessed that he was
a British priest bringing a message from his government. La Romana, fearing a trap, remained cool.
Then Robertson quoted Frere's line of poetry. At
this the Spanish general dropped his mask and became
confidential. The two had a long conversation about
the state of Europe, especially the latest (many months
old) events in Spain, the French invasion, the Madrid
massacre, the Spanish insurrection. La Romana was

terribly excited, and was all eagerness to get out and help his country. Robertson explained that Sir Richard Keates, the Admiral of the Baltic squadron, had orders to co-operate with La Romana and to pick up his troops at Nyborg. La Romana asked for twelve hours to consult his staff.

The chief difficulty was how to communicate with the British fleet cruising outside. Patrolling the narrower waters in the Great Belt was a British frigate which might be reached. Robertson took a leisurely walk toward a lonely spit running into the strait and waved a handkerchief at the frigate only a few hundred yards away. Suddenly a Danish soldier with a pointing musket appeared and arrested the suspiciously-acting commercial traveller. But the quick-witted vendor succeeded in convincing the colonel, who fortunately spoke German, that he was a harmless pedlar, and since his passport was in order he was released.

Now that La Romana was warned to be prepared for sailing it was necessary to make the proper arrangements on the other end. Brother James, having sold his cigars and chocolates, retraced his steps and returned to Hamburg. From here he informed Mackenzie on Heligoland to instruct Admiral Keates to be ready with his fleet at Nyborg on August 7, the day when the Spanish soldiers were to assemble for the ostensible purpose of giving the oath of allegiance to their new King, Joseph Bonaparte. The plan worked without a hitch, although La Romana was able to gather only 9,000 out of his 15,000 soldiers. On the day of the oath the Spaniards embarked, without any difficulty, on the British ships which were waiting in the port. La Romana and his army were transported to Spain where they were of great help to Wellington.

As for Robertson, he doffed the Rohrauer cloak and identity, and assumed the priestly garb once more. For a year the genial monk wandered through Germany, chuckling at the trick he had played on the

French. After the war he returned to his monastery in Regensburg where he occupied himself with philanthropic work and died, undoubtedly in the odour of sanctity, in 1820.[1]

VI

The story of the irrepressible James Robertson is entertaining, but that of Benjamin Bathurst is tragic. In fact, the Bathurst affair is the most baffling mystery on record. It has defied solution for generations.

Shortly before the battle of Wagram in 1809, when Napoleon inflicted a crushing defeat on the Austrians, the twenty-four years old Benjamin Bathurst was sent to Vienna as British ambassador. By the time he reached the Austrian capital, France had compelled Austria to desert her British ally and conclude peace. There was nothing left for Bathurst to do but to pack up and leave. Accompanied by a valet and a messenger named Krause, the young diplomat set out for the north, in the direction of Prussia. On the way, he showed all the symptoms of hysterical fright, as if pursued by some nameless horror. This was inexplicable, especially as Bathurst was well disguised, travelling in the guise of a Hamburg merchant named Koch. Nothing is known of the first part of the journey—which took some two or three weeks—until the party, on the afternoon of November 25, reached the post house of Perleberg, a little Prussian town near Mecklenburg. In Perleberg, Bathurst, shaking with terror, went to call on the Town Major, Captain von Klitzing, for protection. Bathurst may or may not—probably he did—have told von Klitzing what he was afraid of; at any rate, the Town Major gave him two troopers as a guard.

[1] Robertson has written an account of his trip in his *Narrative of a Secret Mission to the Islands in 1808* (ed. by A. C. Fraser; London, 1863). On Robertson see also *Dictionary of National Biography*, XLVIII, 410; Oman, *Studies in the Napoleonic Wars*, 123–40; J. Bagot, *George Canning and His Friends* (London, 1909), I, 273–74.

The following morning, about one hour before the time set for departure, Bathurst dismissed the troopers and went to see the horses in the stable. From that moment he was never again seen dead or alive.

Informed of the strange disappearance, Captain von Klitzing immediately arrested Bathurst's messenger and valet. Was the arrest an act of protection or of justice? No one will ever know. Next day von Klitzing went to Berlin, ostensibly to consult the government, and upon his return he gave the messenger a passport with the name of Kruger and a permit to go to the Prussian capital.

Like Bathurst, the messenger was never again seen dead or alive.

Three weeks later, on December 16, two women found a pair of trousers in the woods near Perleberg. In one pocket there was a paper which was ascertained as having belonged to Bathurst, being a letter to Mrs. Bathurst, telling her of the dangers which surrounded him and putting the guilt of his possible death on Count d'Antraigues (the French *émigré* adventurer in London whom we have already met). Careful search in the woods revealed no other trace of the missing ambassador.

The news of Bathurst's extraordinary disappearance did not reach London until early in January, 1810, because contact between the Continent and Britain was slow and difficult. The London *Morning Post* wrote that Bathurst was " murdered by the French at a town between Berlin and Hamburg. Only a portion of his dress, in which was a letter to his wife, has been found. The Prussian Government upon receiving the intelligence evinced the deepest regret and offered a large reward for the recovery of the body. No success."

The statement that Bathurst was murdered—if he was murdered—by the French was either malice or guesswork. There was not a shred of proof for the assertion. Next year Mrs. Bathurst, supplied with a passport from Napoleon, went to Perleberg with her brother. Their investigation was aided by the French ambassador Saint-Marsan, but not a trace of the missing man was found. Bathurst's wife then went to Paris— she still suspected that the French knew something— and interviewed Foreign Minister Champagny and Minister of Police Savary, but neither could give her any information. Napoleon himself sent her a message giving her his word of honour that he knew absolutely nothing of her husband's disappearance. Though not usually a model of veracity, in this instance Napoleon deserves to be believed. The French were sure that the British Government knew what had happened to Bathurst—which was more than likely.

More than forty years later, in 1852, Mrs. Thistlethwayte, Bathurst's sister, visited Perleberg where a skeleton was discovered in an old house. She examined the skull and assured the authorities that it was not that of her brother. But this testimony, after a lapse of so many years, was of course not very reliable.

What, then, did happen to Bathurst, and why? The mystery will probably never be solved, but certain conjectures are possible. That Bathurst's disappearance had to do with high politics is clear. That Prussian patriots put him out of the way is probable. The lurid background is as follows. After the Treaty of Tilsit, Prussia was practically a French province, but many patriots were scheming for a War of Liberation. In 1809 Colonel von Kleist submitted to Canning a plan of insurrection in north Germany and asked for the aid of the British fleet at the mouth of the Elbe. London sent a German named Maimburg with £30,000 to Kleist with instructions to find out whether the scheme had the consent of the Prussian Government; if so, Britain would give "every assurance of good will and assistance."

Maimburg reported to Canning that Kleist's party was composed of high officers such as Blücher and

Gneisenau, and that King Frederick William III was
" secretly in touch with it." But in Kleist himself
Maimburg had no great confidence, informing Canning
that the colonel was vain, quarrelsome, and a gambler.
At this point Bathurst entered the scene. He was then
in Berlin on the way to Vienna and was in touch with
the plotting Prussian officers. Maimburg, in fact,
asked young Bathurst for further directions.

The threads to the solution of the Bathurst
mystery run, therefore, in two directions : Berlin and
London.

There is considerable evidence that London knew
much, perhaps everything, about the strange fate of
Bathurst. At the time of Maimburg's negotiation
with the Kleist party, indeed at Maimburg's suggestion, George Galway Mills, a former Member of
Parliament, was appointed British consul in Berlin.
Now it is significant that the Mills correspondence of
December, 1809, to January, 1810—the two months
in which the disappearance of and search for Bathurst
took place—is missing in the British archives. Nevertheless, one private letter which Mills wrote at this
time reveals some illuminating details. It seems that
about five days before Bathurst reached Perleberg
(remember we know nothing about Bathurst's journey
to that town) he spent a short time in Berlin, but did
not meet Mills, despite the latter's desire to see him.
Mills explains this on the ground that for some time
Bathurst's mind and health had been " in a very
alarming state." Incidentally, Krause who so completely vanished after he reached Berlin, where he was
interrogated by Mills, made a similar statement about
Bathurst to a Prussian physician.

After Mills had examined Krause, he went to Perleberg to make an investigation, and then he sent his
report, through Maimburg, to London on December
20. This is probably how the London *Morning Post*
got the information that Bathurst was " murdered by
the French." For reasons best known to the

British Foreign Office, Mills' report and Krause's deposition have been suppressed. Apparently both the British and the Prussian Governments tried to shield someone. When I. M. Johnson, a British secret service agent and a friend of Bathurst, went to Perleberg to make an independent investigation, he was discouraged and checked by Mills.

The evidence tends to show that Bathurst was not killed because of his despatches. These were carried by Krause, the messenger. He did not commit suicide, for his body was never found. The French did not do away with him, for if they had, the British Government would not have been so eager to hush up the affair (Why was Mills' report never published?). The most plausible explanation is that the young English diplomat was killed by Kleist's Prussian *Bund*. Bathurst was possibly a member of the secret patriotic society and he may have attended some of the meetings in Berlin. In an abnormal state of mind, he may have committed an imprudence and the officer-conspirators may have concluded that their lives depended upon a man who could not be trusted with their secret. For if Napoleon found out about the military society the Prussian Government would have had to pay for it. If this hypothesis is correct, then it is understandable why Berlin would impress upon London the necessity of keeping silent. There is no other explanation for the mystery of Bathurst.[1]

VII

The struggle against Napoleon continued unabated. Underground movements against French domination were active throughout Europe, even in countries

[1] J. Hall, " The Strange Story of Mr. Bathurst," in his *Four Famous Mysteries*, 34–86; Mrs. Thistlethwayte, *Memoirs and Correspondence of Dr. Henry Bathurst* (1853); Baring-Gould, " The Disappearance of Mr. Bathurst," *Cornhill Magazine*, LV (1887), 278–91; M. W. Call, " The Search for the Lost Mr. Bathurst," *Westminster Review*, CXXXIV (1890), 396–414.

which were formally at peace with France. Separately defeated, the European powers nevertheless had secret contact with one another and were preparing for the final conflict with the conqueror, which reached its climax at Waterloo.

These underground contacts deserve a brief description. In the Austrian Empire, which was defeated by and at peace with Napoleon, Prague and Carlsbad were the two centres of anti-French machinations. To these two Bohemian cities came British agents in large numbers and, well supplied with gold, they organized espionage services and directed propaganda. The Continent being closed to the British, these agents customarily landed in Sweden, had themselves smuggled into Prussia, and then crossed through Saxony to Bohemia.

Despite his treaty with France, Metternich maintained secret relations with Britain. The intermediary between the two countries was the Hanoverian minister in Vienna, Count Hardenberg (not to be confused with the Prussian statesman of the same name). He transmitted his intelligence from Vienna to London through Wessenberg, the Austrian ambassador in Berlin. Such indirect means were necessary because since 1807 Britain and Austria had no representatives in each other's country.

Letters between Vienna and London were carried by bold and hardy agents who often risked their lives. These men, of all nationalities, were frequently aided by friendly Dutch and north German merchants who worked for the Good Cause. Even so, many agents were caught. To outwit the French, English documents were written in the form of business letters and on Continental paper, since English paper was easily detectable.

The couriers and agents took one of two routes. The longest was the southern, with Malta in the Mediterranean as the starting point; from Malta the route led to Constantinople, thence through Albania

—where in Leucadia England had an Ionian Heligoland—to Vienna. A shorter way to the Austrian
capital was the island of Lissa, near the Adriatic coast,
although within the French belt; from here the
British agent Johnson established a regular nine-days'
route to Vienna.

The shortest way from England to Central Europe
was through Holland, where one commercial firm
supplied fishing boats to carry despatches and newspapers to England for £7,000 a year; but after Louis
Bonaparte became King of Holland, that route was no
longer possible. Heligoland, by way of Hamburg,
was, as we have seen in the case of Robertson, fraught
with great danger. Only the Baltic coast proved
comparatively free from Napoleon's domination,
although this route was long and slow. Still, it was
shorter than the Mediterranean route and hence was
most used by the British.

Of all the great powers, only the Russians had the
run of Napoleonic Europe, for Czar and Emperor were
presumably on friendly terms. But it was no secret
that the two empires were preparing for war, and as
usual the preliminary work was done by spies. This
is shown by the adventure of the young Russian
Colonel Tchernichev.

He arrived in Paris early in 1811, having come *via*
Sweden, and installed himself in a sumptuous bache-
lor's apartment in the centre of the city. Tchernichev's only servants were a German domestic and a
silent Russian *moujik* who followed his master like a
shadow. Young, rich, and eccentric, the Russian
soon became a favourite with the ladies, including one
princess of the Bonaparte dynasty, the beautiful
Pauline Borghèse. The heavily perfumed and ostensibly indolent Tchernichev knew how to make his
adoring women friends talk. But women were not
his only source of intelligence. Treated as a colleague
by the diplomatic corps, the colonel had frequent
occasions to " glance " at papers on diplomatic desks.

Tchernichev's chief mission was to keep in touch with Talleyrand who, now that he was out of office, was secretly in Russian service. The colonel brought a personal letter from the Czar to the Duke. "His Highness," Tchernichev reported home, "expressed himself to me as a true friend of Russia." Talleyrand, indeed, helped the Russian make important contacts, especially with high French military men. It was Tchernichev who won over General Jomini. More important still, Tchernichev was the man who informed Marshal Bernadotte, who was then planning to betray Napoleon, that Czar Alexander looked upon him with great favour. This clever Russian colonel, particularly when aided by Talleyrand, was a real menace to Napoleon, who, knowing him to be the Czar's aide-de-camp, treated him with remarkable consideration. The Emperor did not know that Tchernichev was suborning his officers, nor that he was organizing a German legion to start an insurrection in Germany as soon as Russia and France had broken off relations.

Minister of Police Savary, however, grew suspicious of the Russian colonel and reported his doings to the Emperor. Napoleon angrily ordered Savary to permit the colonel "to go, come, see, listen." Savary muttered sullenly: "All that is necessary now is an order that I should give him information myself."

Savary was soon vindicated when Tchernichev was caught receiving information from Michel, a clerk in the War Office. Napoleon ordered the arrest of the colonel, but the latter, warned by a faithful *amie*, escaped across the Rhine. The clerk, however, was arrested at the moment when he was counting 300,000 francs, the price of his treason; he implicated another employé in the War Office. Both were shot. The furious Napoleon caused a virulent article to be published in the French press attacking the Czar and hurting him in his most sensitive spot by reminding the world that the murderers of Czar Paul—Alexander's father—had never been punished.

Napoleon's moral indignation at the Russian espionage is amusing in view of similar French activities in Russia at that moment. While Tchernichev was gathering information in France, the French ambassador in St. Petersburg not only bought accurate data about the position and strength of the Russian forces, " but also the engraved copperplates from which the great map of the Russian Empire had been printed." This heavy mass of metal, stolen from the Russian archives, was secretly transported to Paris where French words were substituted for the Russian and fresh maps printed from this plate ; these maps were distributed among Napoleon's officers.

From these and other indications, particularly Napoleon's readings,[1] it was clear that a Franco-Russian war was imminent.

VIII

The French invasion of Russia was a disastrous failure. Europe now combined against the Emperor whose star was fading, and the battle of the giants, fought on rainy October days, was joined around Dresden. While the cannon were tearing the French troops to pieces, France's German allies deserted the field of battle. The struggle became hopeless. On the fourth day Napoleon ordered a retreat. Of a quarter-million French soldiers, now hardly 80,000

[1] J. W. Thompson, " Napoleon as a Book-Lover," *Atlantic Monthly*, XCVIII (1906), 110–18 : " From December, 1811, Napoleon's book-orders have the importance of state secrets. In that month we find him ordering works giving information concerning the topography of Russia, especially Lithuania, under the head of rivers, roads, forests, marshes, and so forth ; a detailed account in French of the campaigns of Charles XII in Poland and Russia ; a history of Courland ; and anything which could be found of an historical, geographical, and topographical nature, about Riga, Livonia, and the other Baltic provinces of Russia."

dispirited men hurried back toward the Rhine. Around Leipzig lay 100,000 dead bodies, half of them French.

Napoleon was defeated but the allies did not know what to do with their victory. Austria was jealous of Russia. Prussia feared the Czar's plans in Poland. Everybody was in doubt as to the fate of Saxony, Belgium, Italy. No one knew what to do with France.

What troubled the allies most was the problem of Napoleon. Talleyrand hoped to see him dead. " So long as he is alive everything remains uncertain." In London Lord Sheffield thought that if the erstwhile conqueror of Europe could not be borrowed " for the benefit of Pidcock's (wax) museum " then he should " like to see him dead." Lord Grey said that this was a good opportunity to " kill and eat Bonaparte."

Bonaparte could neither be killed nor eaten—to the chagrin of Talleyrand and the British statesmen. The allies entered Paris and Napoleon abdicated in favour of his son. The Czar, however, insisted upon an absolute abdication, forcing the Corsican to resign his throne unconditionally. Napoleon was given the isle of Elba in full sovereignty.

" Is it the intention of the Allies," the British Baron Heytesbury asked, " to leave Bonaparte in Elba ? If there be no other way of getting rid of him, why not give him *un chocolat* ? We shall never feel safe as long as he exists."

CHAPTER XIII

DER KONGRESS TANZT!

WHEN the " Spectre of the West " was banished the powers got together in Vienna, in the autumn of 1814, to settle the affairs of Europe. For the first time in one hundred and sixty-six years a general congress assembled to reconstruct the continent on a monarchical basis and to build a strong dyke against the powerful undercurrents of democracy generated by the French Revolution. After a quarter-century of revolutionary upheavals and wars the rulers of Europe felt they had a hard-earned right to relax. And so they assembled in the beautiful capital on the Danube in all their glittering glory and insolent pomp. The hard work was done, behind the scenes, by a few more or less obscure officials. The big folk, emperors and kings and princes and dukes, enjoyed themselves in this vast diplomatic *mardi gras*. As the good-humoured Viennese said : *Der Kongress tanzt*.

The dancing master and chief impresario of this European show was Prince Metternich, a very remarkable man. Although, as premier minister of the Austrian Empire, Metternich came to be the virtual ruler of Central Europe for the first half of the nineteenth century, he was a typical noble of the *ancien régime*. He had studied in Strasbourg and Mainz under Jacobin teachers, but impervious to ideas, the young aristocrat never learned and never changed. At first he displayed no interest in politics, believing himself destined for a scientific career. " Your Majesty," he told Emperor Francis II, " wishes me to throw myself into a profession which I do not think is mine." But he was a born politician.

Metternich seemed to have taken to diplomacy without the slightest effort or preparation. Like a young duck, he was thrown into the waters and just swam. As Austrian ambassador to Paris, the young man—he was in his thirties—learned to read Napoleon's character so accurately that he could play upon the vain Corsican as if on a chosen instrument. Metternich it was who subtly planted in Napoleon's mind the ambitious idea of marrying Marie Louise, a scion of the haughty house of Habsburg. Too late, the Emperor realized the trap the Austrian had laid for him. " I have committed," Napoleon said in 1813, " a great folly in marrying an Austrian archduchess."

Metternich, so polished and suave and handsome, was not a sordid intriguer like his rival Talleyrand. He had principles and prided himself upon them. A moderate, he hated a " policy of egoism, of good pleasure." Europe he conceived as an entity, a social whole wherein all members must live in harmony—at least if they were good monarchist neighbours. Although an Austrian, he was German enough to believe in universals. " That," he said, " which is called the system of Metternich is not a system, but the application of the laws which govern the world. Revolutions rest upon systems ; the eternal laws are outside and above that which has no other value than that of a system." Always a man of peace, he remained firmly entrenched in power until the Revolution—and how he hated revolutions !—of 1848 destroyed his world and drove him into exile at the age of seventy-five. When parliamentarism won out in Europe, even in Austria, the old prince confessed, and by confessing wrote his epitaph : " I am a man of that which was."

Now when the plenipotentiaries were assembling in Vienna for the congress, Metternich was ready for them with the best-organized secret police in Europe. The chief of the police was Francis Hager, a cultured gentleman, and the most dangerous person in Austria. He co-ordinated all the police activities, created bureaux for the registration of visitors, and invented ingenious methods of censorship and interception.

Hager employed two types of agents, confidential

(*Vertraute*) and professional.   Among the former were
aristocrats and socially prominent persons who
informed the police of the daily doings of men and
women in high society. Diplomatic circles were honey-
combed with these genteel spies, among whom were
the poet Cardani, the litterateur Hebenstreit, and the
papal diplomat Freddi.   There were many others,
nobles and scholars and priests, who betrayed their
hosts and sold out their friends for a salary from
Hager.

The professional agents sent in daily reports—
Materiellen Rapporte, as they are labelled in the Vienna
archives—to the ministry of police.   Oral accounts
from servants and landlords, often given voluntarily,
were also of great help to the police. Lieutenant Klaus,
for example, in whose house lived La Harpe, the tutor
and friend of Czar Alexander, informed Hager of his
conversations with his eminent tenant.   The same
service was performed by Bartsch, the editor of the
Wiener Zeitung, who was friendly with Anstett, the
Czar's confidant.   Neither Klaus nor Bartsch, it must
be added, received any compensation from the police.
Their reports were in the nature of a patriotic
contribution.

Metternich personally had his own staff of confiden-
tial news reporters, or perhaps gossip purveyors.
Among these (paid) men were the Sardinian minister
Saint-Marsan and the French diplomats, Rohan and
Dalberg.

The visiting potentates and diplomats, more or less
aware of Metternich's secret service, had their own confidential agents and paid spies. This was particularly
true of the Czar who, next to Metternich, was the most
important figure in the congress. A beautiful and
brilliant adventuress, Princess Catherine Bagration,
was said to be in the service of the Czar who often
visited her at night, although not necessarily for
political reasons. Viennese gossip had it that the

Russians employed prostitutes as spies—which was probably true, though not original. Hager's agents reported that the well-known courtesan Wolters received a salary from the Czar's adjutant Volkonsky whom she visited in masculine attire (a clever girl, but not clever enough for Hager's spies). Another report to the police contained the information that the courtesan Morel, personally favoured by the amorous Alexander, was also in Russian (political) service.

Talleyrand, who represented the French Bourbons at the congress, was an old hand at espionage. His relations with Gentz, the secretary of the congress, are known from Gentz's diary. Other eminent individuals who sold information to Talleyrand were Count Sickingen, the chamberlain of Emperor Francis II, and Major Martens, a Prussian officer.

The Austrian agents worked with Teutonic thoroughness. Regularly they visited the rooms of the foreign diplomats and searched the waste-paper baskets and fireplaces for every scrap of written stuff. These shreds of paper were labelled *chiffons* by the ministry of police. The *chiffons* were taken to the Black Cabinet, or *Manipulation*, and there pasted together, deciphered, analysed, and copied. From these materials Hager made out a daily report to the Emperor, adding his own observations and comments. The ministry of police received from ten to fifteen *chiffons* daily.

Careful observation taught the secret police the habits and weaknesses of every person under surveillance. Not a chance was neglected, not an error overlooked. The best place to hunt *chiffons*, for example, the agents knew was the fireplace of von Stein, then in Russian service, for that minister often carelessly threw his letters into the grate. The French diplomat Dalberg, on the other hand, was in the habit of throwing his crumpled papers into the waste-paper basket— perhaps deliberately ; an Austrian agent once found there a letter containing information that the French

Government intended to abduct Napoleon from Elba
and remove him to a more inaccessible island.

Visitors to prominent individuals were also closely
watched. When the American inventor, Justus Erich
Bollmann, came to Vienna with projects for a steam-
ship on the Danube and the use of platinum for
coinage, the Austrian agents kept their eyes on his
movements and succeeded in picking up his *chiffons*.

Even more important than *chiffons* were the *intercepta*, that is, intercepted documents, generally in the
post office. The Black Cabinet worked day and night
unsealing and copying the *intercepta*. All post letters
were opened, regardless of addressor or addressee.
Even the correspondence of the Austrian Empress
Ludovica did not escape scrutiny. The same treatment was given to the letters of the Imperial family
and of Secretary Gentz.

Whatever was not entrusted to loyal couriers was
easy prey to the Austrian police; even ciphers were
no protection, for the Black Cabinet had the key to
most of them. Wise people were wary. Castlereagh,
for example, was so suspicious of everybody that he
never employed servants—usually masked spies recommended by Hager. Those unable to employ couriers
took refuge in veiled statements, obscure names,
cryptic signs, or, more childishly, used invisible ink
(which was the easiest thing to detect). Emperor
Francis' sister Theresa, for instance, naïvely
thought that she could mislead the post office Sher-
locks by referring to her august brother as " Venus,"
to Metternich as " Krautfeld " (Cabbage-field : what
malice !), to the Czar as " Piatti," and to the lame
Talleyrand as " Krumpholz " (Crooked timber).

From such an aggregation of emperors and kings
and statesmen the Austrian police was able to gather a
vast amount of confidential information. For, it must
be remembered, everybody was there at the congress,
except Louis XVIII of France, George III of Britain,

and Pope Pius VII. Those who could not come sent
delegates. There were representatives from the Hanseatic cities, the Swiss cantons, the Italian communes.
Vienna also swarmed with lobbyists. The German
book dealers sent a delegation to fight against the
stifling censorship. Napoleon's gallant, and rich, marshals had agents working to save their properties from
expropriation. Inventors and artists peddled their
wares. Evangelists came to save sinful souls. German
Jews sent lobbyists to obtain civic rights ; their paid
spokesman was the famous Prussian statesman,
William von Humboldt. Curiosity seekers, adventurers, and prostitutes added gaiety to the congress
and trouble to the secret police.

So many crowns and medals and uniforms made the
Viennese cynical. With irreverent and penetrating
wit they summarized their reactions. " The Emperor
of Russia loves ; the King of Denmark drinks ; the
King of Württemberg eats ; the King of Prussia
thinks ; the King of Bavaria talks ; and the Emperor
of Austria prays."

Emperor Francis may have prayed but Metternich
danced. The crafty minister was careful to arrange
many balls, parties, festivities. The more the sovereigns and diplomats gave themselves up to pleasures
the less time they had for politics. " We are here," a
diplomat said, " in the midst of emperors, kings, and
Metternich." He was undoubtedly in a class by himself, if for no other reason than that, through his secret
service, he knew virtually everything about everybody.

At the congress Metternich had rivals, but not many.
The chief of these were the inevitable Talleyrand and
the pretentious Czar. Talleyrand the witty was most
detested all around. Being lame, he could not dance,
which made him dangerous, as he had time for
intrigue. He had come to Vienna as the representative
of a defeated power and left the city as the plenipotentiary of a great State. Treated at first as an inferior,
he cleverly supported Britain and Austria against

Russia and Prussia on the question of Poland, and thus he gained the grudging gratitude of Castlereagh and Metternich. When the great powers showed a tendency to put Talleyrand in his proper place as the delegate of a defeated country, the old fox sought out the smaller States and lined them up against the dictatorial big ones. For his services to the Bourbons of Naples, Talleyrand received 6,000,000 livres.

" A worm-eaten heart," Archduke John characterized Talleyrand, " but an excellent head."

Metternich's second rival, Czar Alexander, was hated by everybody, except the professional women, as much as Talleyrand. The Russian autocrat yearned to be considered a man of culture, but succeeded in being regarded as a puerile nobody. General Charles Stewart publicly called him an impostor. A police agent reported that in society the Czar was " considered a swindler who poses as a philanthropist." People repeated Napoleon's characterization of Alexander as " knavish and deceitful." To the Duke of Weimar, Goethe's patron, the Czar was but a " puppet." And Metternich, whom the Russian Emperor detested (jealousy over women ?), remarked that the Czar was nothing but " sound and smoke."

But Alexander certainly had a wonderful time. Fond of dancing and of beautiful women, he paid court to a whole galaxy of sparkling ladies, many of dubious virtue. He deliberately prolonged the congress in order not to part from his women. " Papa," the Czar said to the dour Austrian Emperor, " it is a good thing that Petersburg is so far removed from Vienna ; otherwise I would come here every fortnight." And " Papa " thanked all the saints that Petersburg was almost two thousand kilometres from Vienna, for entertaining the impecunious Czar almost bankrupted the Habsburg privy purse.

" The congress," chuckled the witty old Prince de Ligne, a relic of the *ancien régime,* " does not move : it dances."

II

While the congress danced Napoleon was making plans to escape from Elba. Rumours of his escape were rife. John Burghersh, the British minister in Florence, was warned by a German noble that a Leghorn Jew had shipped to Elba several thousand buttons with the Imperial eagle. " He thinks himself a clever fellow," the incredulous Burghersh laughed at his informant. Yet there were clear indications that Napoleon was planning to break out of his cage. When Lord John Russell visited the Emperor on Elba, Napoleon playfully pinched the Englishman's ear and asked him what his countrymen thought of his chances to return to the French throne. " Sire," Russell replied, " they think you have no chance at all."

" Then," Napoleon smiled, " you can tell them from me that they are wrong."

At the end of February, 1815, Napoleon sailed from Elba with 1,500 men. When he landed on French soil at Cannes the Czar was having a dressing match with a countess in Vienna.

" The congress," Napoleon said upon landing, " is dissolved."

Europe was thrown into consternation. Many Englishmen suspected that their government had helped " Boney " escape. During a vigorous debate in Parliament Lord Grey openly accused the Cabinet of a " great degree of culpable negligence " in regard to the exile on Elba. A motion in the House of Commons to investigate Napoleon's escape was defeated by the Government forces by a vote of 149 to 58.

As Napoleon was victoriously marching towards Paris, Talleyrand in Vienna was a very scared diplomat. He was convinced that this time the Emperor would hang him, and he was, therefore, eager to forestall this. " This man," Talleyrand said, " did not want to end in tragedy and will end up in a ditch." He told the Prussian King, a weak and timid individual, that Napoleon must be hanged.

" One should get him first," His Prussian Majesty muttered.

Things were happening fast in France. Thousands of enthusiastic adherents flocked to the returning Emperor. The way to Paris lay open and Louis XVIII fled from the Tuileries, leaving behind him a list of men to be executed : thirty-four deputies were to be quartered, 103 to be broken on the wheel, 254 to be hanged, and 348 to be sent to the galleys.[1] No wonder Frenchmen welcomed back their glorious Emperor. In his hurry to depart, the Bourbon King stupidly left incriminating documents in the archives, particularly a secret alliance between France, Britain, and Austria aimed against Russia and Prussia. Diplomatically this was a god-send. Napoleon's foreign minister at once communicated the treaty to the Czar. Alexander was outraged, but he had sense enough not to quarrel with his traitorous allies at a moment when all were determined to crush Napoleon anew and permanently.

One hundred exciting days elapsed between Napoleon's landing at Cannes and his decisive defeat at Waterloo. Fouché the realist, Fouché who had the sensitive scent of a hound, knew Napoleon's situation to be hopeless and wanted to assure his own future by being on the winning side. He secretly offered his goodwill to Louis XVIII at Ghent and began to correspond with Metternich. Napoleon intercepted the correspondence, but Fouché, warned by his friend the Prefect of Police, went to see the Emperor and told him that he had contrived to enter into relations with the Austrian minister. The Emperor was not deceived by so transparent a ruse. He knew his Fouché. " Fouché," he roared as he once roared at Talleyrand, " I ought to have you shot."

[1] For the full list see M. Spronck, " Réaction monarchique pendant la révolution," *La révolution francaise*, IX, 44f.

And Fouché replied as calmly as Talleyrand once did : " I can't agree with you, Sire."

Years later General Bertrand admitted that Napoleon, though eager to do so, was " not strong enough " to shoot Fouché.

The end came on June 18, 1815, near a little Belgian town. Fouché, who had arranged a relay system for news from the battlefield, was the first person in Paris to hear of Waterloo and immediately began to intrigue against the defeated Emperor, offering to hand him over to the allies. The Prussian commander, General Blücher, wanted to shoot Napoleon, but the scrupulous and sportsmanlike Wellington advised his Prussian colleague " to have nothing to do with so foul a transaction."

Napoleon was shipped to St. Helena with 4,000 gold napoleons in a concealed box.

Again the fat Louis XVIII entered Paris. Talleyrand and Fouché drove out in the same carriage to pay homage to their new master. " I would like to know," someone whispered, " what makes these two lambs get together."

Talleyrand bowed to Louis XVIII : " Your Majesty has saved Europe at the congress of Vienna."

" No, M. Talleyrand, it was not I ; it was your work."

" Sire," Talleyrand replied ironically, " I have only expressed your august thoughts."

APPENDIX

CRYPTOGRAPHY

" Any one who engages in secret practices against the state must above all things be careful not to communicate by letters ; for these are often intercepted and furnish proof which cannot be controverted. And though nowadays there be many cautious methods of writing, there have also been discovered many aids for their interpretation."—GUICCHIARDINI, *Counsels and Reflections*.

THE use of cryptic symbols for communication is perhaps as old as diplomacy. Biblical scholars pretend to find cryptograms even in Scriptures. This may be true, for we know that some types of shorthand were known in antiquity, while anagrams were part of the Attic tragedies. Authors of Greek tragedies constructed their first eight iambic lines so that they not only made sense but also provided letters to make eight other iambic lines, the first two giving the writer's name, the next two the Olympiad, the third a homage to Athena, and the last couplet a warning that the show was about to begin. This Greek anagram may, possibly, be the earliest systematic cryptography which, by a natural process of transference, came to be applied to statecraft.

Statesman and diplomats in antiquity employed various deceptive means of communication, such as fire-signals, illegible letters, and mystical symbols, but the earliest regular cipher *qua* cipher of which we have any record is that of Julius Cæsar. According to Suetonius, Cæsar's cipher was simple in the extreme ; it consisted of a transposition of the alphabet, *D* standing for *A*, *E* for *B*, *F* for *C*, and so on through all the letters. Octavius Augustus used a similar device, only shifting the second, rather than the fourth letter, as *B* for *A*, *C* for *B*, etc. For a number of centuries, during the early Middle Ages, cipher seems not to have been used as a technique of statecraft, probably because of the general decline in literacy. In an age when most people could neither read nor write the ordinary alphabet was in itself a mystery and there was no need for elaborate disguises. Yet some records show that shorthand was used in the sixth century A.D. Thus we read that the quick-tempered Pope Vigilius (538–555) once struck one of his shorthand secretaries so viciously that the scribe died of the blow.

As Europe gradually emerged from the " dark " ages and literacy began to spread, the ruling élite, both lay and clerical, developed greater sophistication in various governing techniques. Here the papacy led the way, not only in keeping a " register " of all documents and despatches but also in writing in short-hand, or tachygraphy ; the chief reason for the latter seems to have been an intelligible desire to save parchment, which was very expensive. This early medieval tachygraphy was called Tironian, presumably because it was the invention of a Roman named Tiron. In Tironian shorthand every word is represented by a single symbol, originally alphabetical but ultimately ideographical, like Chinese. The oldest use of Tiron-ian in Europe was in the time of Clotaire II (625). Under the Carolingians, especially in the chancery of Louis the Pious (814–840), Tironian tachygraphy was quite common ; but it went out of existence in the tenth century, when an Italian shorthand took its place.

Medieval manuscripts sometimes contain unique systems of writing which are neither Roman nor Italian ; they consist of a suppression of the vowels and their replacement by points or by the succeeding consonants. Thus *i* would be indicated by one point, *a* by two, *e* by three, *o* by four, and *u* by five. Con-sonants like *b*, *f*, *k*, *p*, and *x* preserved their own value and were also substituted for the vowels. So we find *Thfpfklbctxc* for *Theofilactus*, and *Brchkdkbcpnp Bncxlfp* for *Archidiacano Ansculfo*. Quite simple, but it seemed like a big mystery when it was first used by Rabanus Maurus, the learned ninth-century monk who became Archbishop of Mainz.

A CIPHER BASED ON MUSICAL NOTES

There were other ingenious methods of conveying information obscurely. Emperor Lothar I (840–855) once sent a communication to his partisans in the guise of a collection of quotations from the Bible and the canons. Theodore, a ninth-century Greek abbot, when exiled by Emperor Nicephorus, maintained an active correspondence with his flock by means of a cipher in which the twenty-four letters of the alphabet designated the chief members of his community. In the Bamberg Library there is a tenth-century manuscript, which is a copy of a letter written by an Irishman in Britain to his friends at home. He explains that at the court of Merlin, King of Britain, there was an Irish scholar named Dubhtach who had a disconcerting habit of testing his visiting countrymen by means of a cryptogram, which was composed in Greek letters and whose solution was in Latin.

In this connection one should mention Gerbert, that interesting monk from Auvergne. Well educated, Gerbert first became Abbot of Bobbio in Italy, then secretary to two successive archbishops of Rheims, afterwards himself Archbishop of Rheims and of Ravenna, and finally Pope under the name Sylvester II (999–1003). Before he became Pontiff, he had put his pen at the disposal of various distinguished persons, prelates and princes. Many of these Gerbert letters have been preserved, but the difficulty was that they were impenetrable; about fifteen of them are in cipher of such intricacy that they baffled scholars for centuries. Only in recent years has the key to Gerbert's cipher been discovered. His code, it seems, was a tachygraphy developed by Italian notaries; it is possible, in fact, that Gerbert introduced this system into northern Europe.

The Revival of Learning by the Italian humanists in the fifteenth and sixteenth centuries furnished the ruling princes with an example and precedent of a powerful State whose foreign policy was calculatingly cunning and free from scruples. This was particularly true of the aristocratic Venetian Republic where the Council of Ten exercised autocratic powers. Having relations with almost every European and Near Eastern State, Venice, as we have pointed out elsewhere, developed and perfected a refined diplomacy which came to be the model for all Europe. As early as 1290 the Great Council, in order to keep its activities secret, mingled Greek and Hebrew letters with the official Latin in the Government registers. In the middle of the fourteenth century cryptography became an established practice of Venetian diplomacy. When, in 1350, an embassy was sent to Hungary, the diplomats were instructed to designate in their despatches the Doge by *B*, the King of Hungary by *F*, etc. Eight years later a Venetian ambassador in Germany was ordered to refer, in his letters home, to the Duke of Austria as *Meser Antonio*, the Emperor as *Meser Nicoleto*, the city of Friuli as *Modena*. But before the century was over these crude devices gave way to ciphers of real ingenuity.

As the European States extended their contacts with each other simple ciphers were found to be insufficient protection for State secrets. At the end of the fifteenth century the artist-scholar Leon Battista Alberto published the secret of the cipher of Julius Cæsar, then commonly used, and a new code became imperative. One wonders how so disingenuous a code as that of Cæsar ever concealed anything! A number of clever brains now began to devote themselves to constructing intricate series of symbols. The most accomplished of these men were Marco Raphael, a renegade Jew, and Zuan Soro, who may be called the father of scientific cipher (Venetian). Soro became so expert that ciphered despatches were sent to him even from France to be unravelled. Pope Clement VII said that Soro " could decipher any cipher."

After Soro's death in 1544 a number of men competed to develop more and more complicated codes until, in 1547, the Venetian Council of Ten was forced

to decree the use of a single cipher. Two secretaries,
Lodovici and Borgi, were ordered by the Council " to
make a new book of ciphers, stating in detail to whom
they consigned them ; the book to be kept under lock
and key by the secretary charged with the secret
register of the Senate in the Secret Chancery." This
" new book " was so well guarded, and subsequently
it seems so well disposed of, that not a trace of it has
ever been discovered.

The first treatise on ciphers was composed in 1465
by Cicco Simonetta, secretary and counsellor to the
first three Sforza dukes of Milan. Simonetta was disgraced and executed in 1480, and of his work only a
fragment has remained. This bit of *diario* is now
preserved in the National Library at Paris. It gives
thirteen rules for construction and decoding. Simonetta's cipher is based on the single alphabet wherein the
same symbol always represents the same letter. The
first six rules of his treatise deal with the Italian and
Latin languages, pointing out that in Italian the vulner-
able letters are *E* and *L*, and *che* ; in Latin, he wrote,
the words commonly end in *S*, *M*, *T*, or *A*, *E*, *I* and
O. If only one sign is employed the decipherer may
be certain that it stands for a vowel or possibly the
preposition *A*. Simonetta then lists the most common digrams and explains that the most usual trigrams
are *non* and *sis*. A symbol repeated three times
without interval should be a *U*. In four-letter words
a redoubled cipher is equivalent to double ll or ss,
as, for instance, *ille* and *esse*.

The date of Simonetta's little essay on ciphers is
important, for it was the period when cryptography
became the universal practice, when simple ciphers
developed into complicated cryptograms. By the
sixteenth century even the Roman curia followed the
example of secular Governments and communicated
only in cipher with its legates and nuncios. For
example, the cipher of Cardinal Morone, who was
president of the Council of Trent in 1563, was based

on arithmetical numbers, vowels having three numbers and the consonants two; number 8 had no value, being arbitrarily inserted as a blind. When such a ciphered despatch arrived in the Papal chancery, the secretary, in deciphering it, would add from four to twelve consonants to the original letter in order to deceive prying eyes.

In Spain the cipher code was introduced by Miguel Perez Almazan in the time of Ferdinand and Isabella. The Spaniards at first overdid it, or perhaps did not employ clever clerks. For the Spanish archives contain ciphered despatches with such marginal comments, written by some bewildered clerk, as "Nonsense," "Impossible," "Cannot be understood," "Order the ambassador to send another despatch." After 1504, when Isabella died, it became necessary to adopt a simpler cipher; but even at its simplest form the Spanish ciphers were maddening in their subtlety. After four and a half centuries of mystery it took one Anglo-German scholar years of arduous work to find the keys to the Spanish codes. One completed cipher, which was used by De Puebla, the Spanish ambassador in London, for communicating with Madrid, contains 2,400 signs. One may imagine the time it took for the Spanish Foreign Office in the sixteenth century to read all the despatches!

The simplest Spanish cipher of this period was composed of Arabic numerals interspersed with common letters; another code contained Roman numerals and had thousands of signs, the vowels being represented by five different symbols and the consonants by four. In the course of time the number of signs for each letter in the alphabet was increased to fourteen or more; added to this were signs without meaning—*nichil importantia*—which were mixed up in the same sentence or even the same word in order to mislead. Assuredly the Spaniards were a leisurely and ingenious people.

After the emergence of the dynastic States in the

latter part of the fifteenth century, there appeared a series of scientific treatises on cryptography, of which Simonetta's essay was the pioneer. The first comprehensive dissertation was by Abbot Johannes Trithemius, *Polygraphiæ libri sex*, published in Oppenheim in 1518 and dedicated to Emperor Maximilian I. The author, well known as the abbot of Sponheim, was accused by the superstitious of practising diabolical mysteries and his work was burned. In 1563 J. B. Porta published in Naples his *De furtivis literarum notis vulgo de Ziferis ;* and two decades later a Frenchman, Blaise de Vigenère, gave the world a *Traité des chiffres ou secrettes manières d'écrire*. These men, particularly Trithemius, were soon imitated throughout Europe.[1]

J. B. Porta explained clearly the purpose and use of ciphers : " Whenever kings . . . or conspirators find it expedient to set down the hidden counsels of our mind, and want to prevent our letters, when intercepted by spies, patrols, or watches posted in suitable spots . . . from revealing our plans . . . we fly to cipher to afford us some guarantee." Every king, and queen, and conspirator, therefore, sought refuge in cipher in an age of general insecurity. The Public Record Office in London, for example, possesses three volumes containing from 180 to 200 cipher-codes from the reign of Queen Elizabeth.

There were as many types of ciphers as there were inventors. Lord Burghley, the Elizabethan statesman, preferred the signs of the Zodiac. In a cipher he sent to the English agent in the Low Countries we find *Aries* to mean the Duke of Parma ; *Taurus*, Count Mansfeld ; *Gemini*, Count Maurice ; *Cancer*, the Estates-

[1] Trithemius' treatise was republished at Darmstadt in 1621 under the title *Steganographia*. In 1550 A. Glauburg wrote *Additæ sunt etiam aliquot locorum explicationes*. Duke August of Brunswick published *Cryptomenytices et cryptographiæ* (Lunaburg, 1624), based on Trithemius. G. Schott, a Jesuit, wrote *Schola Steganographica* (Nuremberg, 1665) ; another book by a German, Kircher, is *Polygraphiamessai de pasigraphie* (Rome, 1663).

General; *Leo*, the Council of State. In an English cipher of 1588, the Pope is *Beware*; the Emperor, *Doubt*; Catherine de Medici, *Anania*; the Duke of Guise, *Achitophel*; King Henry III, *Ignorant*. A French code of 1563 refers to Catherine de Medici as *Tout*; King Charles IX as *Rien*; Prince de Condé as *Petit*; the Constable Montmorency as *Compère*; Coligny as *Seul*. Another French cipher (1576) is amusing in its malice. Burghley is dubbed *Guillaume le Sage*; Walsingham, *François l'honnête*; King Henry III, *Le marié*; the French queen, *La pucelle*; Catherine de Medici, *M. du Brouillas*; the Duke of Nemours, *Las d'amour*; the Duke of Alva, *Le Brouillon*; the Papists, *Les facheux*. In one English code crowns are *bales of woad*; French cavalry, *ells of velvet*; guns, *barrels of salt*. The cipher of Lord Cobham, the English ambassador to France, had a Latin nomenclature; in it Burghley is *visus*; the Lord High Admiral, *oculus*; Leicester, *auditus*; Francis Drake, *nares*; Walsingham, *olfactus*. The Counsellors are the senses; the men of action, the organs of sense.

The cipher of Henry IV of France, as well as that of Sir Henry Wotton, consisted of symbols and numbers. In Wotton's code England was represented by 39, Genoa by 43, war by 29, ammunition by 67, the Queen of Spain by 55. In a communication between Henry IV and Maurice of Nassau, Germany was referred to as 70, Holland as 96, Brandenburg as 45, United Provinces as 53, Brunswick as 51; the Pope was 31, the Emperor 33, money 78, alliance 71, army 79, ambassador 73, the King of Spain 35.

"There are," Lord Bacon wrote, "several kinds of cyphers; as the simple; those mixed with non-significants; those consisting of two kinds of characters; wheel-cyphers, word-cyphers. There are three properties required in cyphers, viz.: (1) that they be easy to write and read; (2) that they be trusty and undecypherable; and (3), if possible, clear of suspicion. . . . To prevent all suspicion, we shall

"THE QUEEN'S CIPHER," AN EXAMPLE FROM
SIXTEENTH-CENTURY ENGLAND

annex a cypher of our own, which has the highest perfection."

Bacon then invented the following cipher, as an example :

A	aaaaa	N	abbaa
B	aaaab	O	abbab
C	aaaba	P	abbba
D	aaabb	Q	abbbb
E	aabaa	R	baaaa
F	aabab	S	baaab
G	aabba	T	baaba
H	aabbb	V	baabb
I	abaaa	W	babaa
K	abaab	X	babab
L	ababa	Y	babba
M	ababb	Z	babbb

" Thus, in order to write an *A*, you write five *a*'s, or *aaaaa ;* and to write a *B*, you write four *a*'s and one *b*, or *aaaab*."

King Charles I, who was decapitated in 1649, was likewise an adept in the use of ciphers, mainly based on complicated numerals. " I was confident," Hyde, the friend of the Stuarts, wrote in 1659, " that the devil himself cannot decypher a letter that is well written. . . . Nor did I ever hear that more of the king's letters that were found at Naseby, than those which they found decyphered, or found the cyphers in which they were writ, were decyphered. And I very well remember that in the volume they published there was much left in cypher which could not be understood." In fact, it was not until over two hundred years later, in 1858, that Wheatstone, an English professor who invented the ingenious crypto-machine, was able to unravel some of the King Charles' ciphers.

In the seventeenth century the customary method of constructing ciphers was by means of numerals and letters written upwards and downwards, Chinese-wise, or from left to right, as the Semites do ; of course various combinations were applied within this general framework. Words or letters were inserted here and there in order to mislead; others were placed at regular or systematically irregular intervals. This type, connected with the name of Jerome Cardan, the great Italian mathematician, is sometimes called the trellis or cardboard cipher.

The following is a simple illustration of this kind of cipher; it should be read downwards vertically and then upwards again:

```
t   i   l   w   e   l   d   f   r   e
h   t   l   s   s   o   o   t   e   i
e   s   e   u   h   h   u   u   s   l
p   h   n   t   a   o   t   o   h   p
e   t   c   s   l   t   t   h   a   p
s   o   r   g   l   e   h   t   n   u
t   d   e   n   n   l   e   i   d   s
i   e   a   o   o   b   s   w   s   y
l   c   s   m   t   a   i   e   p   d
e   n   e   a   b   e   e   g   e   e
```

Beginning with the first letter on the top and read downwards, and then up the line and down again, the message spells: " The pestilence doth still encrease amongst us; we shall not be able to hold out the siege without fresh and speedy supplie."

In the course of the centuries every Foreign Office came to employ ciphers for communication with its confidential representatives. Accumulated diplomatic experience, as well as an increase in scientific knowledge, helped to create codes of amazing complexity, although few ciphers are, in the long run, really invulnerable. " All persons," Dr. Wallis, an English expert, confessed to his friend Leibniz in 1699, " are not qualified or capable of acquiring the art of deciphering." There are, however, certain principles which help to solve codes. The decipherer must discover first what letters, words, or symbols occur most frequently. According to one authority, the letters of the alphabet fall in the following order of popularity: *E T O A*

NISHRDLCUFMPWGYBVK Z.   Another frequency is: *ETAONISHRDLCUF MPWGYBVKJZ.* Perhaps fifteen per cent of the letters in any given message will be *E,* and only two per cent *K, X, Q, J, Z.*

One may conclude with a code instruction given in the World War:

"Write the message in clear, letter by letter, left to right on the page, with a prearranged number of letters on each line. Each letter must be placed directly under the corresponding letter of the preceding line. You now have a number of columns of letters equal to the number of letters per line. Copy from top down, taking the columns in a prearranged order. Divide the letters thus arranged into groups of ten. To decipher, count the number of letters and the number in the column, write the columns in the original order, and read the message in clear from left to right."

There are, however, easier ways of making a living.

BIBLIOGRAPHY

GENERAL

Adair, E. R.
The Extraterritoriality of Ambassadors in the Sixteenth and Seventeenth Centuries (1929)

Andreas, W.
"Italien und die Anfaenge der neuzeitlichen Diplomatie," in *Historische Zeitschrift* (1942-43)

Bailey, T. A.
A Diplomatic History of the American People (1940), Ch.1-10

Cambon, J.
Le diplomate (1922)

Cecil, A.
"The Foreign Office," in A. W. Ward and G. P. Gooch, *The Cambridge History of British Foreign Policy, 1783-1919* (1923), III, Ch. 8

Clemens, S.
Der Beruf der Diplomaten (1926)

Dolet, E.
De officio legati (1541)

Ernst, F.
"Ueber Gesandschaftschaftswesen und Diplomatie an der Wende vom Mittelalter zur Neuzeit," in *Archiv fuer Kulturgeschichte* (1950)

Ferrero, G.
The Reconstruction of Europe: Talleyrand and the Congress of Vienna, 1814-1815 (1941)

Ganshof, F. L.
Le Moyen Age, in P. Renouvin, *Histoire des relations internationales* (1953)

Garden, G. de
Traité complet de diplomatie (1833)

Genet, R.
　　Traité de diplomatie (1930)

Gentilis, A.
　　De legationibus (1583)

Germonius
　　De legatis principum et populorum (1627)

Grenville-Murray, E. C.
　　Embassies and Foreign Courts. A History of Diplomacy (2d ed., 1856)

Gundissalvus (Gonsalvo de Villadiego)
　　Tractatus de legato (1485)

Horn, D. B.
　　The British Diplomatic Service, 1689-1789 (1961)

Hotman, J.
　　The Ambassador (1603)

Hrabar, V. E.
　　De legatis et legationibus tractatus varii (1906)

Ilchman, W. F.
　　Professional Diplomacy in the United States, 1779-1939 (1961), Ch. 1

Jusserand, J. A. A. J.
　　L'école des ambassadeurs (new ed., 1934)

la Mothe le Vayer, F. de
　　Legatus (1579)

Luxardo
　　Das vordekretalische Gesandschäftsrecht der Paepste (1878)

Maggi, O.
　　De legato (1596)

Mann, G.
　　Secretary of Europe: The Life of Friedrich Gentz, Enemy of Napoleon (1946)

Marselaer, F.
　　Κηρύκειον *sive legationum insigne* (1618)

Martens, C. de
  Guide diplomatique, 2 vols. (rev. ed., 1866)

Mattingly, G.
  "The First Resident Embassies: Medieval Origins of Italian Diplomacy," in *Speculum*, XII (1937)

Mattingly, G.
  Renaissance Diplomacy (1955)

Maulde-la-Claviere, M. A. R. de
  La diplomatie au temps de Machiavel, 3 vols. (1892-93)

Mendelssohn-Bartholdi, A.
  Diplomatie (1927)

Mennevée, R.
  L'espionnage international en temps de paix, 2 vols. (1929)

Mowat, R. B.
  A History of European Diplomacy, 1451-1789 (1928)

Nicolson, H.
  Diplomacy (1939)

Nicolson, H.
  The Evolution of Diplomatic Method (1954)

Padover, S. K.
  "Prince Kaunitz and the First Partition of Poland," in *The Slavonic Review*, 1935

Paschalius
  Legatus (1598)

Pradier-Fodéré, P.
  Cours de droit diplomatique, 2 vols. (1881)

Reumont, A. von
  Della diplomazia italiano dal secolo XIII al XVII (1857)

Rodd, J. R.
  Diplomacy (1929)

Rowan, R. W.
>   *Spy and Counter-Spy: the Development of Modern Espionage* (1928)

Rowan, R. W.
>   *The Story of the Secret Service* (1937)

Satow, E.
>   *Guide to Diplomatic Practice,* 2 vols., 1917

Schaube, A.
>   "Zur Entstehungsgeschichte des staendigen Gesandschaften," in *Mittheilungen des Instituts fuer Oesterreichische Geschichtsforschung,* X (1889), 501-52

Singer, K.
>   *Three Thousand Years of Espionage* (1948)

Spaulding, E. W.
>   *Ambassadors Ordinary and Extraordinary* (1961)

Wicquefort, A.
>   *L'ambassadeur et ses fonctions* (1730)

BIBLIOGRAPHY

CHAPTER I

Calendar of State Papers, Venetian, 1202–1509, Introduction and *passim*; E. Nys, "Les commencements de la diplomatie et le droit d'ambassade jusqu'à Grotius," *Revue de droit international*, XV, 577–86; Gachard, "Les monuments de la diplomatie vénitienne," *Mémoires de l'académie de Belgique*, XXVII (1853); O. Krauske, "Die Entwickelung der ständigen Diplomatie vom fünfzehnten Jahrhundert bis zu den Beschlüssen von 1815 und 1818," in Schmoller's *Staats- und Socialwissenschaftliche Forschungen*, V (1885), No. 3; A. Baschet, *La diplomatie vénitienne* (Paris, 1862); "Contemporary Literature," *North British Review*, LI (1869–70), 233–35, 545–46; R. Brown, ed., *Four Years at the Court of Henry VIII. Selection and Despatches written by the Venetian Ambassador, Sebastian Giustinian* (2 vols., London, 1854); *cf.* the review in *British Quarterly Review*, XXI (1855), 457 f.; E. Albèri, *Relazioni degli ambasciatori Veneti al senato* (Florence, 1840); J. W. Zinkeisen, *Geschichte des osmanischen Reiches in Europa* (Gotha, 1854); V. Tormene, *Il balaggio a Constantinopolidi Girolamo Lippomano* (Venice, 1903); see the review in *Edinburgh Review*, CCIII (1906), 387–409; M. N. Tommaseo, ed., *Relations des ambassadeurs Vénétiens sur les affaires de France au 16me siècle* (2 vols., Paris, 1838); *cf.* the review in *Quarterly Review*, XCVI (1854–55), 373 f.; *ibid.*, CLXII (1886), 379–82.

CHAPTER II

L. Pastor, *History of the Popes* (St. Louis, 1908), VIII, 84–89; *Calendar State Papers, Foreign*, 1553–1558, No. 240; *ibid., Venetian*, 1509–1519, Introduction and Nos. 100, 39, 40, 56; *ibid., Spanish*, I, Introduction; E. Vehse, *Memoirs of the Court, Aristocracy, and Diplomacy of Austria* (London, 1856), I, *passim*; R. Ehrenberg, *Das Zeitalter der Fugger* (Jena, 1912), I, 100–10; J. Zeller, *La diplomatie française vers le milieu du XVIe siècle, d'après la correspondance de Guillaume Pellicier, évèque de Montpellier, ambassadeur de François Ier à Venise* (1539–1542) (Paris, 1880); *The Life and Letters of Ogier Ghiselin de Busbecq* (transl. by C. T. Forster and F. H. B. Daniell; 2 vols., London, 1881).

CHAPTER III

Calendar State Papers, Foreign, I, No. 1116; III, Nos. 194, 236, 252; III, No. 84; XI, No. 1072; XIV, Introduction and No. 302; VIII, Introduction and No. 1230; XV, Introduction and No. 379; XVIII, Nos. 715, 721, 728, 184, 313, 540; XX, p. 361–62; XIX, p. 239 and No. 248; XX, Introduction and p. 616–17; XXI, Pt. 1, p. 49, 92–3, 140–41, 231–32; XXI, Pt. 3, 391–93; Pt. 2, 210–11, and p. 334; Calendar State Papers, Rome, II, Introduction; Venetian, VII, Introduction. See also F. C. Dietz, "The Exchequer in Elizabeth's Reign," in Smith College Studies in History, VIII (1923), No. 2; P. J. Blok, Bijdr. voor vaderl. gesch. en oudheidk., 6th Ser., iv–v; C. Read, "The Fame of Sir Edward Stafford," American Historical Review, XX (1915), 292–313; L. Ranke, Civil Wars and Monarchy in France in the Sixteenth and Seventeenth Centuries (tr. M. A. Garvey; New York, 1854), 329–32; F. v. Raumer, History of the Sixteenth and Seventeenth Centuries (London, 1835), I, 288–93.

CHAPTER IV

E. Bourgeois, Manuel historique de politique étrangère (2 vols.; Paris, 1901), I, 19 f.; Cambridge History of Modern Europe, IV, 802; C. Seignobos, "Histoire générale des XVIIe et XVIIIe siècles," Revue des cours et conferences, IV (1895–96), Pt. 1, 368–69; Calendar State Papers, Venetian, XII, Nos. 492, 568, 569, 631; L. P. Smith, Life and Letters of Sir Henry Wotton (2 vols.; Oxford, 1907); H. M. Sutton, ed., The Lexington Papers (1851); see the review in Quarterly Review, LXXXIX (1851), 393–412; G. Pagès, Le grand electeur et Louis XIV (Paris, 1905), 266 and passim; A. v. Reumont, The Carafas of Maddaloni (1854), 48 and passim; J. Y. Akerman, Moneys received and paid for secret services of Charles II and James II, from 30th March, 1679, to 25th December, 1688 (Camden Society, 1851); H. J. Chaytor, ed., Embajada Espanola, An Anonymous Contemporary Spanish Guide to Diplomatic Procedure in the Last Quarter of the Seventeenth Century (Camden Miscellany, XIV; London, 1926; Spanish and English texts), see the Preface.

Chapter V

J. D. Mackie, *Negotiations between King James VI and I and Ferdinand Grand Duke of Tuscany* (Oxford, 1927); *Calendar State Papers, Venetian*, XI, Nos. 554, 578; X, Nos. 166, 81, 90, 162, 191, 127, and Introduction; XI, Nos. 365, 366, 342, 365, 391, 204, 376, 725, 750, 798, 813, and Introduction; XIV, Nos. 152, 741, 785, 52; XV, p. 391-92, No. 691; XVI, No. 526; XVII, Nos. 70, 658, 677; XIX, Nos. 431, 499, 379, 584, and Introduction; XX, Nos. 100, 145, 289, 327, 402, 377, and Introduction; XXVII, Introduction and *passim*; *Calendar State Papers, Foreign*, XIV, No. 302; X, No. 165. See also Lubimenko, "A Project for the Acquisition of Russia by James I," *English Historical Review*, XXIX (1914), 246-56; G. Fagniez, *Le père Joseph et Richelieu* (1577-1538) (2 vols.; Paris, 1894); cf. the reviews in *Revue historique*, LV (1894), 119 f., and *Quarterly Review*, CLXXXIII (1896), 339-73; *Cambridge Modern History*, IV, 38-39, 41, 59; Bourgeois, *Manuel diplomatique*, I, 25-34.

On Mazarin see de Laborde, *Le palais Mazarin et les grandes habitations de ville et de campagne au dix-septième siècle* (1846); R. Chantelauze, *Louis XIV et Marie Mancini, d'après de nouveaux documents* (1880); A. Cheruel, *Lettres du cardinal Mazarin à la reine, à la princesse Palatine* . . . (1836); J. Michelet, *Histoire de France. Richelieu et la Fronde* (1858); A. Renée, *Les nièces de Mazarin* (1857); P. Clément, *Lettres, instructions, et mémoires de Colbert* (Paris, 1861); cf. the review in *Quarterly Review*, CLV (1883), 75-105. See also C. H. Firth, "England and Austria in 1657," *English Historical Review*, XXXII (1917), 407-11; Firth, *The Last Years of the Protectorate*, 1656-1658 (2 vols.; London, 1909), II, 245-49 and *passim*; J. Valfrey, *Hugues de Lionne, ses ambassades en Espagne et en Allemagne* (Paris, 1881); D. J. Hill, *A History of Diplomacy in the International Development of Europe* (London 1925), II, 32-38 and *passim*; A. F. Pribram, *Franz Paul Freiherr von Lisola, 1614-1674, und die Politik seiner Zeit* (Leipzig, 1894), ch. 7; D. Bigby, "An Unknown Treaty between England and France, 1644," *English Historical Review*, XXVIII (1913), 337-41; G. L. Beer, "Cromwell's Policy in its Economic Aspects," *Political Science Quarterly*, XVII (1902); C. H. Firth, "Secretary Thurloe on the

Relations of England and Holland," *English Historical Review*, XXI (1906), 319–27; S. R. Gardiner, *History of the Commonwealth and Protectorate* (1901), III, 218 and *passim*; R. Vaughan, *The Protectorate of Oliver Cromwell and the State of Europe during the early Part of the Reign of Louis XIV* (1839), II, 45–46 n.; C. H. Firth, " Thomas Scot's Account of his Actions as Intelligencer during the Commonwealth," *English Historical Review*, XII (1897), 116–26; E. Jenks, " Some Correspondence of Thurloe and Meadowe," *English Historical Review*, VII (1892), 72 f.; " Mr. Secretary Thurloe," *Macmillan's Magazine*, LXX (1894), 291–303; S. V. Bischoffshausen, *Die Politik des Protektors Oliver Cromwell . . . und Thaetigkeit seines Ministers des Staatssecretaers John Thurloe* (1899); C. H. Firth, " Cromwell's Instructions to Colonel Lockhart in 1655," *English Historical Review*, XXI (1906), 742–46.

CHAPTER VI

A. Chéruel, " Politique extérieure de Louis XIV au début de son gouvernement personnel, 1661," *Revue d'histoire diplomatique*, IV (1890), 161 f.; Hill, *History of Diplomacy*, III, 59–60; J. J. Jusserand, *Recueil des instructions . . . aux ambassadeurs de France, Angleterre*, I and II (1930); G. B. de Puchesse, " Les introducteurs des ambassadeurs (1585–1900)," *Revue d'histoire diplomatique*, XV (1901), 252 f.; *Calendar State Papers, Venetian*, XXXI, No. 246; XXXIII, No. 238 and Introduction; A. I. Dasent, *The Private Life of Charles the Second* (1927), vii f., 146; C. Rousset, *Histoire de Louvois et de son administration politique et militaire* (1886), II, 555 and *passim*; V. Barbour, *Henry Bennet, Earl of Arlington, Secretary of State to Charles II* (1914), 44, 111, and *passim*; C. L. Grose, " The Anglo-Dutch Alliance of 1678," *English Historical Review*, XXXIX (1924), 349–72, 526–51; J. Walker, " The Secret Service under Charles II and James II," *Transactions of the Royal Historical Society*, 4th Ser., XV (1932), 211–35; S. Rosenfeld, ed., *The Letter Book of Sir George Etherege* (1929); *cf.* review in London *Times Literary Supplement*, March 7, 1929; H. Omont, " Projets de prise de Constantinople et de fondation d'un empire française d'Orient sous Louis XIV," *Revue d'histoire diplomatique*, VII (1893), 195–246; L. Drapeyron,

" Le grand dessein secret de Louis XIV contre l'empire Ottoman en 1688," *Académie des sciences morales et politiques, compte-rendu,* CVII (1877), 740–74; W. T. Morgan, "Economic Aspects of the Negotiations at Ryswick," *Transactions of the Royal Historical Society,* 4th Ser., XIV (1931), 225–49; Ranke, *Histoire de France principalement pendant le XVIe et le XVIIe siècle* (tr. J. J. Porchat; Paris, 1888), V, 303–19; A. C. Wood, " The English Embassy at Constantinople 1660–1762," *English Historical Review,* XL (1925), 533–61; M. Lane, " The Diplomatic Service Under William III," *Transactions of the Royal Historical Society,* 4th Ser., X (1927), 87–109; L. G. W. Legg, *Matthew Prior : A Study of his Public Career and Correspondence* (Cambridge, 1921); Earl Stanhope, *History of England, comprising the Reign of Queen Anne until the Peace of Utrecht* (London, 1870); *cf.* review in *Quarterly Review,* CXXIX (1870), 1–39; Lord Mahon, *History of England from the Peace of Utrecht to the Peace of Aix-la-Chapelle* (I ; London, 1836); *cf.* review in *Quarterly Review,* LVII (1836), 330–49; A. Hassall, *Life of Viscount Bolingbroke* (Oxford, 1915); B. Williams, *Stanhope, A Study in Eighteenth-Century War and Diplomacy* (Oxford, 1932).

CHAPTER VII

A. Sorel, *L'Europe et la révolution française* (Paris, 1908), I, 70, 70 n., 74–75, and *passim* ; S. Brunner, *Der Humor in der Diplomatie und Regierungskunde des 18 Jahrhunderts* (2 vols. ; Vienna, 1882) ; G. Smyth, ed., *Memoirs and Correspondence of Sir Robert Murray Keith* (2 vols. ; London, 1849) ; M. D. Conway, *The Life of Thomas Paine, with a history of his literary, political and religious career in America, France and England* (New York, 1893), I, 146; Hist. MSS. Comm., *Stuart Papers,* V, Introduction, xx–xxi, 96, 173, 181, 318 ; VI, Introduction ; D. B. Horn, " The Cost of the Diplomatic Service, 1747–52," *English Historical Review,* XLII (1928), 606–11 ; F. Masson, *Le departement des affaires étrangères pendant la révolution,* 1787–1804 (Paris, 1903), 48–53 and *passim* ; *Politisches Journal,* 1786, 56–57 ; Bielfield, *Institutions politiques* (The Hague, 1760), II, ch. 3, sec. 18 ; E. Boutaric, *Correspondance secrète inédite de Louis XV sur la politique étrangère avec le comte de Broglie, Tercier, etc.* (2 vols. ; Paris, 1886).

CHAPTER VIII

J. B. Perkins, *France under the Regency* (Boston, 1892), 384–88 ; Aubertin, *L'esprit public au XVIIIe siècle* (Paris, 1873) ; Sévelinges, ed., *Abrégé de la correspondance diplomatique de Dubois* (2 vols. ; 1815) ; E. Bourgeois, *La diplomatie secrète au XVIIIe siècle* (Paris, 1911) ; *cf.* Armstrong in *English Historical Review*, XXVII (1912), 167–69 ; Mahon, *History of England*, I, 162 f., 236–38 ; F. S. Oliver, *The Endless Adventure* (London, 1931), I, 210–11, 227–37 ; L. G. W. Legg, *British Diplomatic Instructions, France, 1721–1727* (London, 1927), Introduction ; E. Armstrong, *Elisabeth Farnese, 'The Termagant of Spain'* (London, 1892) ; *cf. English Historical Review*, VIII (1893), 162–64 ; *Cambridge Modern History*, VI, 141 f. ; Hill, *A History of Diplomacy*, III, 413–24 ; R. Lodge, *The Private Correspondence of Sir Benjamin Keene* (Cambridge, 1933) ; *cf.* London *Times Literary Supplement*, January 7, 1932, 11 ; Brunner, *Der Humor in der Diplomatie*, II, 433–34.

CHAPTER IX

A. Hayward, *Biographical and Critical Essays*, 3rd Ser. (London, 1874), 96–104 ; W. H. Craig, *Life of Lord Chesterfield, An Account of the Ancestry, Personal Character and Public Services of the Fourth Earl of Chesterfield* (London and New York, n.d.), 114–15 ; R. Lodge, *Great Britain and Prussia in the Eighteenth Century* (Oxford, 1923), 7, 25–28, and *passim* ; W. L. Dorn, "The Prussian Bureaucracy in the Eighteenth Century," *Political Science Quarterly*, XLVI (1931), 403–23 ; Broglie, *Frederick the Great and Maria Theresa. From hitherto unpublished documents, 1740–1742* (Engl. tr. ; London, 1883), I, 68–78 and *passim* ; Earl of Ilchester and Mrs. Langford-Brooke, ed., *Correspondence of Catherine the Great when Grand Duchess with Sir Charles Hanbury-Williams* (London, 1928) ; see review in London *Times Literary Supplement*, August 9, 1928 ; Ilchester and Langford-Brooke, *The Life of Sir Charles Hanbury-Williams* (London, 1929), see review in London *Times Literary Supplement*, February 28, 1929 ; A. Rambaud, ed., *Recueil des instructions données aux ambassadeurs et ministres de France*

*depuis les traités de Westphalie jusqu'à la révolution française,
Russie* (Paris, 1890), 427–40 and *passim*; D. B. Horn, *Sir
Charles Hanbury-Williams and European Diplomacy* (1747–
1758) (London, 1930); C. Whibley, *Political Portraits*
(London, 1917), 85–87, 90–97, and *passim*; A. R. Ropes,
"The Causes of the Seven Years' War," *Transactions of the
Royal Historical Society* (London, 1889), new Ser., IV, 143–
70; R. Waddington, *Louis XV et le renversement des alliances
et préliminaires de la guerre de sept ans*, 1754–1756 (Paris,
1896); *cf.* Ward, *Collected Essays*, II, Pt. 2, 88–89; E. E.
Cuthell, *The Scottish Friend of Frederic the Great, The Last
Earl Marischall* (London, 1915), II, 81–82 and *passim*;
Arneth, *Geschichte Maria Theresias* (10 vols.; Vienna,
1863–79), IV, 475–78 and *passim*; H. Tuttle, *History of
Prussia under Frederick the Great* (New York, 1888), III,
186–87; R. Koser, *Geschichte Friedrichs des Grossen* (3
vols.; Stuttgart, 1913), II, 407; Bedford, *Correspondence,*
II, 197–98; *Die Geheimnisse des saechsischen Cabinets. Ende
1745 bis Ende 1756. Archivarische Vorstudien zur Geschichte
des siebeniaehrigen Krieges* (2 vols.; Stuttgart, 1866); *cf.*
Ward, *Collected Papers*, II, Pt. 2, 100–08; *Pologne 1752–1764*
(a manuscript copy from the French ministry of Foreign
Affairs, in possession of J. W. Thompson, the co-author of
this book); Hill, *A History of Diplomacy*, III, 501–02, 644;
L. B. de Marsangy, *Le Chevalier de Vergennes, son ambassade
à Constantinople* (Paris, 1894); E. Boutaric, *Correspondance
secrète inédite de Louis XV*, II, 429–33; I, 312, 188–90;
*Recuil des instructions données aux ambassadeurs et ministres de
France* . . . , *Pologne*, II, 235–37, 239–41, 243–44, 245–46,
and *passim*; Broglie, *The King's Secret* (2 vols.), II, 200–01,
204, 206, 213–14, 215–16, 217–18, 218–19, and *passim*; P.
Coquelle, "Le Cabinet secret de Louis XV en Hollande,"
Revue d'histoire diplomatique, XV (1901), 275–92; Abbé
Georgel, *Mémoires pour servir à l'histoire des évènemens de la fin
du dix-huitième siècle depuis 1760 jusqu'en 1806–1810* (Paris,
1817), I, 272–79; *Quarterly Review*, CXLVII (1879), 250–
73; *Journal des savants*, September, 1879, 550–60, 581–89;
Broglie, "La diplomatie secrète de Louis XV," *Revue des
deux mondes*, LXXXVII (1870), 769–820, 257–311;
LXXXVIII, 257–93; *Cambridge Modern History*, VI, 903;
J. S. Corbett, *England in the Seven Years' War, A Study in
Combined Strategy* (London, 1907), I, 81, 84–85, 148–54;
II, 184–85, 229 n.; P. Coquelle, "L'espionage en Angle-

terre pendant la guerre de sept ans," *Revue d'histoire diplo-matique*, XIV (1900), 508–33; *Despatches of . . . Bucking-hamshire*, II, vii, 199 n., 189, 253; J. F. Chance, *British Diplomatic Instructions*, V, *Sweden*, 1727–1789 (Royal Historical Society; London, 1928), Preface and Intro-duction; M. C. Morison, " The Duc of Choiseul and the Invasion of England, 1768–1770," *Transactions of the Royal Historical Society*, 3rd Ser., IV (1910), 83–115; Countess of Minto, *A Memoir of the Right Hon. Hugh Elliot* (Edinburgh, 1868); *cf.* review in *Quarterly Review*, CXXV (1868), 329–66; H. Temperley, *Frederic the Great and Kaiser Joseph* (London, 1915), 97–98 and note, 255–65; O. Browning, " Hugh Elliot in Berlin," *Transactions of the Royal Historical Society*, New Ser., IV (1889), 85–99; O. d'Haussonville, " Souvenirs d'un diplomate anglais," *Revue des deux mondes*, LXXXI (1869), 405–40; *Quarterly Review*, CXXV (1868), 46–49; F. Wharton, ed., *The Revolutionary diplomatic Correspondence of the United States* (Washington, 1889), II, 351–54 and note, 358; H. B. Wheatley, ed., *The Historical and Posthumous Memoirs of Sir Nathaniel William Wraxall, 1772–1784* (London, 1884), V, 186–88.

CHAPTER X

Diaries and Correspondence of James Harris, First Earl of Malmesbury (London, 1844), I, 83–84, 148–49, 527–28; III, 7, 32, 44–46, 119–20, and *passim*; Masson, *op. cit.*, 261–63; A. v. Vivenot, *Quellen zur Geschichte der deutschen Kaiser-politik Oesterreichs waehrend der franzoesischen Revolutionskriege, 1790–1801* (Vienna, 1874), II, 440–44, 437–39; M. D. Conway, *The Life of Thomas Paine* (New York, 1893), I, 377–78; F. A. Aulard, " Organisation du service des agents secrets dans la première république," *La révolution française*, XII (1887), 1117–1128; *ibid.*, " Instructions générales aux agents diplomatiques de la république française," *La révolution française*, XIII (1887), 66–73; Auckland, *Journal*, III, 329–31; 151–52 n., 57, 370; Malmesbury, *op. cit.*, III, 76, 83–84 n., 76 n., 91–92, 261 n., 259–60, 273, 333–34; A. v. Vivenot, *Vertrauliche Briefe des Freiherrn von Thugut, oesterr. Ministers des aeussern* (Vienna, 1872), I, 91 and *passim*; Hist. MSS. Comm., *Fortescue Manuscripts*, II, 497; A. B. Paget, ed., *The Paget Papers, Diplomatic and other Corre-*

spondence of the Right Hon. Sir Arthur Paget, G.C.B., 1794–
1807 (2 vols. ; London, 1896), I, 27, 31, 39–40, 63, 70, 70–71
76, 85–86, 87, 99–100, 274 n., and *passim* ; *cf.* review in
Edinburgh Review, CLXXXIV (1896), 135–60 ; H. E.
Egerton, *British Foreign Policy in Europe to the End of the
Nineteenth Century,* 106–07 ; W. Wickham, *The Correspondence of the Right Honourable William Wickham from the Year*
1794 (2 vols. ; London, 1870), I, 19–20, 24–25, 42, 67, 63,
95, 125–26, 208, 184–85, 438–39, 492, 493–94, 496, 356–57 ;
II, 1, 2, 10, 48, 49, 34–35 ; J. Hall, *General Pichegru's Treason,
1761 to 1804* (London, 1915) ; E. Driault, " Les dernières
thèses d'histoire sur la politique extérieur de Napoléon,"
Séances et trav. de l'acad. d. sc. mor. et pol., compte-rendu, CXCI
(1919), Pt. 1, 630–47 ; C. A. Fyffe, *A History of Modern
Europe* (New York, 1891), I, 189–90 n. ; *Arkhiv Kniazia
Vorontzova* (Moscow, 1880), XVI, 322 ; XVII, 166 ; VIII
(1876), 52–3, Pt. 1, 276–77, 286–87 ; XI, Pt. 1, 96, 97 ; E.
Vehse, *Memoirs of the Court, Aristocracy, and Diplomacy of
Austria,* II, 381–88 ; A. v. Vivenot, *Zur Geschichte des
Rastadter Congresses* (Vienna, 1871), 311–12 ; H. Hüffer,
" L'assassinat des plénipotentiaires française à Rastadt,"
Revue historique, LXI (1896), 307–21 ; *ibid., Der Rastadter
Gesandtenmord* (Bonn, 1896) ; *ibid.,* " A propos de l'assassinat
des plénipotentiaires de Rastadt," *Revue historique,* LXXI
(1899), 141–42 ; *La révolution française,* XXXVI (1899),
565–66 ; R. B. Mowat, *The Diplomacy of Napoleon* (London,
1924), 33 n. ; K. Waliszewski, *Paul the First of Russia*
(London, 1913), 329–30 ; Broglie, " Mémoire à l'empereur
Paul," *Revue d'histoire diplomatique,* III (1889), 1–12 ; A.
Tratchevski, " L'empereur Paul et Bonaparte, premier
consul," in *ibid.,* III (1889), 281–86 ; Weil, " L'assassinat de
Paul Ier," *Annales historiques de la révolution française,* New
Ser., III (1926), 363–83 ; *cf. English Historical Review,* XI
(1896), 171–75.

CHAPTER XI

L. Madelin, *Le consulate et l'empire* (2 vols. ; Paris, 1932–
33) ; *cf.* review in *American Historical Review,* XXXIX
(1934), 323–26 ; O. Wolff, *Die Geschaefte des Herrn Ouvrard.
Aus dem Leben eines genialen Spekulanten* (Frankfort, 1932),
80 and *passim* ; H. W. V. Temperley, *Life of Canning*

(London, 1905), 55–57 and *passim*; L. V. Harcourt, ed., *The Diaries and Correspondence of the Right Honourable George Rose* (2 vols.; London, 1860), II, 49–50; *Bath Archives*, I, 239; Lord Broughton, *Recollections of a Long Life* (ed. Lady Dorchester; 4 vols.; London, 1910), IV, 11–12; Rose, *Pitt and National Revival*, 24; B. Frere, "Memoir on J. H. Frere," in *Works of the Right Honourable John Hookham Frere* (London, 1874), I, 69–70, 47–48 n., and *passim*; G. W. E. Russell, *Collections and Recollections* (London, 1903), 99, 102; *Paget Papers*, I, 196; II, 14, 96–97, 109; A. Fournier, "Die Mission des Grafen Saint-Julien im Jahre 1800," *Historische Studien und Skizzen* (Prague and Leipzig, 1885), 181–218; L. M. Roberts, "The Negotiations Preceding the Peace of Lunéville," *Transactions of the Royal Historical Society*, New Ser., XV (1901), 47–130; *Diaries of Sylvester Douglas*, I, 305 f.; Auckland, *Journal*, IV, 147–48; Lady Jackson, ed., *The Diaries and Letters of Sir George Jackson* (2 vols.; London, 1872), I, 65–66, 78–79, and *passim*; Wortley, *Highcliffe and the Stuarts*, 43–44, 198–200; A. Vandal, *L'avènement de Bonaparte* (Paris, 1907), II, 77–90; *Mémoires de Joseph Fouché, duc d'Otrante, ministre de la police générale* (Paris, 1824); *cf.* review in *Edinburgh Review*, XLII (1825), 94 f.; *Quarterly Review*, CLXXXVII (1897), 375 f.; "Political Spies," *Quarterly Review*, CLXXVII (1893), 239 f.; Mowat, *Diplomacy of Napoleon*, 12, 121–22 n., 107; A. Sorel, "Une agence d'espionage sous le consulat," in his *Lectures historiques* (Paris, 1909), 113–51; L. Pingaud, *Un agent secret sous la révolution et l'empire. Le comte d'Antraigues* (Paris, 1893); C. F. de Méneval, *Mémoires pour servir à l'histoire de Napoléon Ier depuis 1802 jusqu'à 1815* (Paris, 1894), II, 516 and *passim*; L. Lécestre, *Lettres inédites de Napoléon Ier* (2 vols.; Paris, 1897); M. Loyd, *New Letters of Napoleon I* (London, 1898); *cf.* review in *Quarterly Review*, CLXXXVII (1897), 357–83; Broglie, ed., *Mémoires de Talleyrand* (I and II; Paris, 1891); *cf.* review in *Quarterly Review*, CLXXIII (1891), 131–58; *Edinburgh Review*, CLXXIV (1891), 1–31; P. Bertrand, ed., *Lettres inédites de Talleyrand, 1800–1809* (Paris, 1889); G. Pallain, *La mission de Talleyrand à Londres en 1792* (Paris, 1889); H. de Neufville, *Mémoires et souvenirs* (Paris, 1889); *cf.* review in *Edinburgh Review*, CLXXI (1890), 546–65; "Talleyrand," *Fraser's Magazine*, XIX (1839), 127–51, 287–309; XLII (1850), 522–37; D. Cooper, *Talleyrand* (London, 1932);

cf. London *Times Literary Supplement*, January 29, 1933; Masson, *op. cit.*, 402–06; Whibley, *Political Portraits*, 173–86; W. Ekedahl, "The Principal Causes of the Renewal of the War between England and France in 1803," *Transactions of the Royal Historical Society*, New Ser., VIII (1894), 181–201; Rose, *Diaries*, II, 11–12, 13, 18–21, 25, 26, 41–42, 43–44, 46, 177; P. M. Thornton, *Foreign Secretaries of the XIXth Century to* 1834 (London, 1881), I, 59–61; Malmesbury, *op. cit.*, IV, 246–47, 287, 293 n.; *Jackson Diaries*, I, 198, 200–01, 205, 206 f., 211, 229–30.

CHAPTER XII

Paget Papers, II, 135–36, 265, 320 n., 321–22; *Jackson Diaries*, I, 252; II, 163–66; *The Memoirs of Baron de Marbot late Lieutenant-General in the French Army* (tr. A. J. Butler; 2 vols.; London, 1892), I, 193–95; II, 125–26, 139–40, 200–02, 203, 363–64; R. Adair, *Historical Memoir of a Mission to the Court of Vienna in* 1806 (London, 1844); Wortley, *op. cit.*, 89–90, 92, 93–94, 97–99, 101, 102, 106–07, 134–35, and *passim*; H. Butterfield, *The Peace Tactics of Napoleon* 1806–1808 (Cambridge, 1929), 18, 195, 287, and *passim*; H. Randolph, ed., *Life of General Sir Robert Wilson* (2 vols.; London, 1862), II, 163–64 and *passim*; *Arkhiv Kniazia Vorontzova*, XIX, 166–67; XVII, 159, 165, 159 n.; Rose, "A British Agent at Tilsit," *English Historical Review*, XVI (1901), 712–18; *cf.* criticism in *Athenæum*, June 15, 1907, 730–31; Mowat, *op. cit.*, 186–87; *Revue historique*, CXII (1913), 178–79; J. H. Rose, *Napoleonic Studies*, 133–52; Earl of Ilchester, *The Journal of Lady Holland* (1791-1811) (2 vols.; London, 1908), II, 239–40; Earl of Malmesbury, *Memoirs of an Ex-Minister, An Autobiography* (2 vols.; London, 1884), I, 2; Auckland, *Journal*, IV, 315; Temperley, *Canning*, 75 n.; J. Rydjord, "Napoleon and the Independence of New Spain," *New Spain and the Anglo-American West* (Historical Contributions Presented to Herbert Eugene Bolton; Los Angeles, 1932), I, 289 f.; A. G. Macdonell, "Napoleon's Marshals as Artists," *London Mercury*, XXIX (1933), 37 f.; J. Fortescue, *Historical and Military Essays* (London, 1928), 226; Rose, *Napoleonic Studies*, 386–89; F. Ellesmere, *Personal Reminiscences of the Duke of Wellington* (London, 1904), 148–49, 109, 144;

C. Oman, *Studies in the Napleonic Wars* (London, 1929),
161–74, 123–40; C. S. B. Buckland, *Metternich and the
British Government from 1809 to 1813* (London, 1932), 31–32,
36, 34 n., 44–46, 71–73, 78–116, 261–334, 145–48, 123–25,
125–44, 151–56, and *passim*; Vandal, *Napoléon et Alexander
Ier*, III, 41–46, 133–37; S. Tasticheff, *Alexandre et Napoléon*
(Paris, 1891); *cf.* review in *Quarterly Review*, CLXXVII
(1893), 416–42; K. de Lettenhove, "1814. Talleyrand,"
Revue d'histoire diplomatique, I (1887), 247; Auckland,
Journal, IV, 405, 407.

<h2 style="text-align:center">Chapter XIII</h2>

Whibley, *Political Portraits*, 187–201; A. Fournier, *Die
Geheimpolizei auf dem Wiener Kongress* (Vienna and Leipzig,
1913); M. H. Weil, *Les dessous du congrès de Vienne, d'après
les documents originaux des archives du ministère impérial et
royal de l'intérieur à Vienne* (2 vols.; Paris, 1917); C. K.
Webster, *The Congress of Vienna. 1814–1815* (Oxford,
1918); *Letters of Alexander von Humboldt, written between the
Years 1827 and 1858, to Varnhagen von Ense* (London, 1860),
229; Wortley, *op. cit.*, 215; *Bath Archives*, II, 464; Sainte-
Beuve, *Nouveaux lundis* (Paris, 1884), XII, 79–80 and n.;
F. Krones, *Aus dem Tagebuche Erzherzog Johanns von Oester-
reich 1810–1815* (Innsbruck, 1891), 181; Broughton,
Recollections, II, 63–64; I, 212; Russell, *Collections and
Recollections*, 14; T. C. Hansard, *Parliamentary Debates*
(1815), XXX, 545–83; J. R. Hall, *The Bourbon Restoration*
(London, 1909), 79, 81–82, 114–15; N. Young, *Napoleon
in Exile: St. Helena* (London, 1915), I, 162; Rose,
Napoleonic Studies, 326; Ellesmere, *Wellington*, 169.

<h2 style="text-align:center">BIBLIOGRAPHY TO APPENDIX ON
CRYPTOGRAPHY</h2>

Perhaps the earliest English book on the subject is John
Wilkins' *Mercury the Secret and Swift Messenger* (London,
1641). Wilkins was followed by John Falconer who wrote
a *Cryptomensysis patefacta* in 1685. In 1704 Colonel Parsons
published a *New Book of Cyphers, more Compleat and Regular
than Any Yet Extant*. In 1772 P. Thicknesse issued *A*

Treatise on the Art of Decyphering and of Writing in Cypher.
The list of later works is much too long to be enumerated.
For some special and general studies, see S. M. Drach,
" Viceroy Joseph's Official Despatches," *Transactions of the
Society of Biblical Archæology*, VI (1878), Pt. 1, 244–48 ; see
also *Saturday Review*, CXXVI (1924), 418 ; " Concerning
Anagrams," *Living Age*, CCCXXI (1924), 1115–16 ;
Calendar of State Papers, Venetian, I, Appendix II ; *Calendar
of State Papers, Spanish*, 1485–1509, I, xi–xiii, cxxxvii–
cxlvi ; *Calendar of State Papers, Foreign*, 1577–1578, XII,
Nos. 38, 104, and *passim* ; A. J. Butler, " Some Elizabethan
Cipher-Books," *Transactions of the Bibliographical Society*
(1900–1902), VI, 129 f. ; *Historical Manuscripts Com-
mission*, XI, Appendix I ; also *ibid.*, *Reports*, I, 1–10 ; II,
183, 188 ; III, 74, 197, 248, 266 ; VI, 638–40 and *passim* ;
Shaw's edition of Bacon's *Works*, I, 141–45 ; A. Rees,
Cyclopedia (London, 1819), VIII, article " Cipher." The
indices to the various volumes of the *Calendar of State
Papers* should be consulted for much detailed information.
The best studies on cryptography are to be found in
foreign languages. Only a few may be mentioned here :
A. Giry, *Manuel de diplomatique* (1894), 519–23, gives
bibliography ; P. W. Finsterwalder, " Eine parteipolitische
Kundgebung eines Abhängers Lothars I," *Neues Archiv*,
XLVII (1928), 393–415 ; J. Havet, in *Académie des in-
scriptions et belles-lettres, comptes-rendu*, XV (1887), 4th Ser.,
94–112, 351–374 ; G. Gandy, " Venise et sa diplomatie,"
Revue des questions historiques, X (1871), 246 f. ; L. Pasini,
" Delle scritture in cifra usate dall republica Veneta," *Il
regio archivio generale di Venezia*, 1873, 292–93 ; Cesschetti,
" Le scritture occulte nella diplomazia Veneziana," *Memorie
del R. instituto Veneto di scienze, lettere et arti*, IV (1869),
3rd Ser., 1185–1211 ; *Operette di Jacopo Norelli, Bibliotecario
di S. Marco* (Venice, 1820), II, 253–72 ; A. Meister, " Die
Anfänge der modernen diplomatischen Geheimschrift,"
*Beiträge zur Geschichte der italienischen Kryptographie des XV
Jahrhunderts* (Paderborn, 1902) ; F. Argelatti, *Biblioteca
scriptorum mediolanesium* (Milan, 1745), II, col. 2166–68 ;
P. M. Perret, " Les règles de Cicco Simonetta pour le
déchiffrement des écritures secrètes," *Bibliothèque de l'école des
chartes*, LI (1890), 516–25 ; J. Susta, " Eine päpstliche
Geheimschrift aus dem 16 Jahrhundert," *Mittheilung des
Instituts für Oesterreichische Geschichtsforschung*, XVIII (1897),

367–71 ; J. L. Klüber, *Kryptographik* (Tübingen, 1809) ;
H. Omont, " Traité de physique et d'alchémie du XVe
siècle, en écriture chryptographique," *Bibliothèque de l'école
des chartes*, 1897 ; " Dispacci in cifre de R. Archivio di Stato
di Firenze," *Archivio storico italiano*, 3rd Ser., XIV (1871),
473–76 ; *Allgemeine Zeitschrift für Geschichte*, V (1846),
402–04.

INDEX

A

Adams, John Quincy, 178–79
Aix-la-Chapelle, Peace of, 145
Alberto, Leon Battista, 256
Alexander I, Emperor of Russia, 180, 193, 194, 195, 206, 213–14, 215, 218–22, 239, 240–42, 245–51
Alexander VII, Pope, 80
Almazan, Miguel Perez, 258
Alsace, 79, 110, 111, 116
Alva, Duke of, 44, 45, 260
America, North, 111, 113, 114, 115, 162, 169, 177, 182, 197, 227–28
America, Spanish, 40, 226–28
Amiens, Treaty of, 201–2, 209
Antwerp, 36, 41, 69, 196
Archives, 19
Austria, 25, 26, 31, 34, 35, 56, 58, 69, 72, 75, 79–82, 87, 95, 96, 108, 112, 113, 114, 116–19, 121, 122, 126–28, 136–37, 141, 145, 146, 147, 148, 151, 169, 181, 182, 188, 189–90, 191–92, 198–201, 204, 212, 215, 233, 238, 242, 244

B

Bacon, Francis, 260–61
Badoer, Andrew, 20, 31–32
Badoer, Luigi, 37
Barbarigo, Antonio, 21
Barneveld, John van Olden, 67
Bassompière, Marshal François de, 76
Bathurst, Benjamin, 220, 233–37
Bavaria, 62, 80, 99, 113, 144, 200, 248
Belgium, see Netherlands, Austrian

Bennigsen, General Levin August von, 194–95, 216
Bernadotte, Marshal Jean Baptiste Jules, 215, 229, 240
Bernis, Cardinal, 112, 163
Bestuchev, Chancellor, 142–44, 146
Beville, Lieutenant-Colonel de, 173–74
Blake, Admiral Robert, 84, 85
Blücher, General Gebhard von, 235, 252
Bohemia, 56, 78, 238
Bolingbroke, Lord Henry St. John, 109–10
Bonaparte, Joseph, 222, 224, 226–28, 232
Bonaparte, Letitia, 222
Bonaparte, Louis, 239
Bonaparte, Napoleon, see Napoleon
Bonnac, Marquis François Armand de, 158–60
Brandenburg, see also Prussia, 56, 58, 69, 80, 81, 92, 133, 260
Breteuil, Baron Louis de, 151, 167, 182
Broughton, John Cam Hobhouse, Baron, 197
Brussels, 44, 70, 116, 118
Burghley, Lord William Cecil, 259, 260
Busbecq, Ogier Ghiselin de, 25–27
Bute, John Stuart, Earl, 157, 178

C

Cæsar, Julius, 253, 256
Callières, François de, 59–63
Canning, George, 180, 215–22, 229, 235, 236

283